HB (49) GAN 4556

JAMES BOSWELL
UNOFFICIAL WAR ARTIST

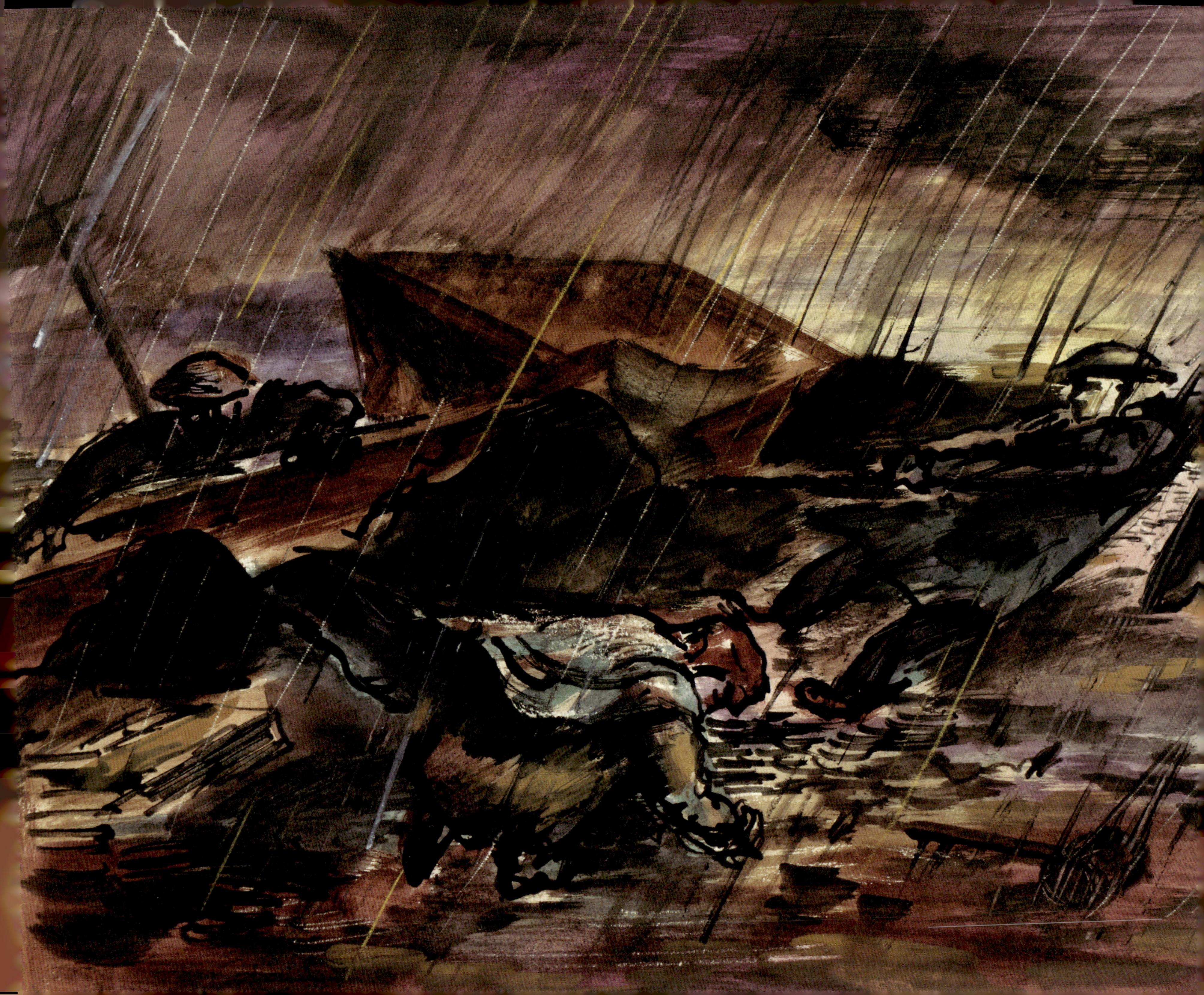

JAMES BOSWELL
UNOFFICIAL WAR ARTIST

William Feaver

Drawings and paintings by James Boswell from the collections of
The British Museum, The Imperial War Museum and The Tate Gallery.

Muswell
Press

JAMES BOSWELL UNOFFICIAL WAR ARTIST

First published in Great Britain 2007 by The Muswell Press
129 Rosebery Road London N10 2LD

ISBN 10. 0-9547959-2-X
ISBN 13. 0-978-0-9547959-2-4

British Library Cataloguing-in-Publication Data
A catalogue record for this book is available from the British Library.

Book consultant Phil Abel, Hand and Eye Letterpress
Book design and art direction Brian Webb and Dan Smith of Webb & Webb Design Limited, London
Printed in England by Empress Litho

Frontispiece Making Camp

Published by Ruth Boswell, The Muswell Press

ACKNOWLEDGEMENTS

I would like to thank Anthony Griffiths, Stephen Coppel and the Staff of the Prints & Drawings Department of the British Museum, the Staff of the Art Department of The Imperial War Museum and Heather Birchall and the Staff of the Tate Archive Department for their support and help.

I would also like to thank Lord Sainsbury of Preston Candover KG, Mr Simon Sainsbury and the late Sir Timothy Sainsbury for their generous support, reflecting James Boswell's long association with J Sainbury; also Philip Lawson for his role in making it happen.

My thanks too to Sal Shuel and Simon Shuel who have been of immeasurable help.

Ruth Boswell

In dreams, waking, suddenly in the night and in daylight moments of evocation that say what to paint. The lorry lights along the palings, the shadows and cords of the hammocks at night in the belly of the ship, the faces in the hurricane lamps – light and the blue crude letters on the ration boxes. And the worn wooden floors of trucks and railway wagons – all that is worn and used until it has grown a patina of humanity like the dining tables scrubbed yellow in the sun or the mallets and spades and the tents whose textures ensnares soldiers' dreams. The comforting look of a petrol tin grey with soap and the bridal colour of the nets. And a hundred things.

James Boswell, Iraq 1943

CONTENTS

LONDON 1939

Eyeing us, Neville Chamberlain bares his teeth and raises one arm in fascist salute. The occasion is a foreign policy presentation coupled with the disclosure of plans for national security. *Design for Dying*, the main cartoon in *Left Review's* April 1938 issue, reveals that the Prime Minister has in mind a diplomatic strategy endorsed with a swastika and a type of air raid shelter for the British masses composed of a sheet of paper resting on four twigs.

April 1938: not long to go before prevarication and worse at Munich and, as usual in *Left Review*, the knives are out. Cast as Asinine Toff in the class war, Chamberlain spouts blithering nonsense with a crazy wing-collared self-assurance. Sadly, *Left Review* had ceased publication by the following autumn when newsreels recorded his triumphant arrival at Heston aerodrome fresh from discussions with Herr Hitler and waving another piece of paper.

To James Boswell, New Zealand-born and unimpressed by the way things were going in the Mother Country, this cod statesman was representative of bad government in all its posturing absurdity. Where James Fitton, his colleague on *Left Review*, made Chamberlain 'Chambermaid', an idiotic Mrs Mop off to clean the WC with a bucketful of 'Peace', Boswell drew him dishevelled: the seedy con-artist always insisting – in collusion with fat-headed Military and City types – that, in ever-worsening circumstances, he most certainly knew best.

Left Review had a small circulation and, it so happened, folded immediately after *Design for Dying* appeared, but for Boswell, a contributor throughout its four years, the magazine was a prime spot for graphic skewerings. He and Fitton, together with James Holland, became the magazine's 'Three Jameses', celebrated for their herd of prize stereotypes. These were related, clearly, to the grotesques created by George Grosz in Weimar, Germany, a decade before but anglicised, naturally. Besides Chamberlain – so keenly ghastly – and his grasping cronies there were middling-dim men-in-the-street such as those who, accompanied by their ladyfolk, enter the New Burlington Galleries in the summer of 1936 to view the *International Surrealist Exhibition*. Hitting out in two directions at once Boswell mocked both them (such suits, such neat teeth, such expressions of baffled deference) and the silly rhetoric of Herbert Read's catalogue introduction, a quote from which he pasted across his drawing: 'Do not judge

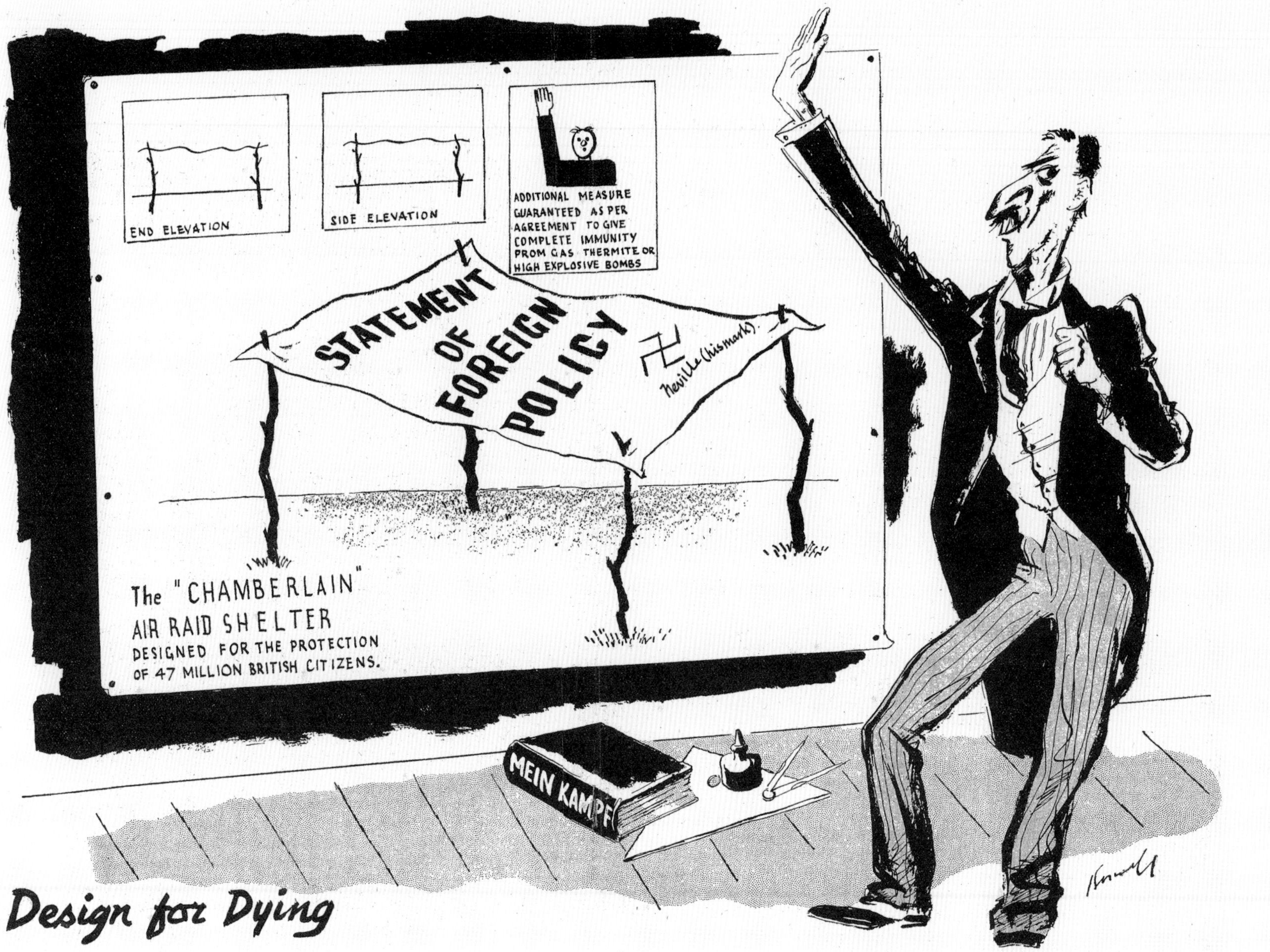

Design for Dying

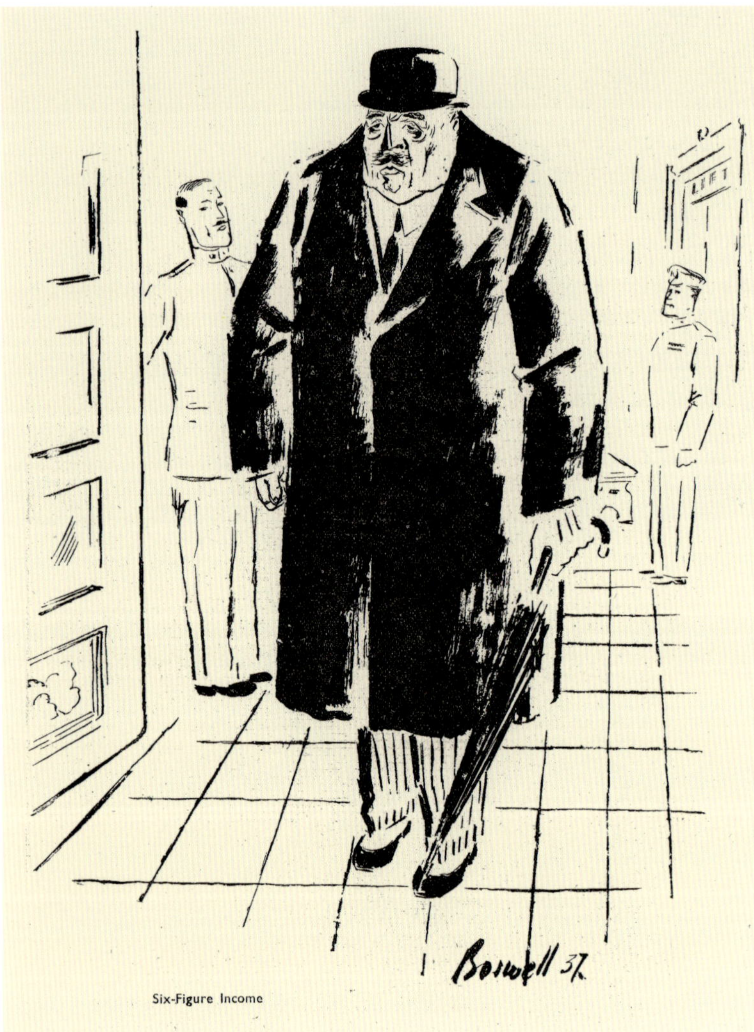

Six-Figure Income

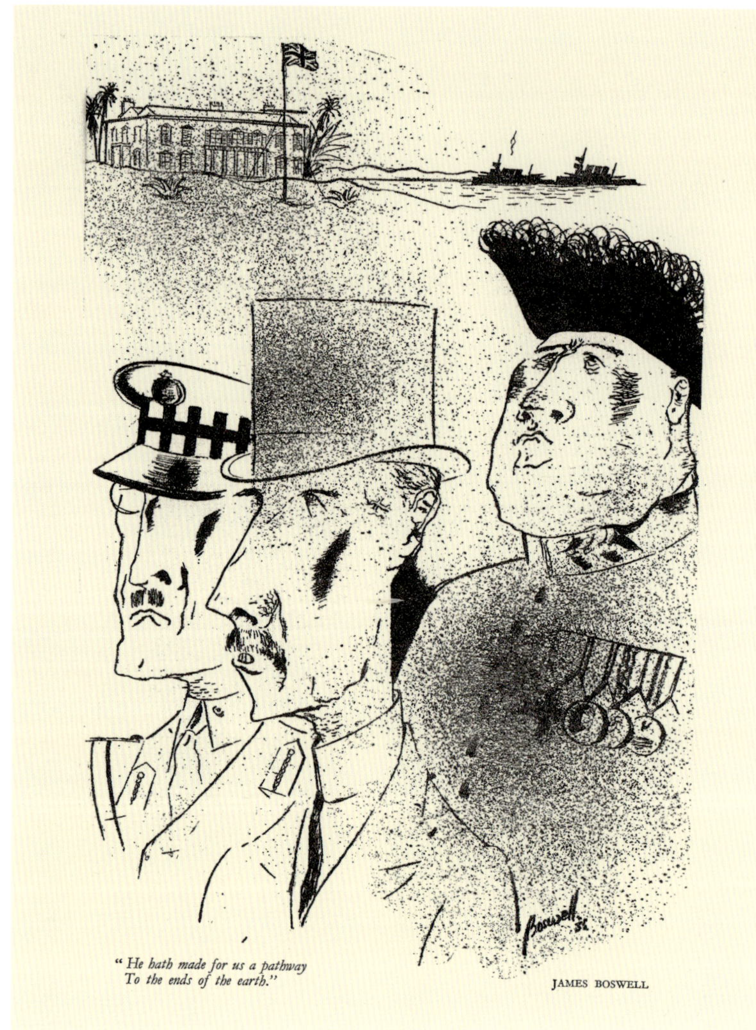

" He hath made for us a pathway
To the ends of the earth."

JAMES BOSWELL

Chapter opener **Design for Dying**

Far left **Six Figure Income**

Left **A Pathway to the Ends of the Earth**

this movement kindly. It is not just another amusing stunt. It is defiant – the desperate act of men too profoundly convinced of the rottenness of our civilisation to want to save a shred of its respectability.'

Boswell on rottenness was in another league from Read, the quintessential Hampstead intellectual. To him, any villain was easy game and, as a member of the Artists' International Association, he felt that Surrealism really wasn't desperate enough to be profoundly convincing. At this stage he believed that art was weaponry in the war of the ideologies and that the sharpest art was propaganda.

Montagu Slater the writer, and contributor to *Left Review*, first met Boswell in 1929. He was impressed by his attitude, 'a colonial and proud of it, something quite unusual in a colonial

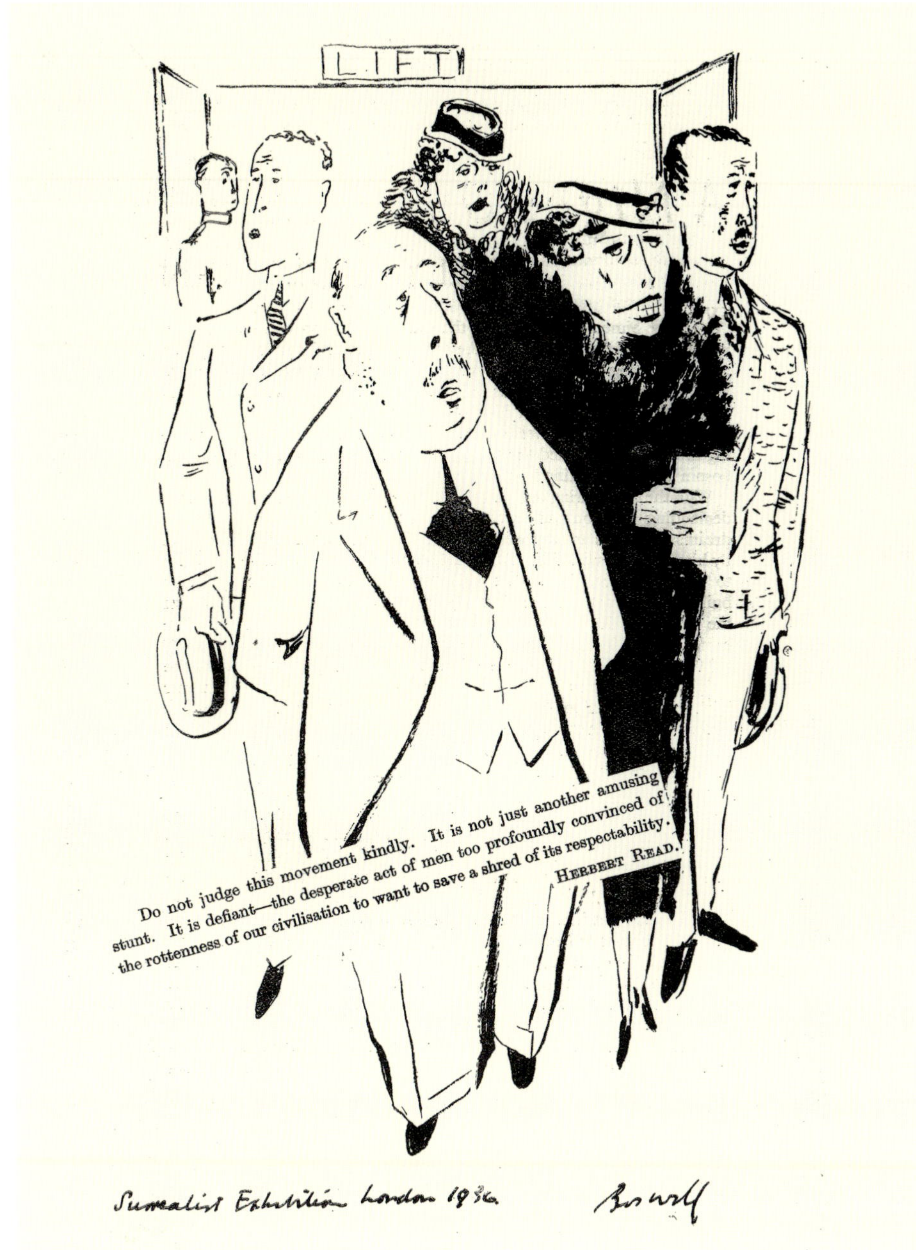

Surrealist Exhibition, London 1936. *Left Review*

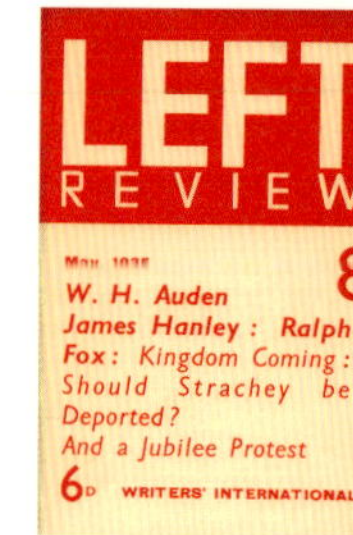

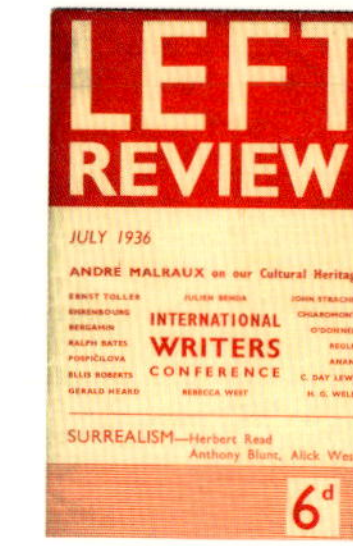

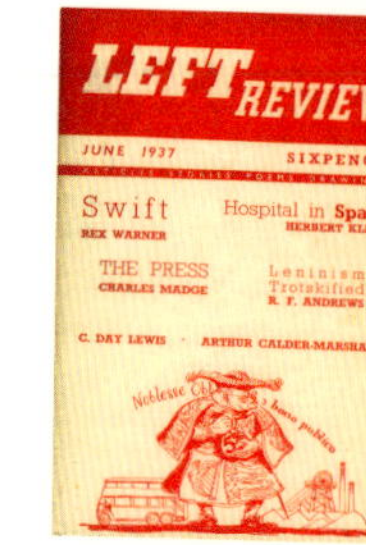

art student.' Boswell had been brought up in a bookish family (his father was a teacher) and had come to England when he was nineteen. Having just left the Royal College of Art, thrown out for the second time, he was keen for a cause to adhere to. Slater remembered playing chess with him. 'For days on end with all-too-human chess men drawn – by Boswell – on cardboard, making fantastic prophecies, many since fulfilled, about the progress of world crisis, and talking about the fall of the Roman Empire and how Roman art and literature were refreshed by the colonials like Martial in the last phase.'

In 1933, a year after he joined the Communist Party, Boswell became a founder member of the Artists' International Association, (later the AIA), a group of mainly young artists enthused with political evangelism and hopes of exhibiting accordingly. 'We only had the crudest ideas about Art and Marxism and we nearly all felt the need to do something practical,' he later wrote. 'It did an excellent job at the time.' In Germany, the Nazis had come to power. Events to agitate about kept the AIA busy. There were banners to paint for the support of hunger marchers, for 'Artists against Fascism and War' and 'Aid for Spain'.

'The time has now come when we can expect art to be something more positive,' the then progressive critic Anthony Blunt wrote in *Left Review*, July 1936. 'A new art is beginning to arise, the product of the proletariat, which is again performing its true function, that of propaganda.' More exhortation than objective statement, his words were echoed in W H Auden's mock-epic poem in *Letters from Iceland* of 1937, a teasing mention of a meeting in a Lyons Corner House – typical AIA – where, he said, they 'scrapped Significant Form and voted for Subject.'

From 1936 Boswell had a day job as graphic designer and art director of the Asiatic Petroleum Company (subsequently Shell) Publicity Department; in his spare time, besides drawing for *Left Review*, he did cartoons for the *Daily Mirror* and the *Daily Worker* using the name Buchan and developing a manner attuned to the style of another New Zealander, David Low. He had a further pseudonym: Boz. Same as the young Dickens, whose *Sketches by Boz* were illustrated by George Cruikshank in the Camden Town street-wise detail that Boswell himself now aspired to. Boswell's London was also the Thirties London of Patrick Hamilton and George Orwell, a London of woebegone tea rooms and sinister bed-sits. Subject was all. Monty Slater remarked that

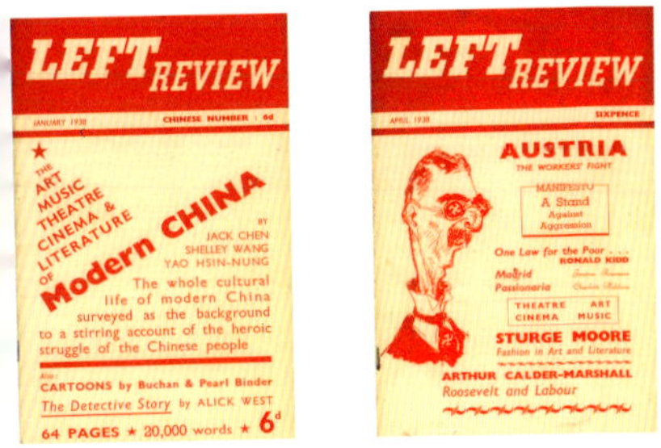

Left Review
1935–38

around then he and Boswell, conscious of being 'still from the outside looking in…were busy in the streets of Kentish Town getting to know people.' If the City was the Heart of Empire, Kentish Town and Soho were two of its lousiest extremities. Here lives were led at a shilling a day for a wretched couple, squaddie and wife, expecting twins by the look of it. Grim prospects too in the outermost spec-built suburbs where little more than a shilling a day could secure one of the dismal Desirable Residence, the sort featured in Orwell's *Keep the Aspidistra Flying*.

By May Day 1938, there was a degree of mutuality between radical factions. A mass demonstration streamed along the Thames embankment towards Whitehall with an AIA banner proclaiming Unity and a Surrealist loudspeaker van blaring the *Internationale*, accompanied by leading Surrealists in Neville Chamberlain masks.

A year later, outside the gents on the corner of the St Giles's Circus and Charing Cross Road, a man in a bowler with a bow-tie moustache hisses a proposition and the streetwalker, a regular client of the Hygenic Stores, we may suppose, feigns gentility. Boswell – Boz – is hardly on friendly terms with these stock figures but, having also done a series of drawings in Le Sphinx, the celebrated Paris brothel, he feels confident that he can close in on life in the raw. The traffic light has gone red; the Chamberlain era will soon be over; the drawing technique is now assured.

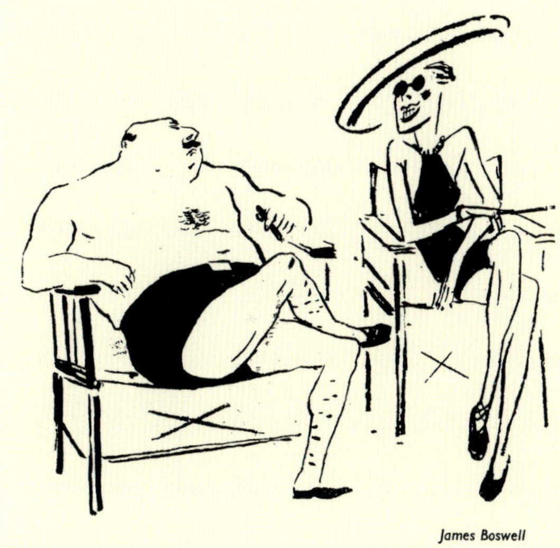

LET'S GET SENSIBLE, WHAT?

My dear old chap, it's just a farce
To talk about the working clarce,
They don't exist, or if they do
They're better off than me and you.
Of course we've got some unemployed
But that's a thing we can't avoid,
And what is more, it doesn't stop
The Man who Means to Get on Top.
The chaps with guts, old fellow, guts
Jump to White Houses from Log Huts.
My dear old boy, it's plain enough
That Socialism's so much blough.

MILES TOMALIN

Left Review, July 1937

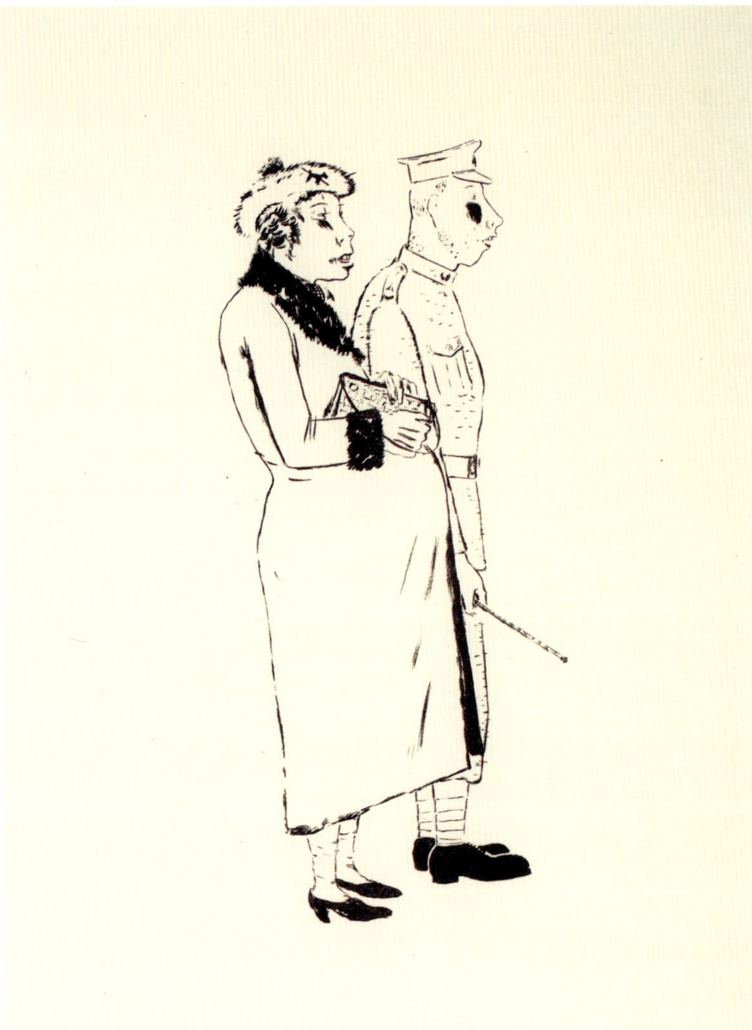

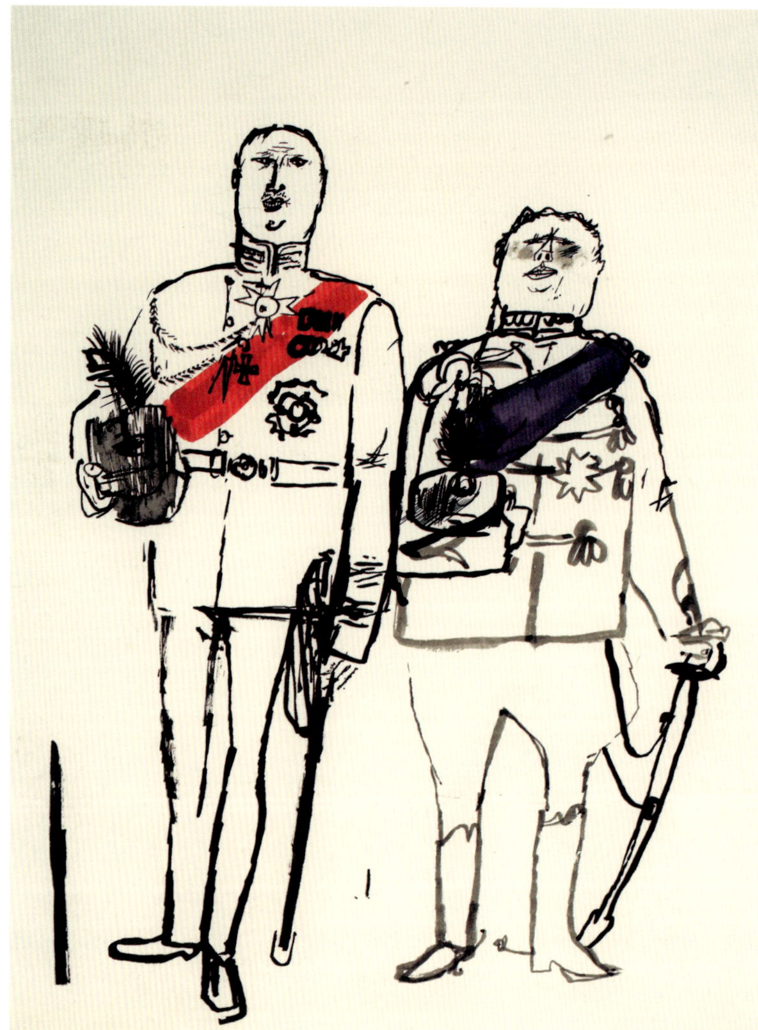

Far left **A Shilling A Day**
Left **The Two Generals**

Opposite **Daily Worker 1938**

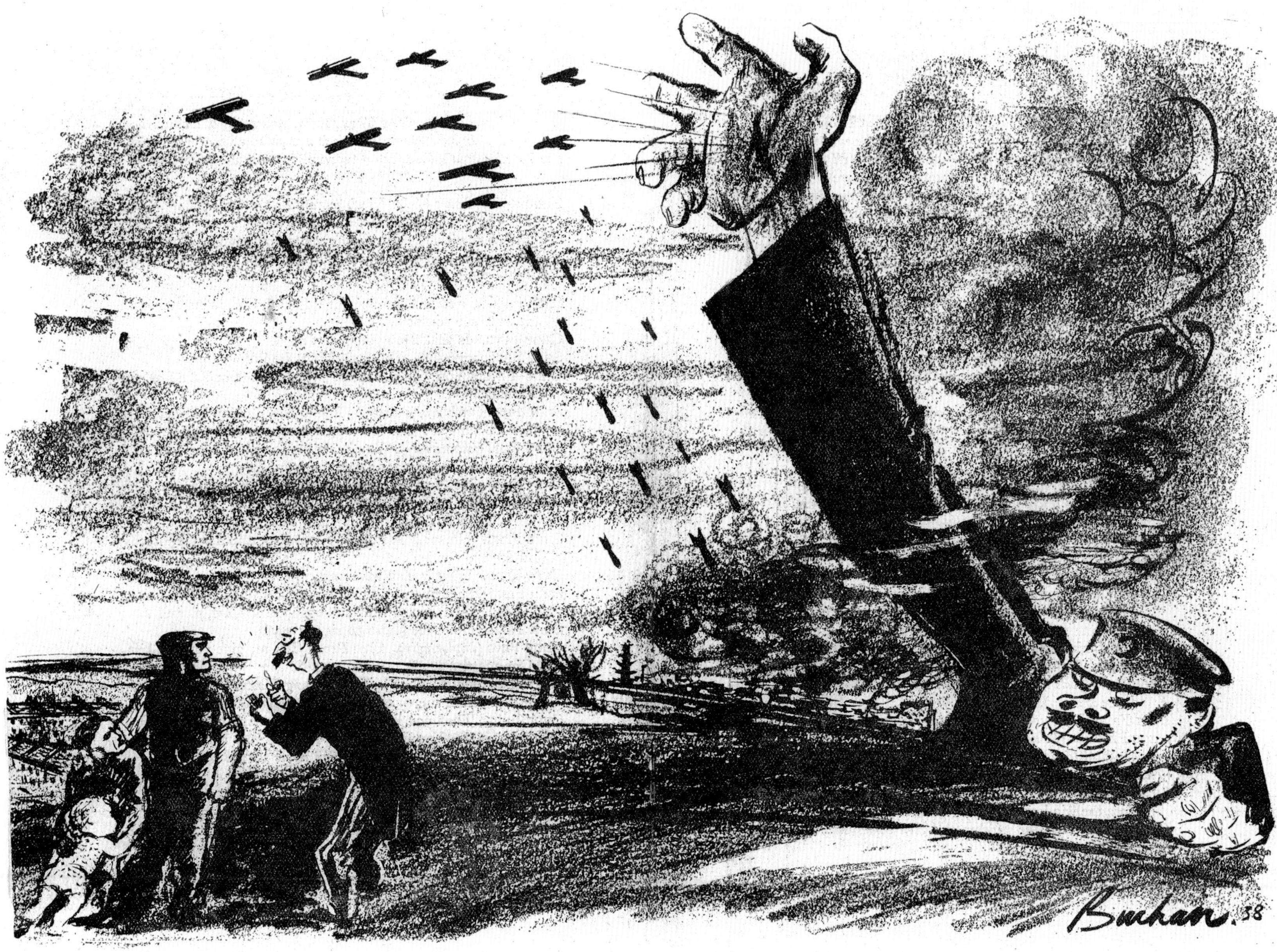
Buchan. 38

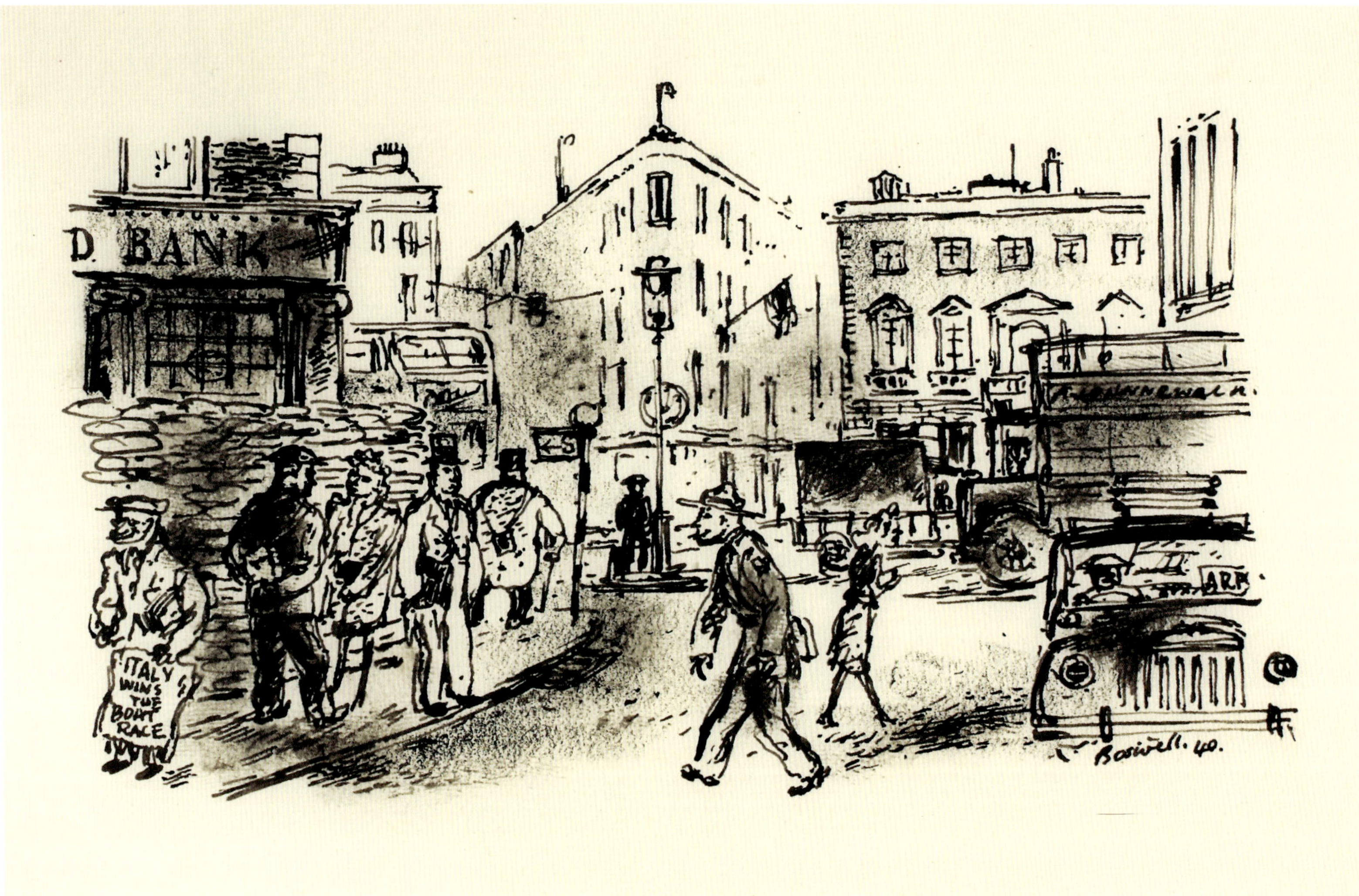

Left **Wartime Street Scene**

Opposite **Cambridge Circus**

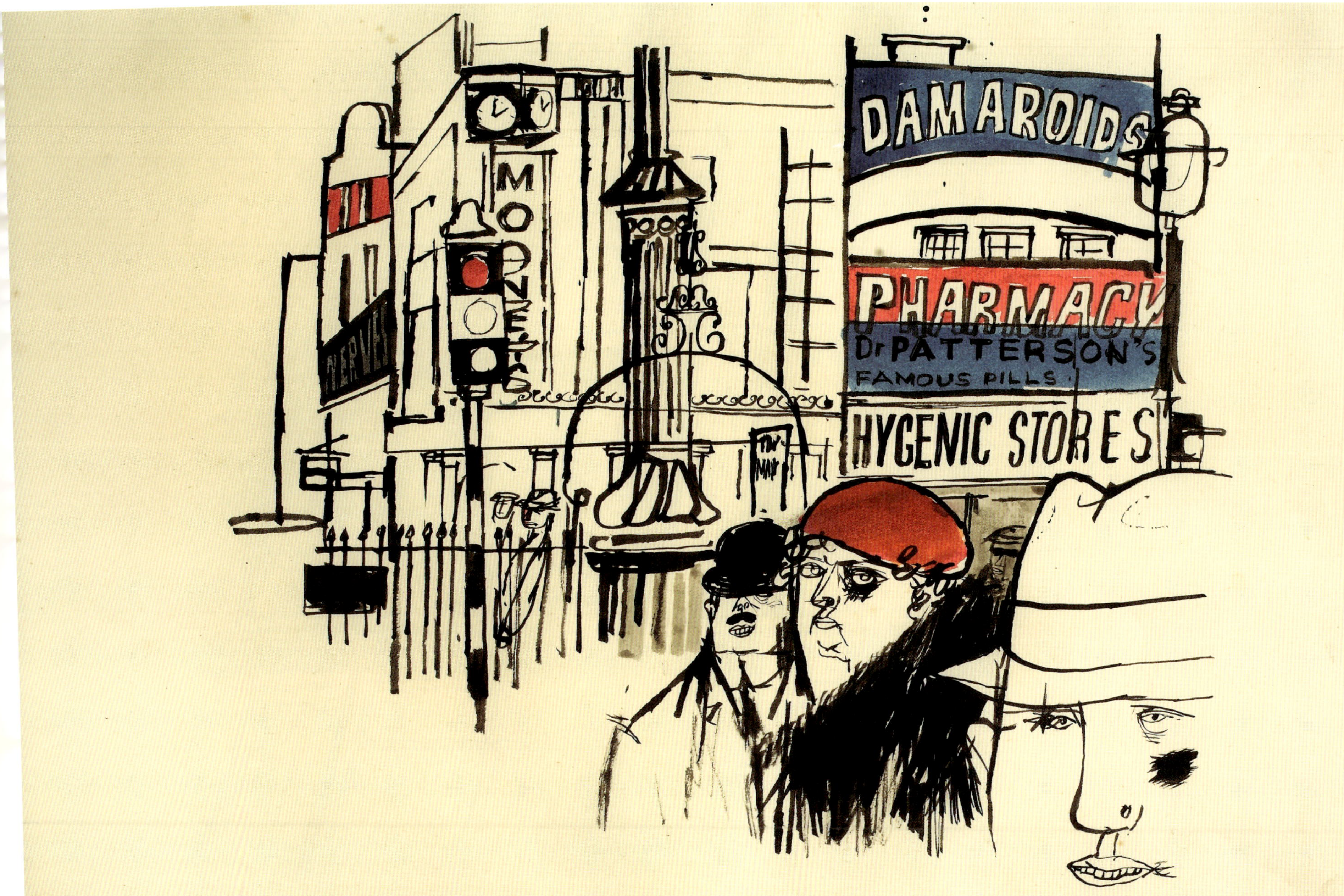
DAMAROIDS
PHARMACY
Dr PATTERSON'S
FAMOUS PILLS
HYGENIC STORES

SCOTLAND 1940

***Everyman Prints*, published by the AIA at a shilling each in black and white, one and six for those printed in two colours, were launched in January 1940. Opening a display of them – several by Boswell – at Picture Hire Ltd, the Director of the National Gallery, Kenneth Clark, remarked that the modest price 'has enabled artists to become a little less high hat in their choice of subjects.'**

Six months earlier, shortly before the German invasion of Poland, Clark had taken steps to ensure that certain artists should be employed to make a visual record of the imminent war. His aim was 'simply to keep artists at work on any pretext and, as far as possible, to prevent them from being killed.' Those he especially favoured, such as Henry Moore, John Piper and Graham Sutherland, were eminent high hat artists but accommodatingly so.

During 1940, Orwell observed in his essay *The English People*, 'class feeling slipped into the background, only reappearing when the immediate danger had passed.' Come the Blitz and the front line became anywhere between Kentish Town and Woolwich and, given the urgency to record incidents and consequences, distinctions between illustrators and easel artists lapsed to some degree. Clark's War Artists' Advisory Committee found that those who responded most competently, not to say impressively, to their demands were those trained to draw and design to order, notably Edward Bawden, Edward Ardizzone, Eric Ravilious and Anthony Gross. The choice of subjects was generally agreed between artist and committee with an emphasis on straight reportage involving human interest. Eric Kennington did brawny pastel portraits of typical heroes and service chiefs; Piper was directed to bombed churches, aggravated examples of what, in pre-war life he had identified as 'pleasing decay'. For others, less well placed, there was the possibility of occasional commissions or purchases. For the rest, Boswell among them, (whose membership of the Communist Party was a disqualification, presumably, for Official War Artist work), the war offered few, if any, professional opportunities.

Boswell's work at Shell dwindled. Enlisted in ARP (Air Raid Precautions) he drew the new normality, sandbags fortifying a bank branch, tidied rubble, a smashed (and redundant anyway) car lot, barrage balloons dotting the sky and an ATS ingenue venturing onto a parade ground where women in uniform stride purposefully by. Through into the autumn of 1940 and the start of the Blitz he

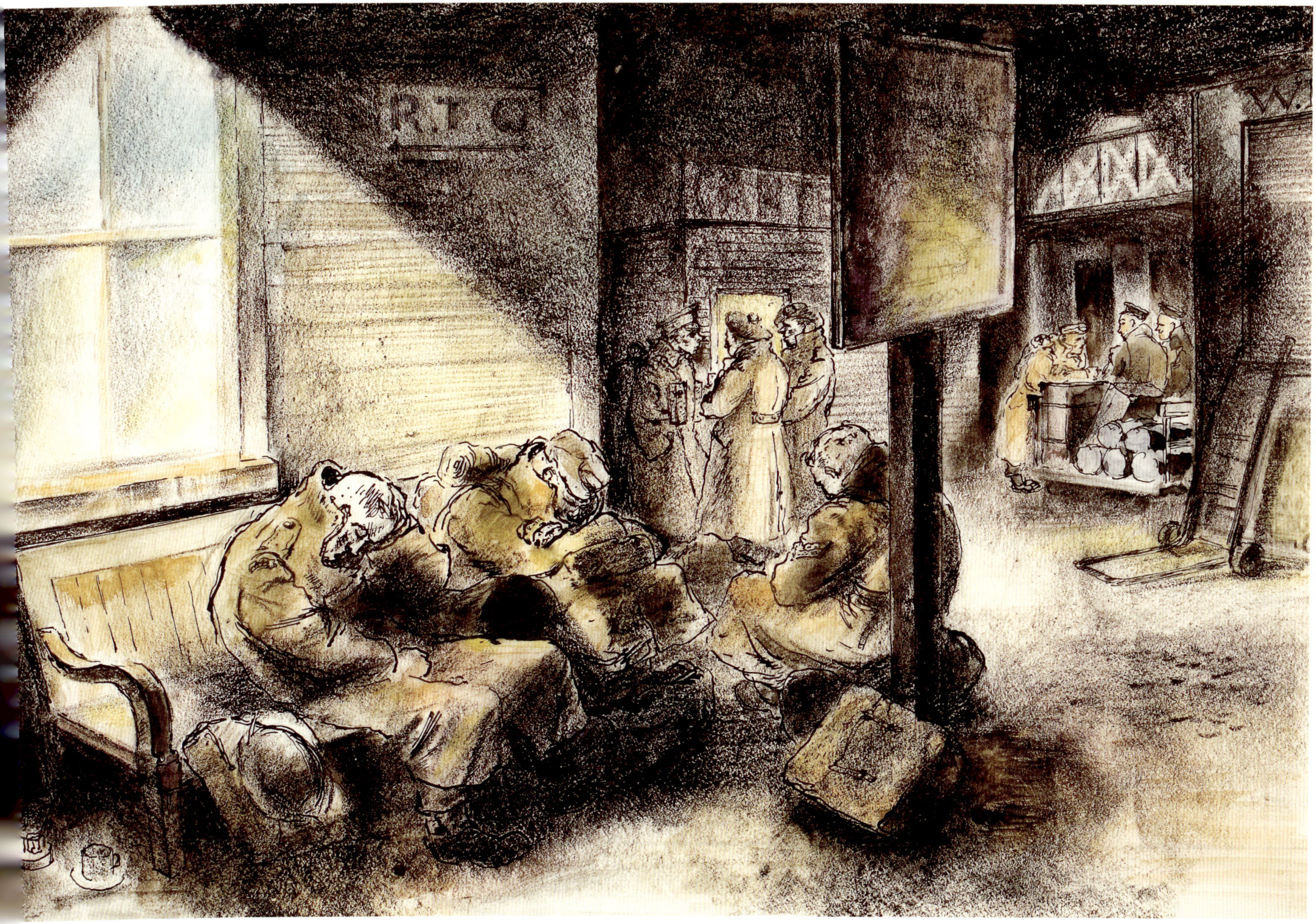
R.T.O

saw streets baited with touts on every night club door and troops from all over, dazed New Zealanders accosted by peroxide blondes in the Charing Cross Road.

The first issue of a new magazine, *Our Time*, February 1941, carried a frontispiece by 'Buchan' of a woman and a child, her grandchild possibly (hard to tell the age of the war-weary); the drawing accompanies an account of *Blitz Nights and Days* by Randall Swingler: 'People go below ground at sunfall as resignedly as if they were going to lay themselves down for ever in their graves.' Overleaf a bedraggled mother with a pram, boy with bundle and dad with Timothy White's carrier bag, trudge along a flattened street, off to try their luck with the Billeting Officer. Boswell saw new habits established, prams and push chairs left outside tube entrances while their owners descended to shelter. What he noticed, fact rather than arty generalisation, amounted, he said, to 'a kind of graphic social realism.' In Holborn tube station (one of the deepest) he drew families settling down, each blanket a territory, same as on a Bank Holiday beach. Unlike Henry Moore's larvae-like underground sleepers, Boswell's people look individual.

Boswell was called up in early 1941 as a private in the Royal Army Medical Corps posted to No.1 Depot, Church Crookham, near Aldershot. *The Draft* shows others like him cramming the pavement outside a Southern Railways station. A corporal is about to bawl them onto lorries and despatch them to base. Initiation was a shock. Class-conscious army strictures disgusted him but he was equally disconcerted by the loutishness it helped provoke.

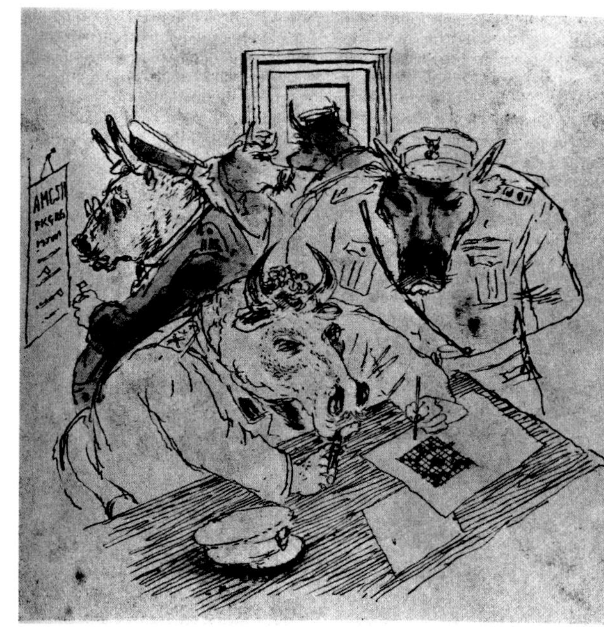

Chapter opener **'Waiting'**

Above ***Our Time*** **1942**

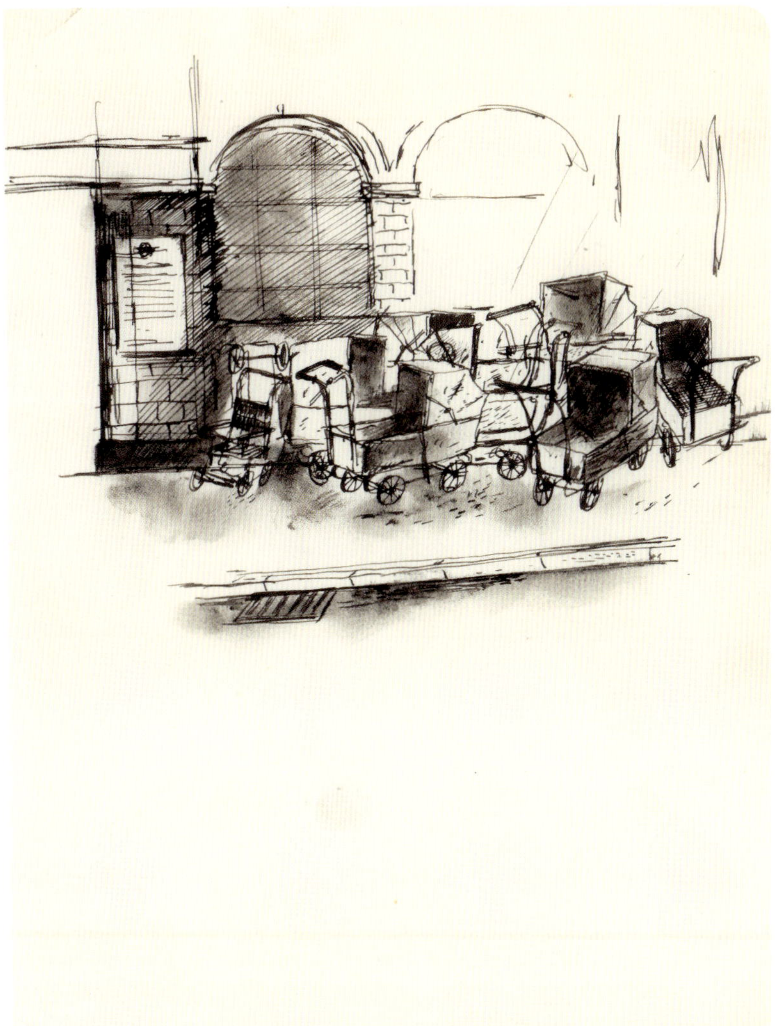

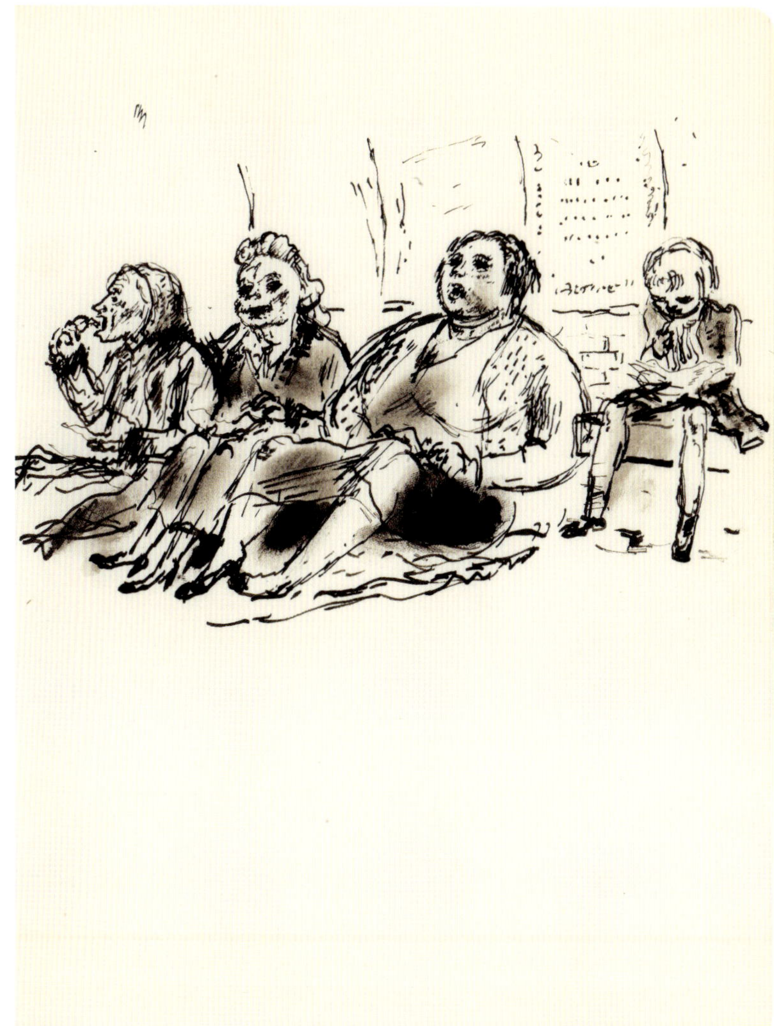

Right **Prams outside the Tube Shelter**

Far right **Tube Shelter, London**

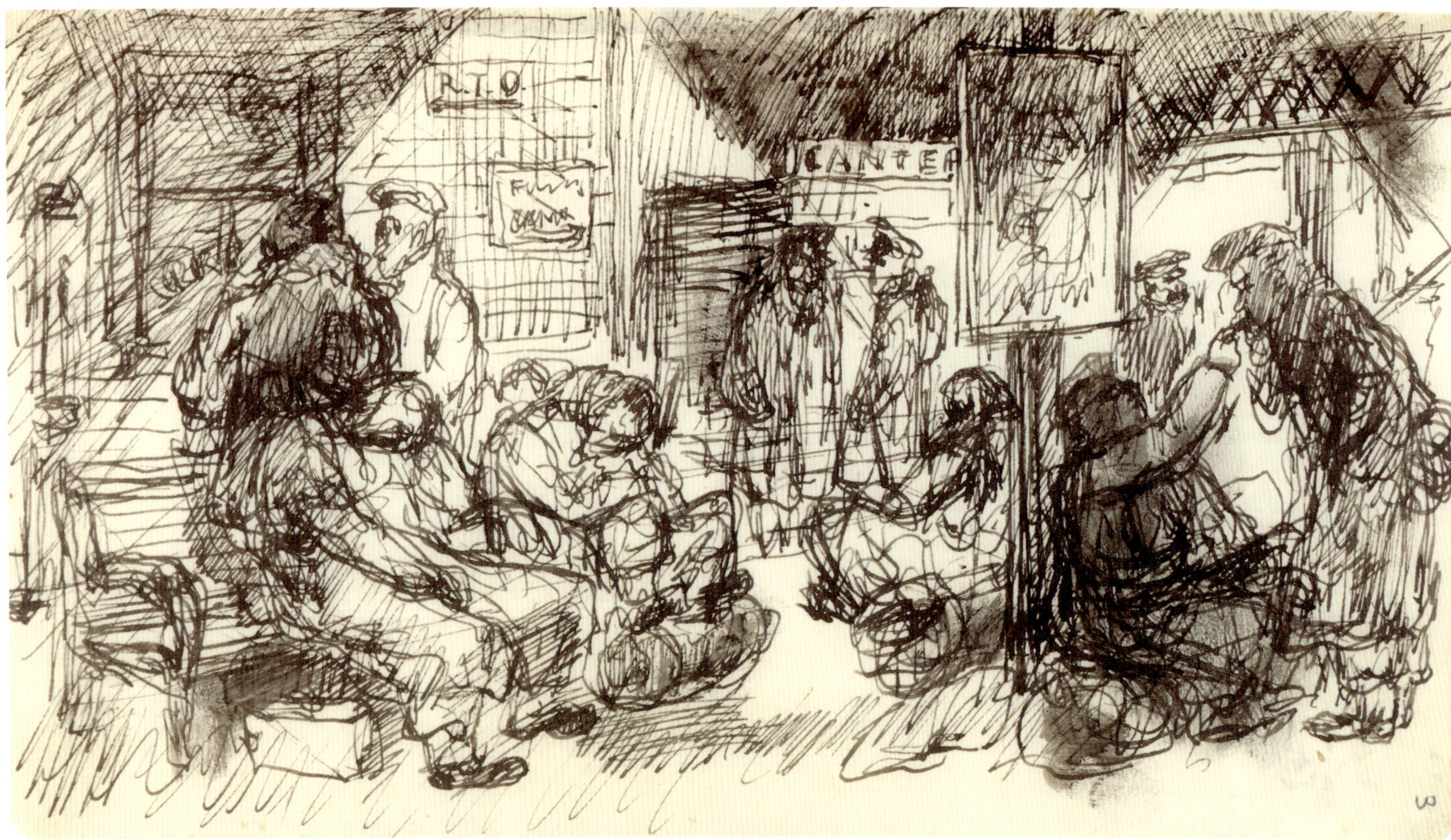

Right **Sketch for Waiting**

Opposite **Waiting, Crewe 2am**

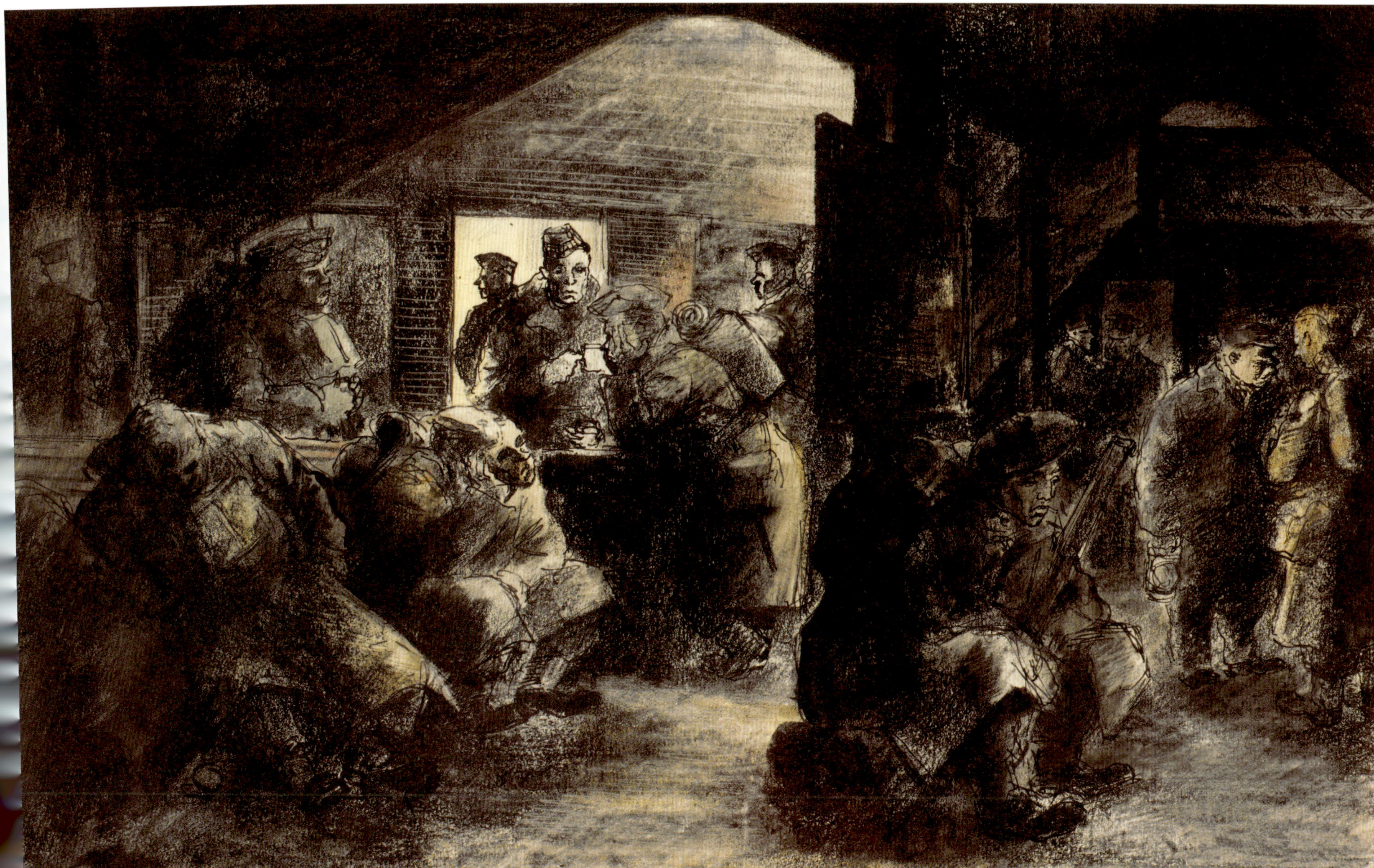

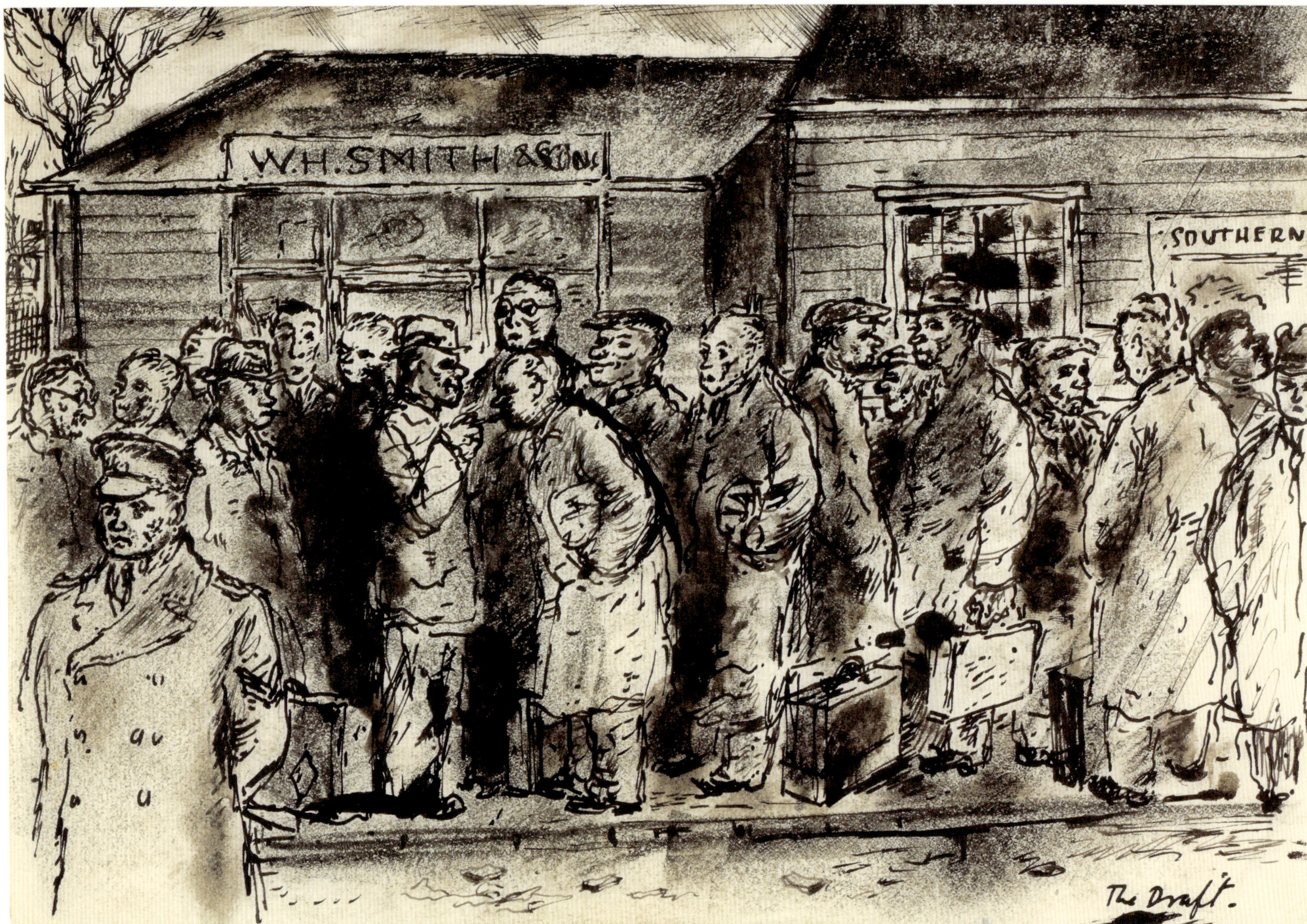

The Draft, *Lilliput* September 1942

After radiography training at the army hospital on Millbank he was posted to a camp near Peebles in the Scottish Lowlands. This was a setting for training and manoeuvres and day to day time-wasting. The threat of invasion had receded; the war was now normality.

Crewe, 2am: darkened platform, no train in sight, and slumped figures dead to the world. In the Reinforcement Camp near Peebles something of a frontier town atmosphere prevailed. Boswell drew stores being unloaded, trees felled, fatigue parties slithering in the rain, outbreaks of football, boredom and more boredom interspersed with the snip of the barber's scissors and the attractions of Peebles High Street, shelter in the tea room and the High Class Drapery Store, shop doorways for clinches, a knee trembler, possibly, and unlucky consequences, maybe, followed by enrolment as one of the 'College Boys' on the VD ward.

On hand to watch Medical Officers discussing a radiograph, Boswell saw the pointing finger in the darkened room, murmurings and nods of agreement. Sick parade: trousers dropped, lungs listened to, a tattoo of a topless girl gracing a skinny arm. He drew ambulance drivers chatted up by officers (only better class women had driving licences, they assumed) and the Officers' Mess with its chandelier and properly-appointed bar where quiet, banal, conversations were sustained. Back in the barracks there were long afternoons and evenings when colleagues were happy to pose for him, one with his accordion, another writing home and another – Eric – just sitting there.

In September 1941 the AIA displayed war pictures in the ticket hall of Charing Cross Underground. Boswell was prominent among those taking part – they included Clifford Rowe, Julian Trevelyan, Percy Horton and Carel Weight – and the subjects ranged across the home front, from *Art Lesson in a School Shelter* to *Reproachful Cat*. Holding the exhibition in an underground station was 'in accordance with the AIA policy of popularising art', Horton of the Royal College of Art explained. 'Is it enough to make a slight perfunctory sketch of a bombed building or to paint a peaceful landscape with an unobtrusive barrage-balloon somewhere in the sky? Or does the war demand more than this?' He recommended intensity of expression. 'James Boswell's racy commentaries on life in the army', he wrote 'are in the English tradition which goes back through Rowlandson to Hogarth'.

His Depot Barber Shop, *Fatigue Party* and *The Night the Sergeant Copped It*, were subjects worked up over the previous nine months.

In March 1942 *Our Time* published an article by Montagu Slater, 'Private James Boswell', saluting 'the Good Soldier Boswell' for his account of army life so far: 'three fat notebooks crammed with mere God's plenty.' He reproduced *Nursing Orderlies at Play* (chairs smashed, a woman screaming) and, predictably perhaps, the private's view of the officer class: bulls the lot of them, arrogant, short-sighted, obtuse.

Like creatures from nursery rhymes, four bull generals encounter high seas on a cake of Blanco. Others ride piggy-back on stumbling foot soldiers. A telescope is jabbed into a wheezing squaddie's chest. These caricatures are barrack room harangue, men as beasts

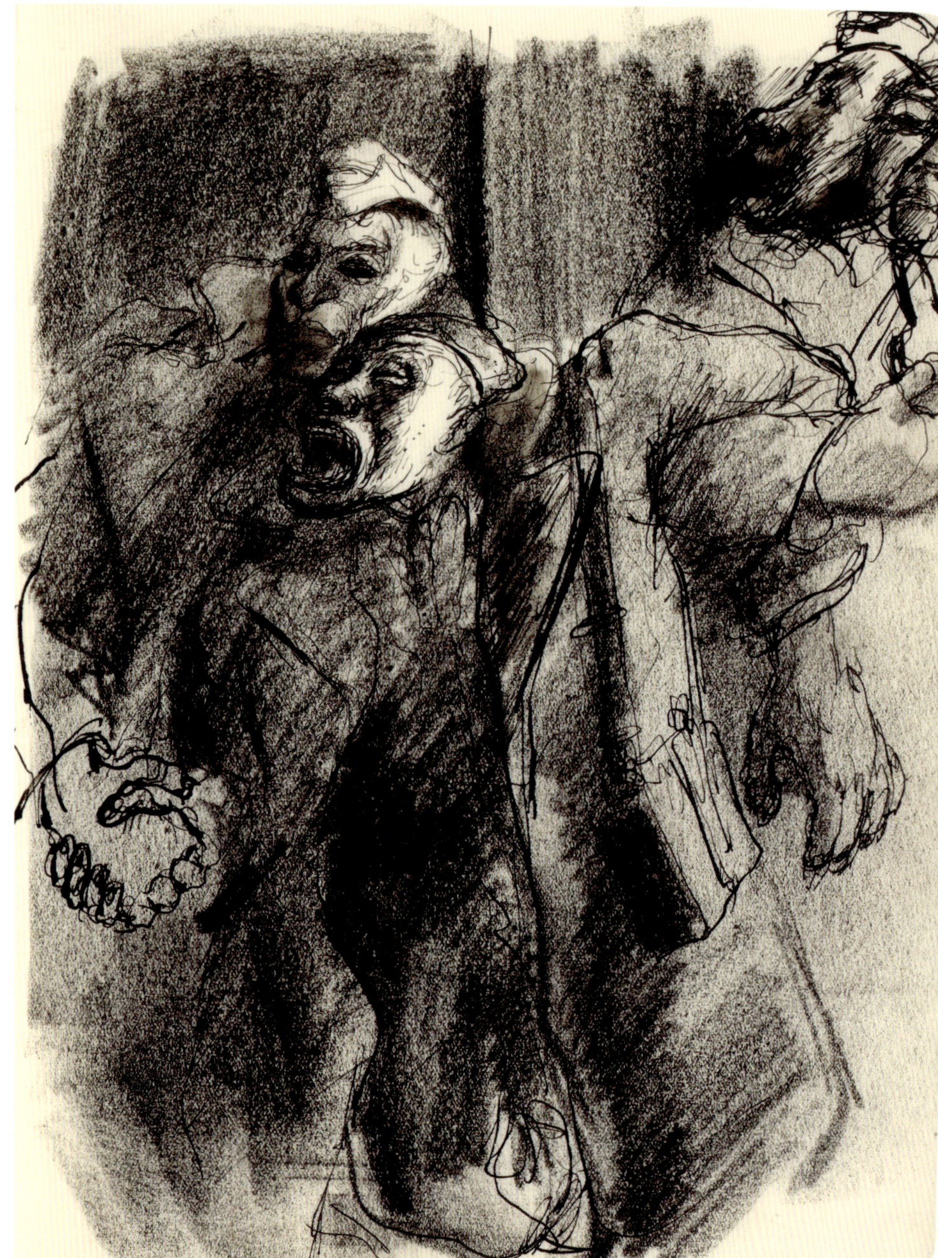

Right **Night Out**

Opposite
Right **Women at War**
Far Right **The Blitz**

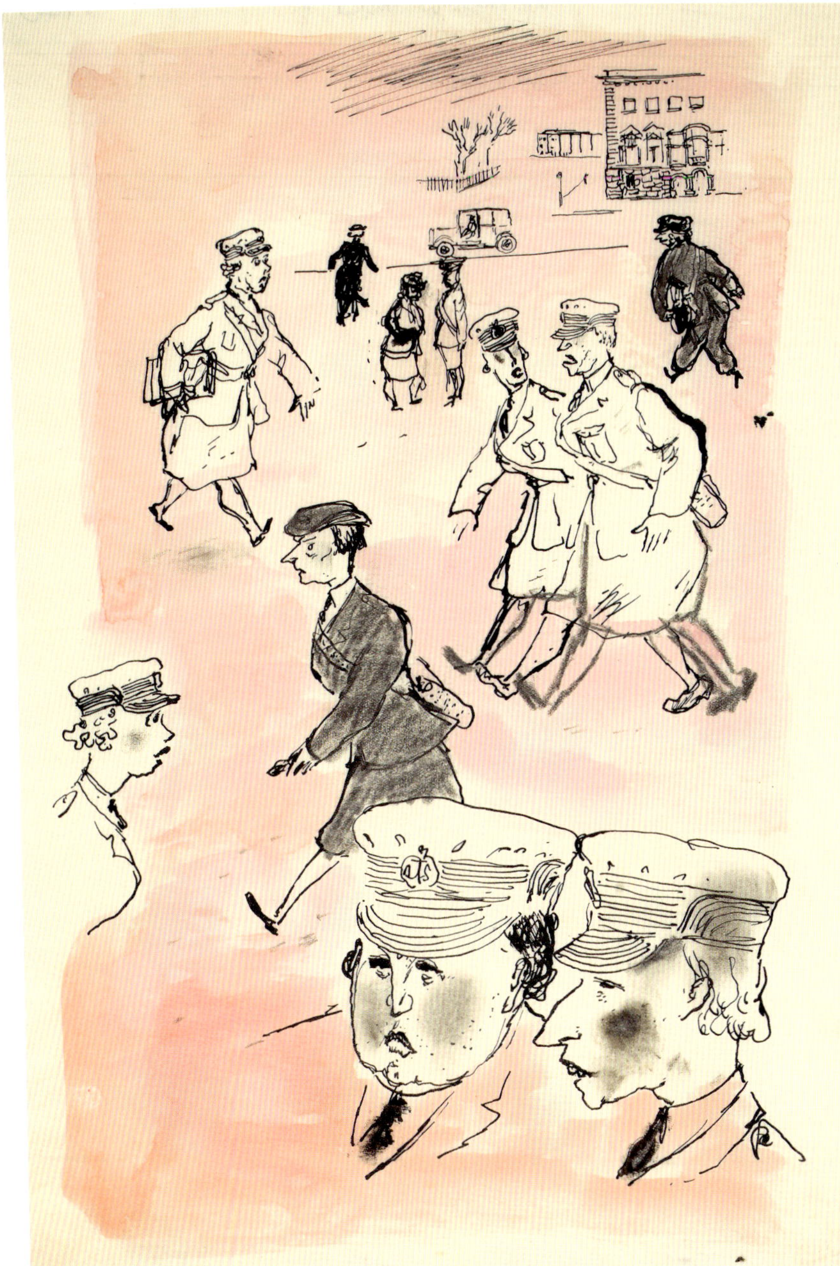

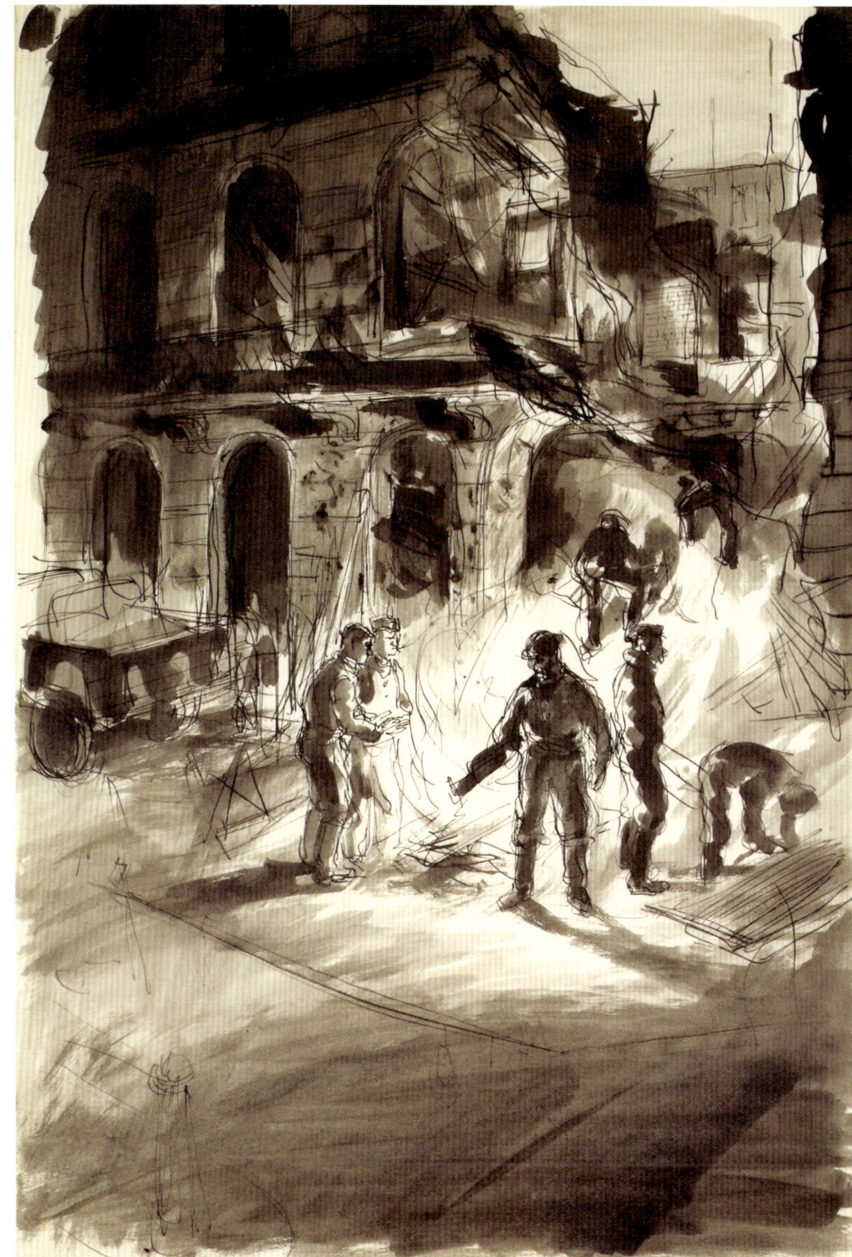

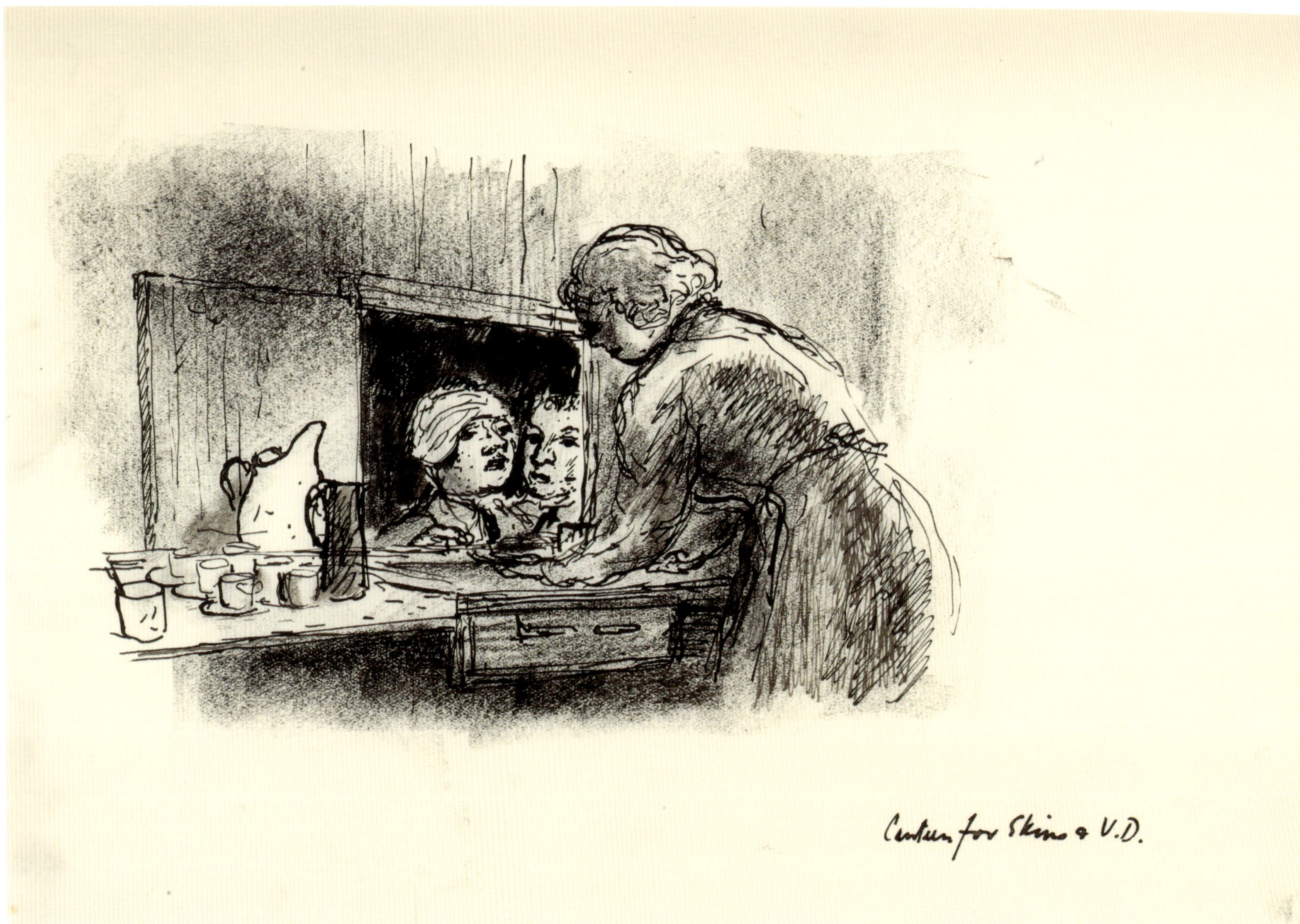

Centre for Skins and VD

– anticipating the livestock of *Animal Farm* by a couple of years – conducting a war in which bumf issues from top-ranking arses and bull heads confer, fixing the next move on a crossword campaign map.

For Boswell, the Peebles months were a period of acclimatisation to army ways before being posted. Military dictates – chance, not to say fate – determined what subject matter would be arrived at and what could be accomplished. Simultaneously, it so happened, in early 1942, the young ex-art student Sapper Ronald Searle arrived in Malaya, just in time to be caught up in the surrender of Singapore. A prisoner of war for four years, including six months on the Burma Railway, he drew surreptitiously to create evidence and help see himself through, saving scraps of witness that nobody else could provide. Boswell did not experience any such test of stamina or nerve. Like many other conscripts, among them the scene-painter Stanley Haughton and the advertising man Keith Vaughan, he kept a sketchbook account of his military life for no greater purpose than occupying himself, venting feelings and keeping his hand in. Where after Peebles? Russia was now in the war – simplifying issues for Party members – Japan and the United States too. The most likely overseas destination had to be the Middle East or beyond.

Preparing for travel Boswell wrote out a list of requisites: 'Set Brushes. Cap Comforter. Pants, cell short, Holdall complete. Housewife, K.O. suit. Overalls 1 suit, one shirt angora, canvas shoes, socks, towels, pullover, gym kit.' Next thing he was on a troopship. The tedium of weeks at sea going around the Cape of Good Hope then heading north again was not much relieved by drawing. Subject: monotony. *Our Mess Deck*, Section 10, Messing 120, Hammocks 89. No Smoking.

It could have been a posting to Singapore. Instead it was Iraq.

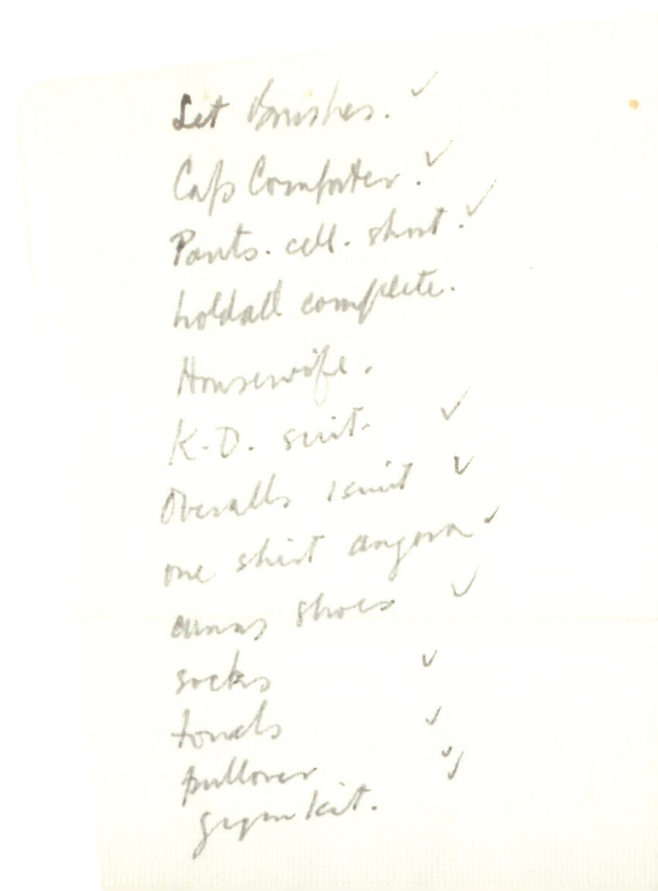
Set Brushes. ✓
Cap Comforter. ✓
Pants. cell. short. ✓
holdall complete.
Housewife.
K.D. suit. ✓
Overalls 1 suit ✓
one shirt angora ✓
canvas shoes ✓
socks ✓
towels ✓
pullover ✓
gym kit.

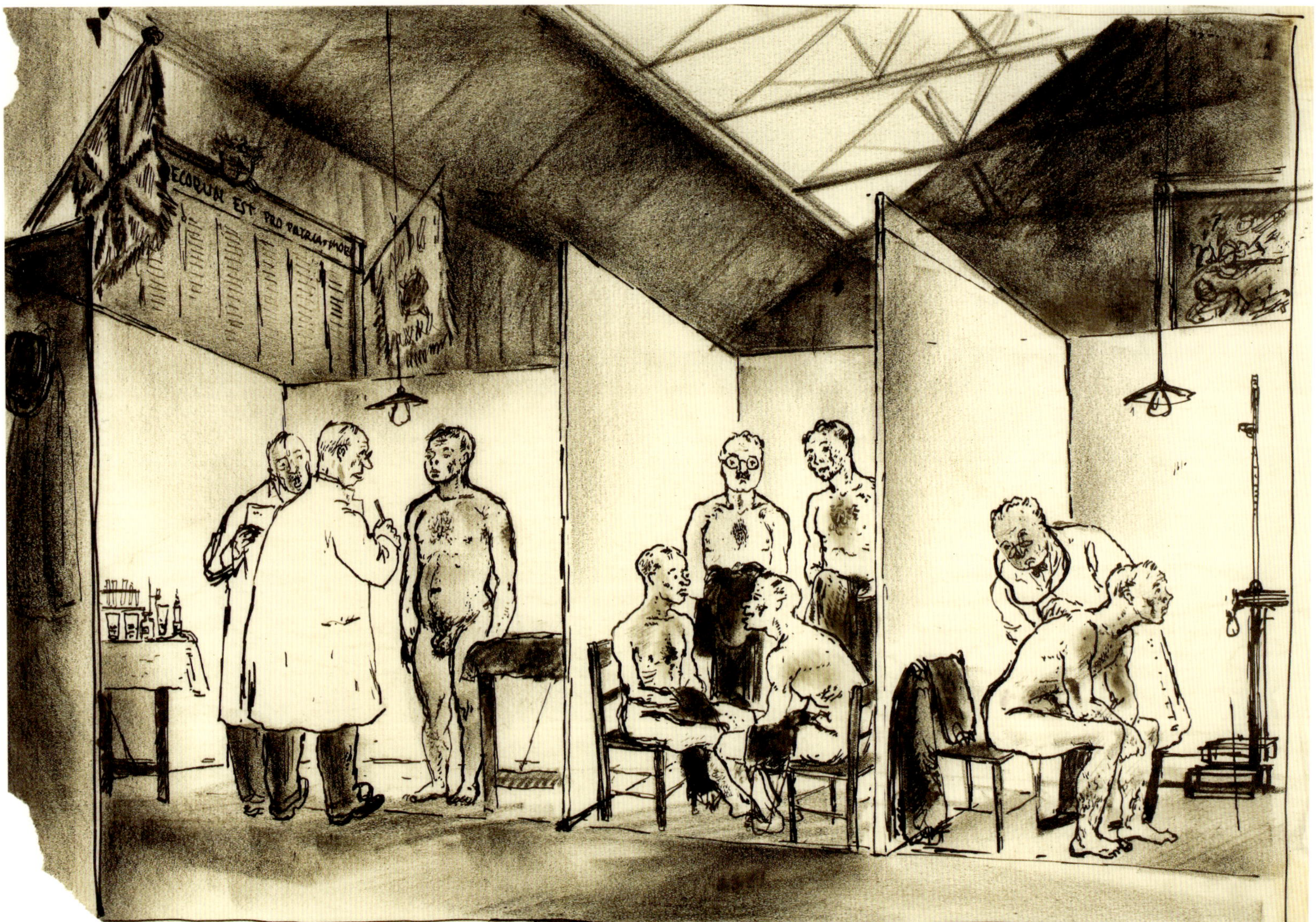

Left **Medical Inspection before Call Up, Drill Hall, Marylebone**

Opposite **London Wall 1940**

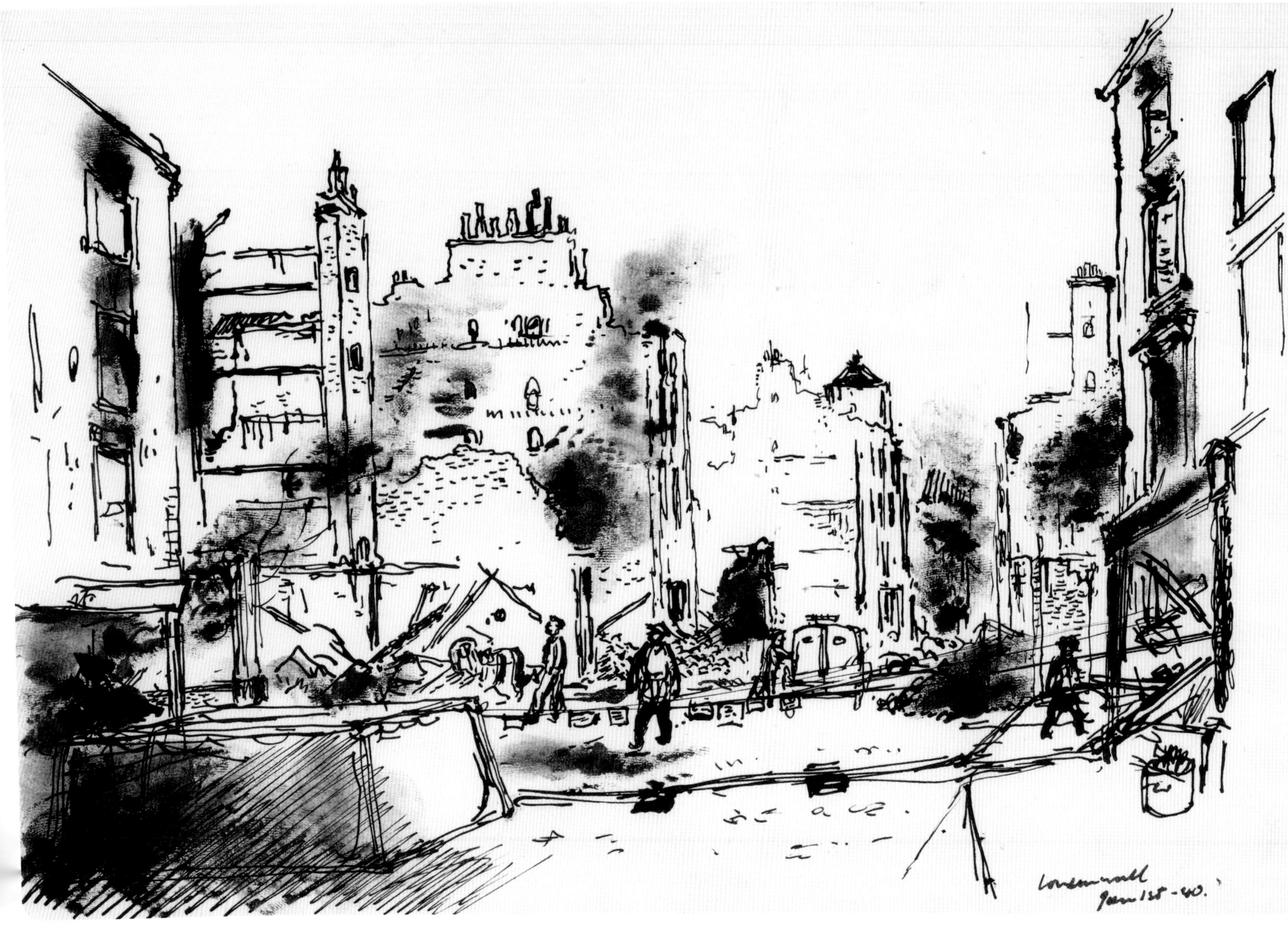
Londonwall
Jan 1st - 40.

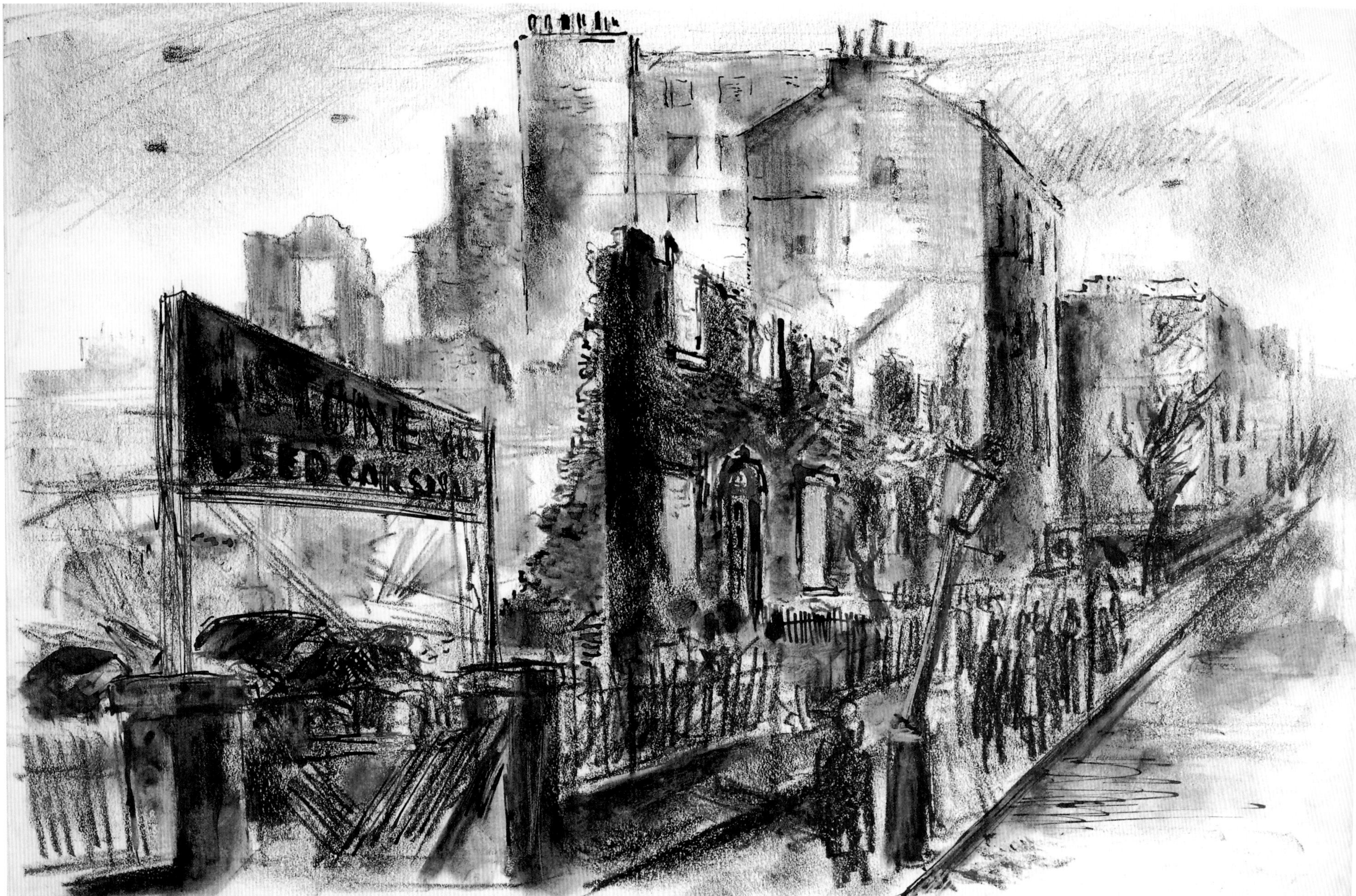

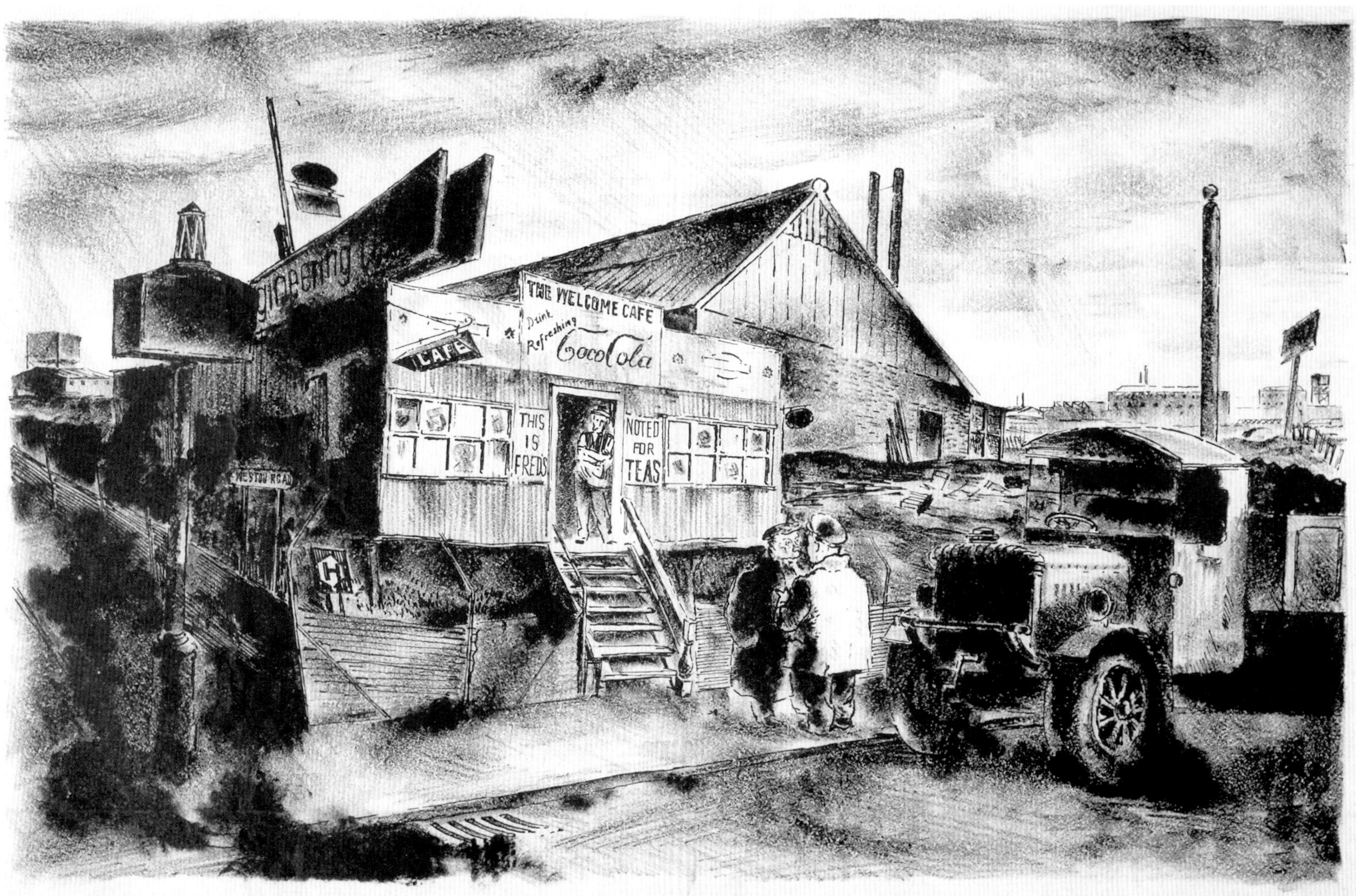

Opposite Bomb Site, London

Right This is Fred's

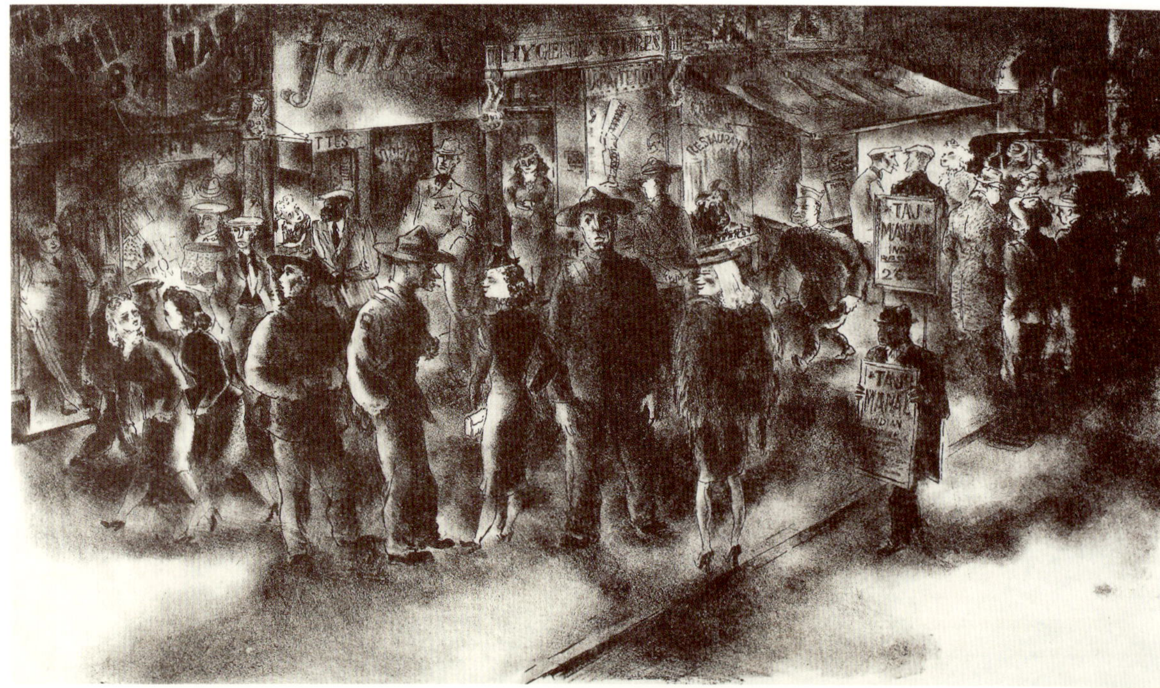

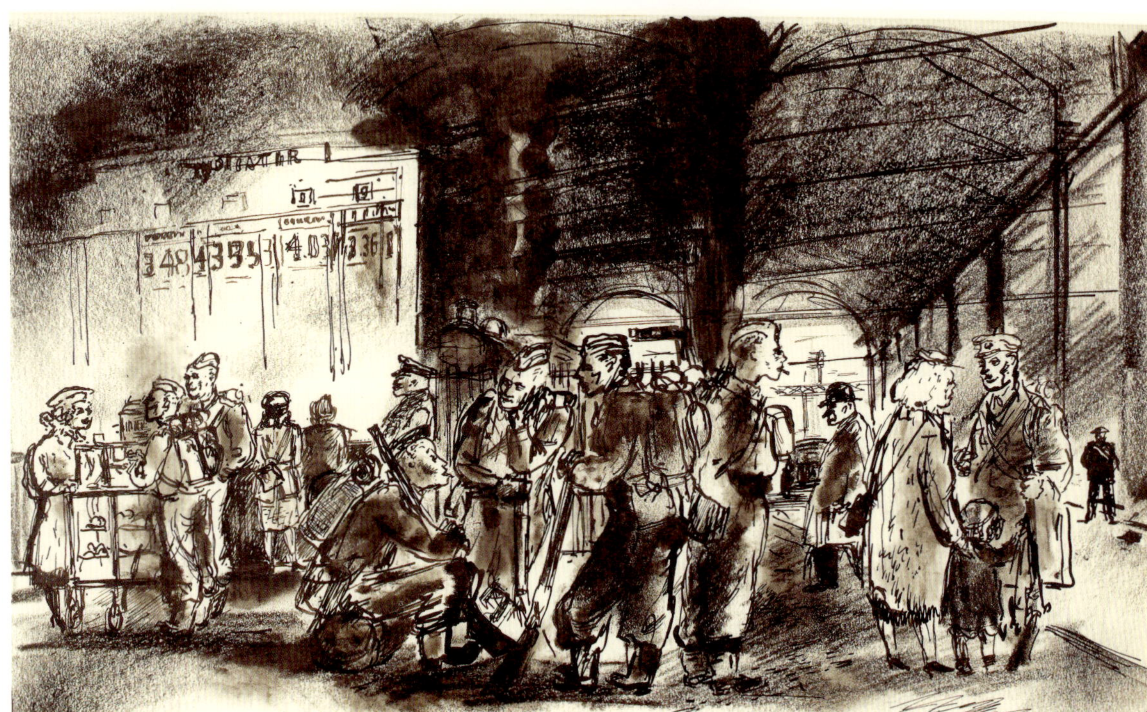

Top **Diggers at Dusk**
Bottom **Waterloo Station**

Opposite **Holborn Underground, London**

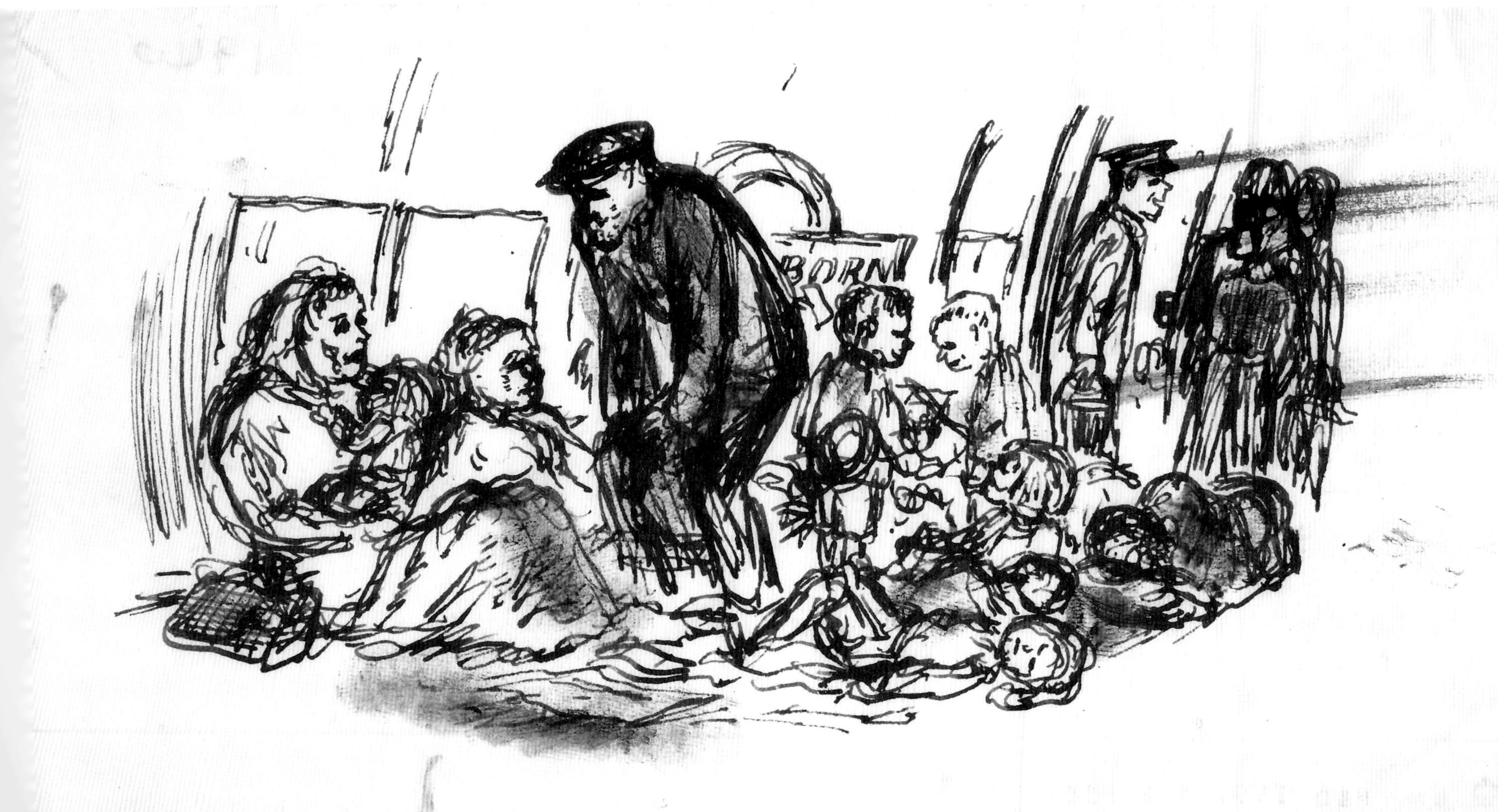
BORN

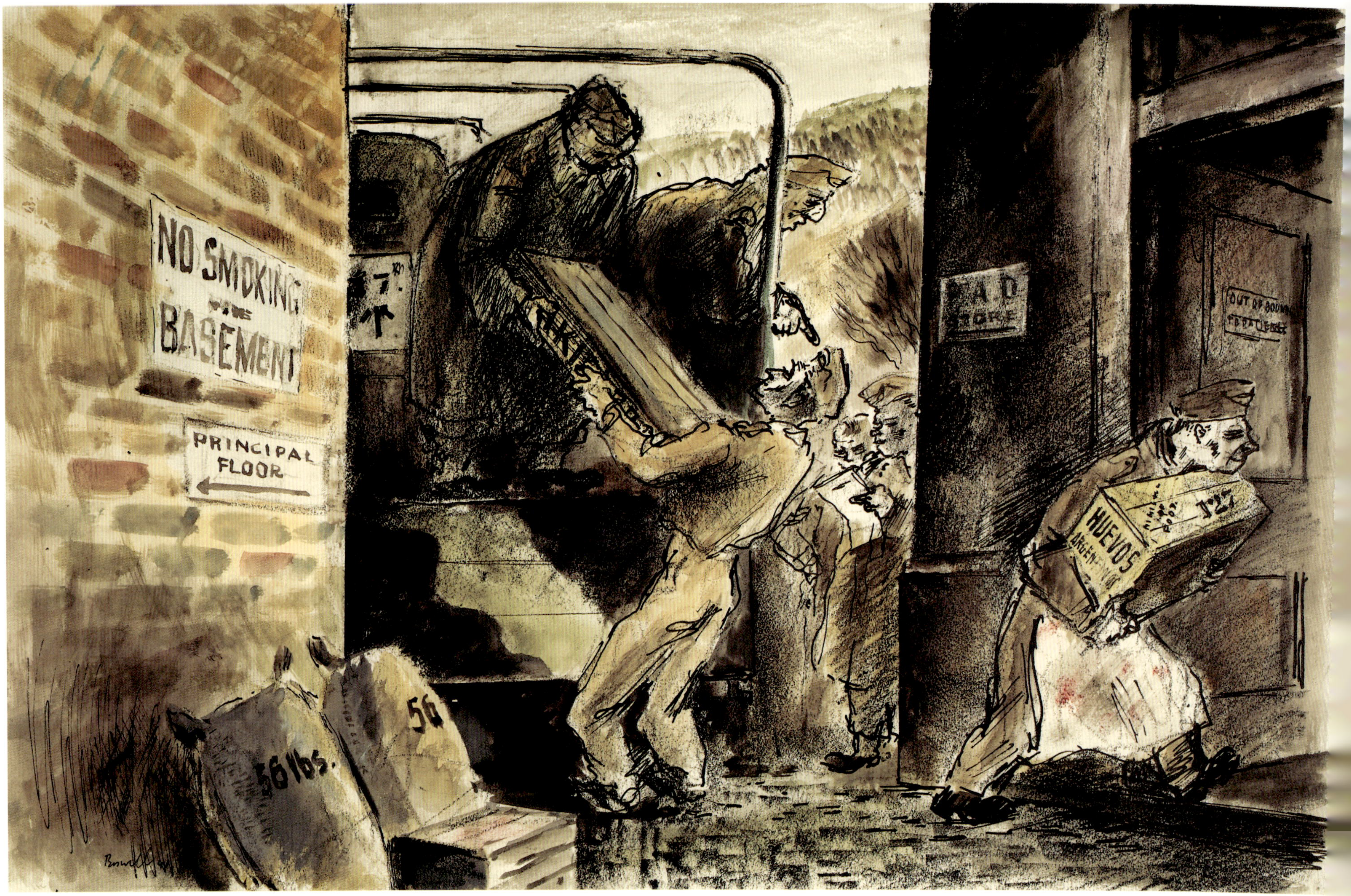
NO SMOKING
BASEMENT
PRINCIPAL
FLOOR
HUEVOS
56 lbs.
56

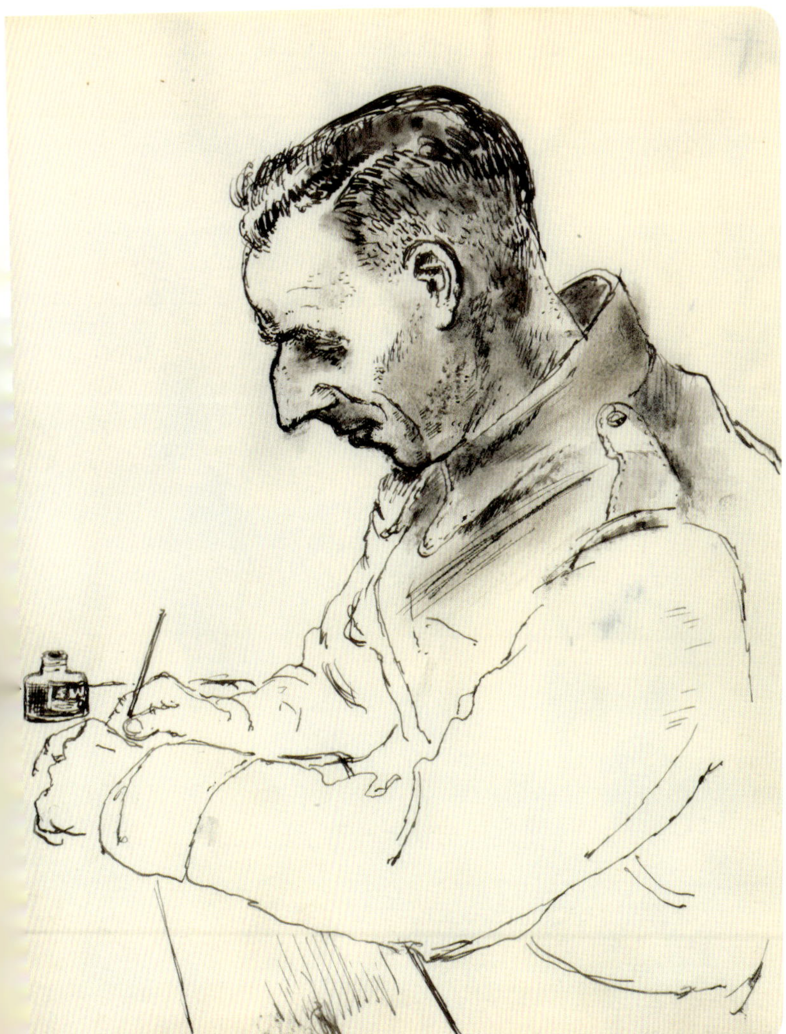

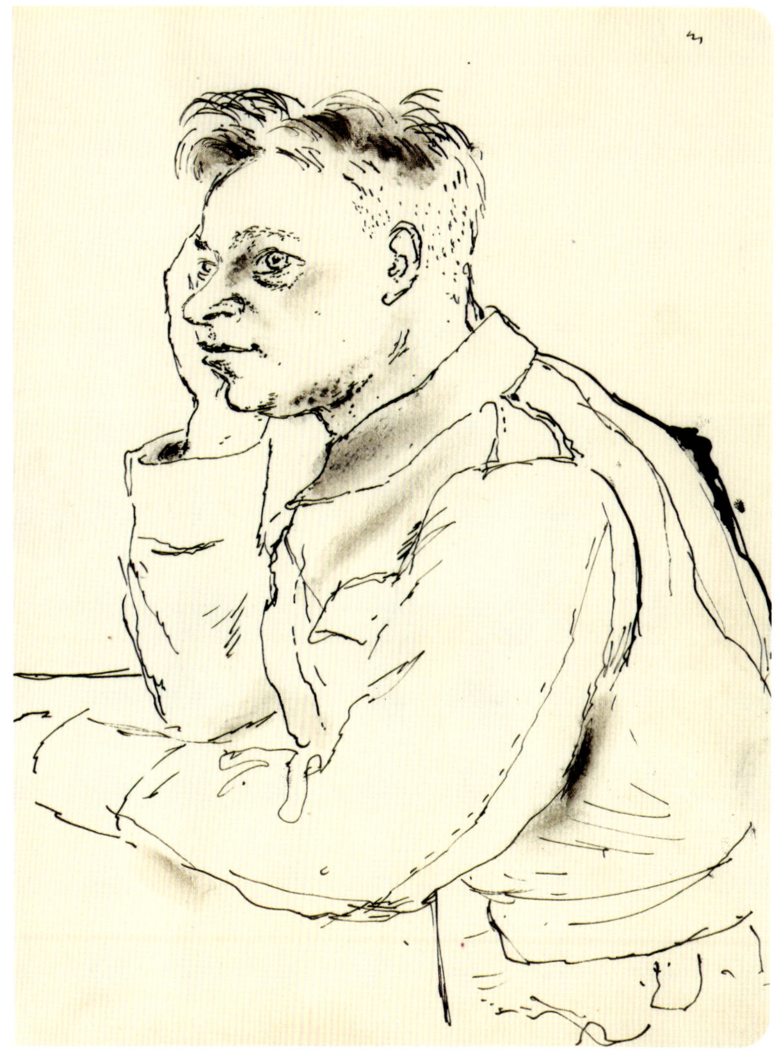

Opposite **Bringing in the Rations**

Far left **Writing Home**
Left **Eric**

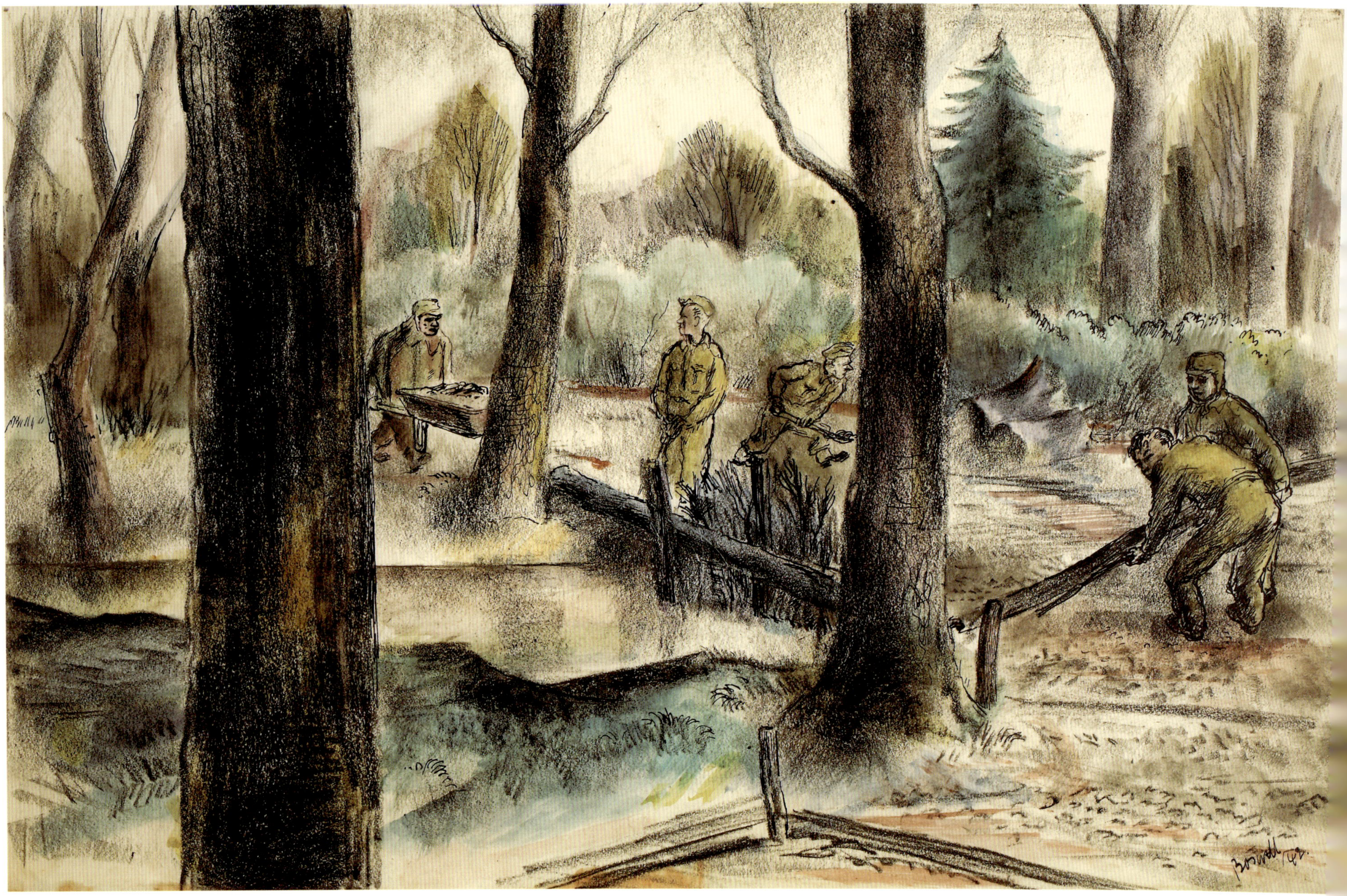

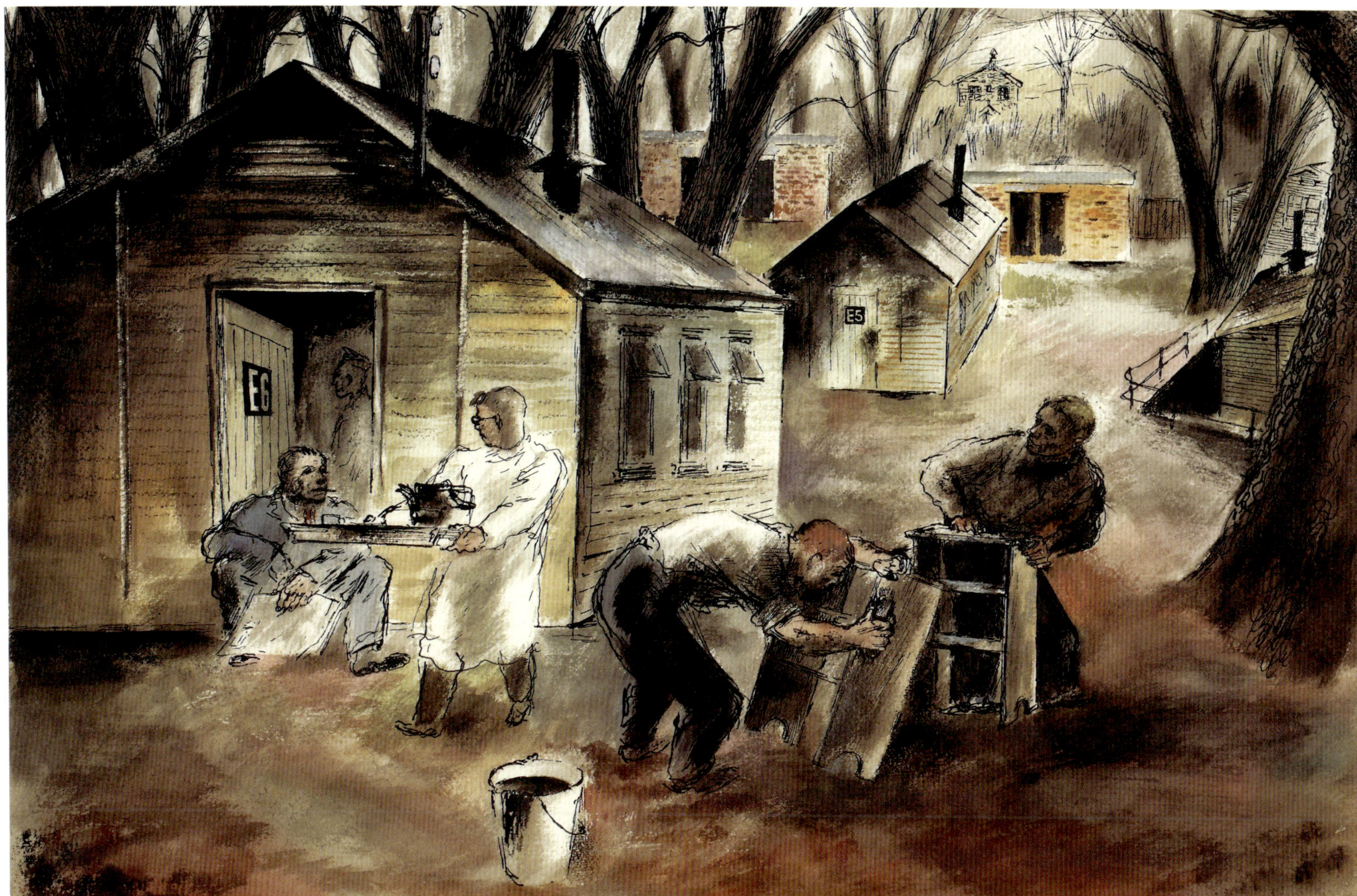

Opposite Roadmaking by RAMC, Peebles, Scotland

Right The Camp, Peebles, Scotland

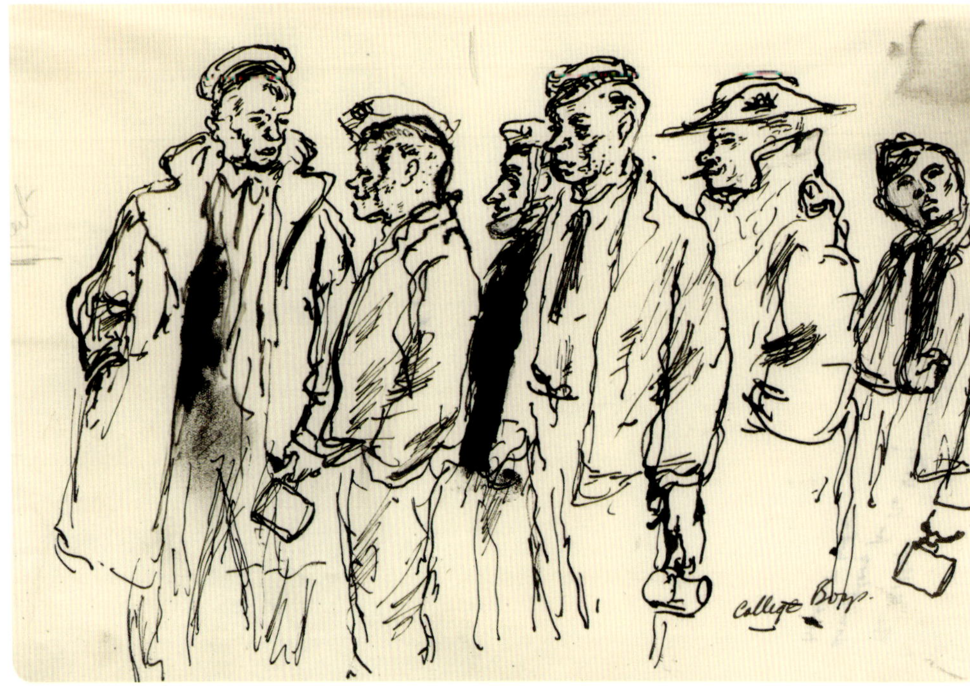

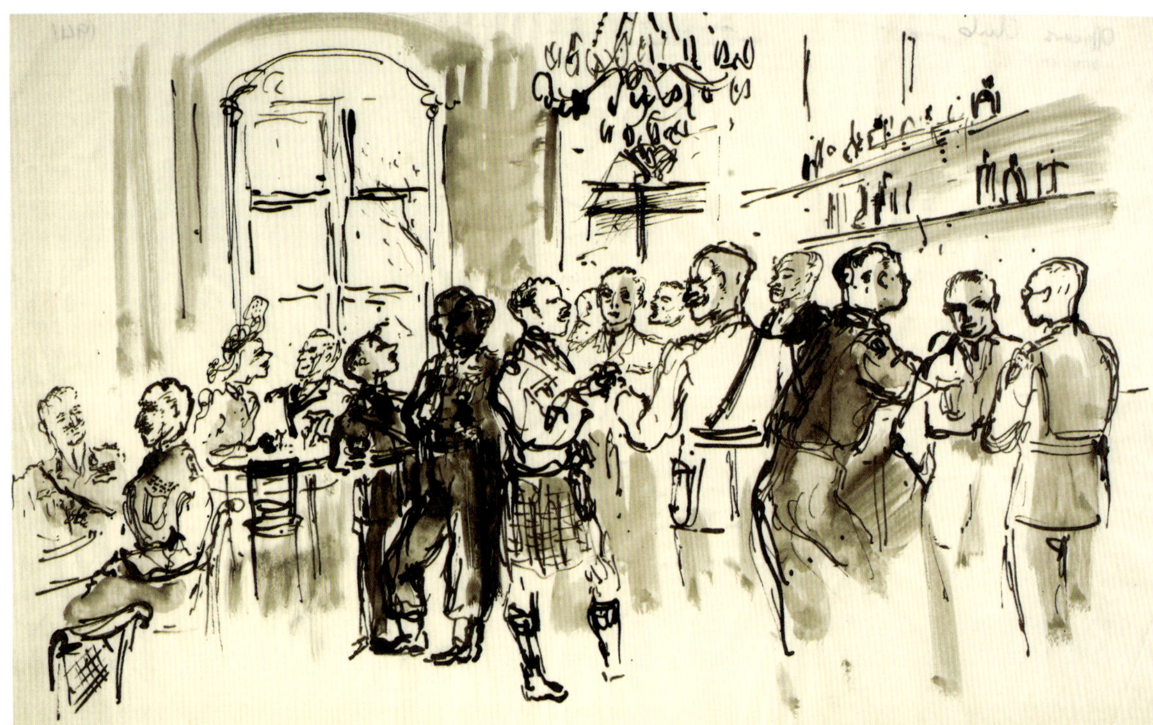

Top College Boys
(Army slang for the VD wards treatment unit.)
Bottom Officers' Club

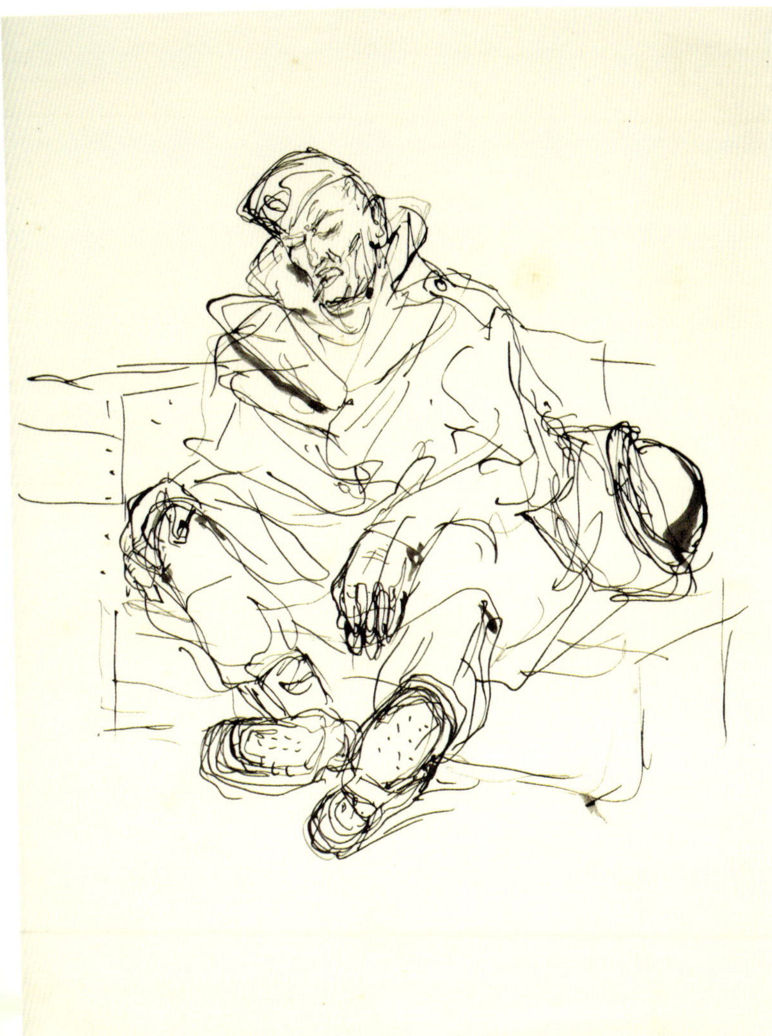

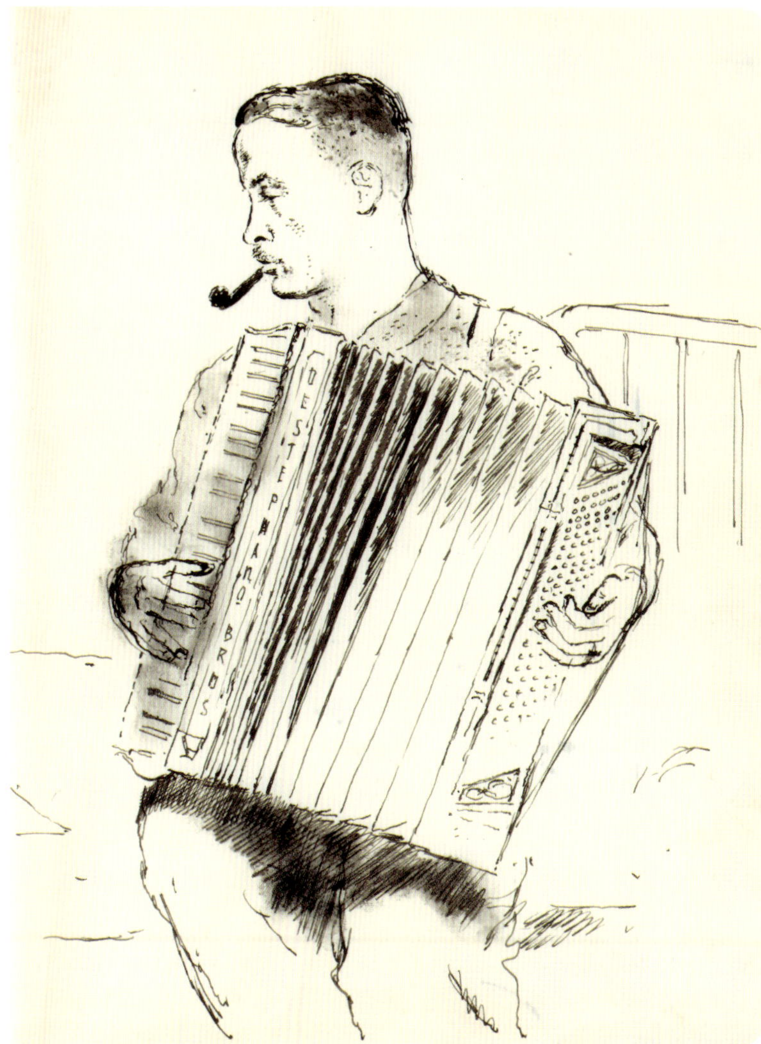

Far left **Time Out**

Left **Time Off**

Overleaf **Army Football**

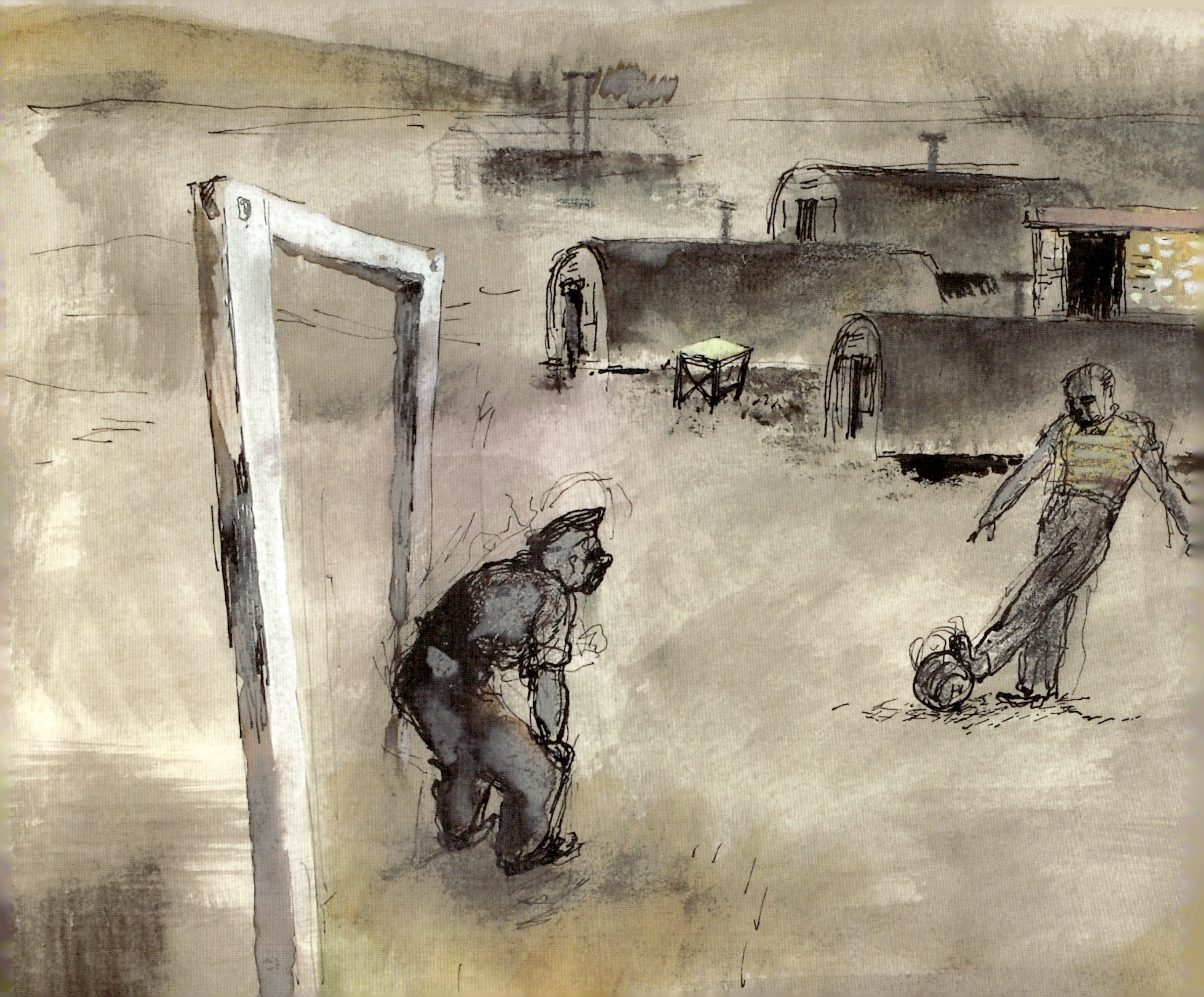

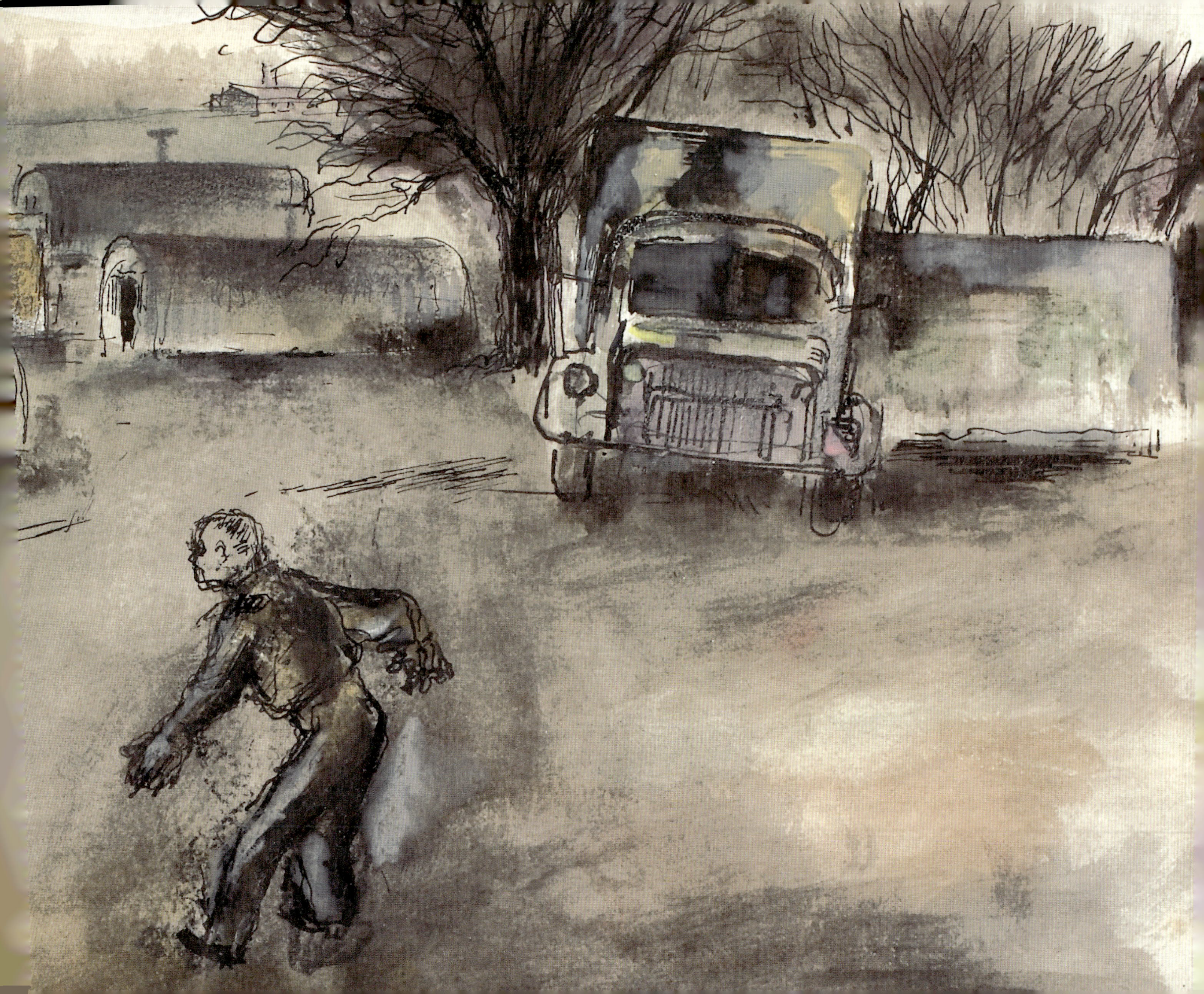

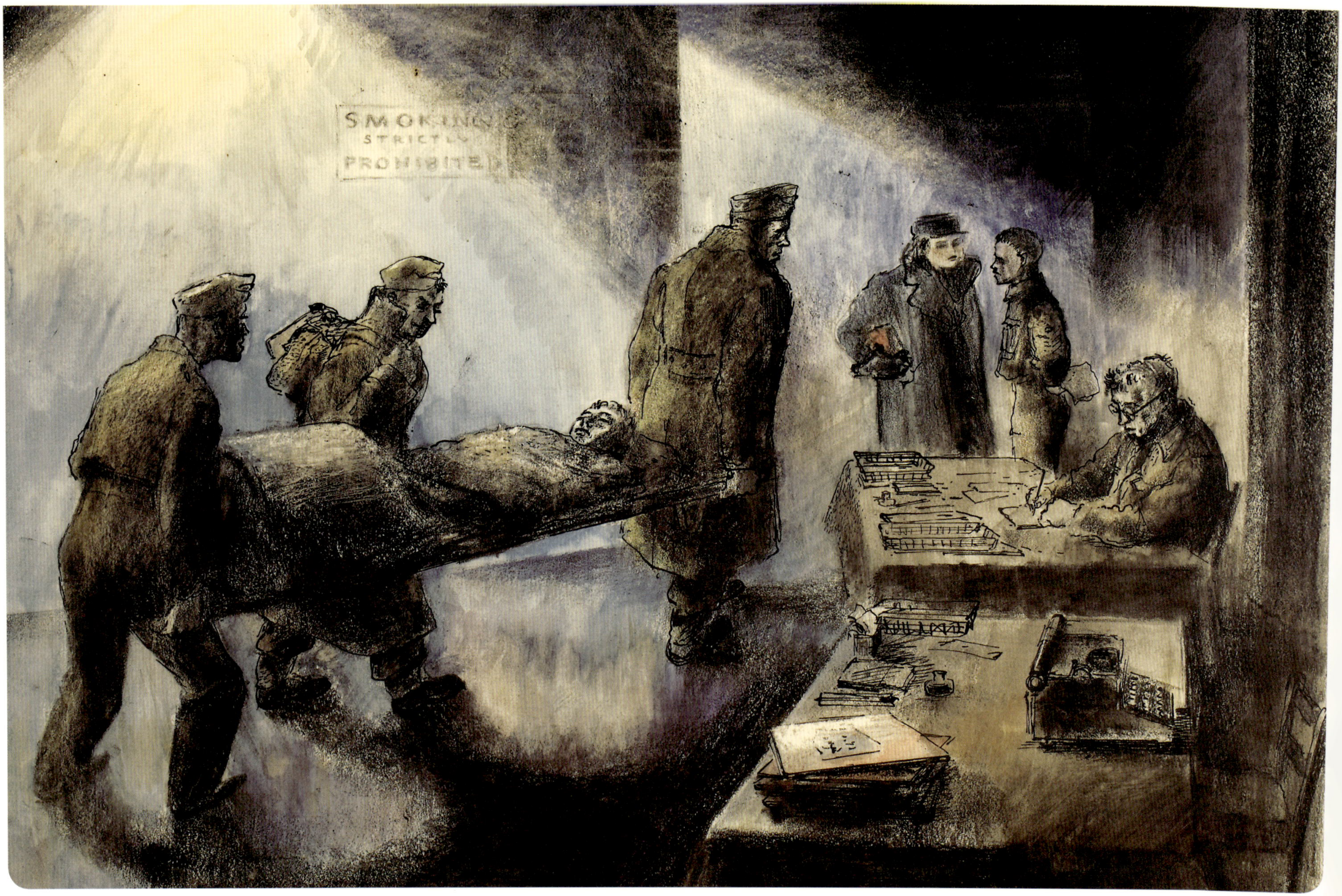
SMOKING
STRICTLY
PROHIBITED

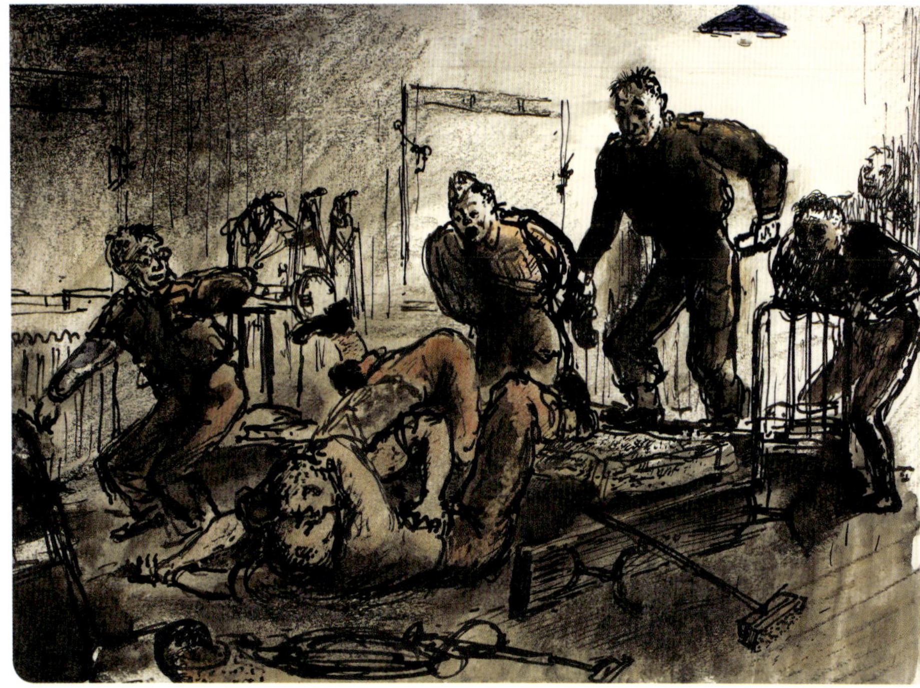

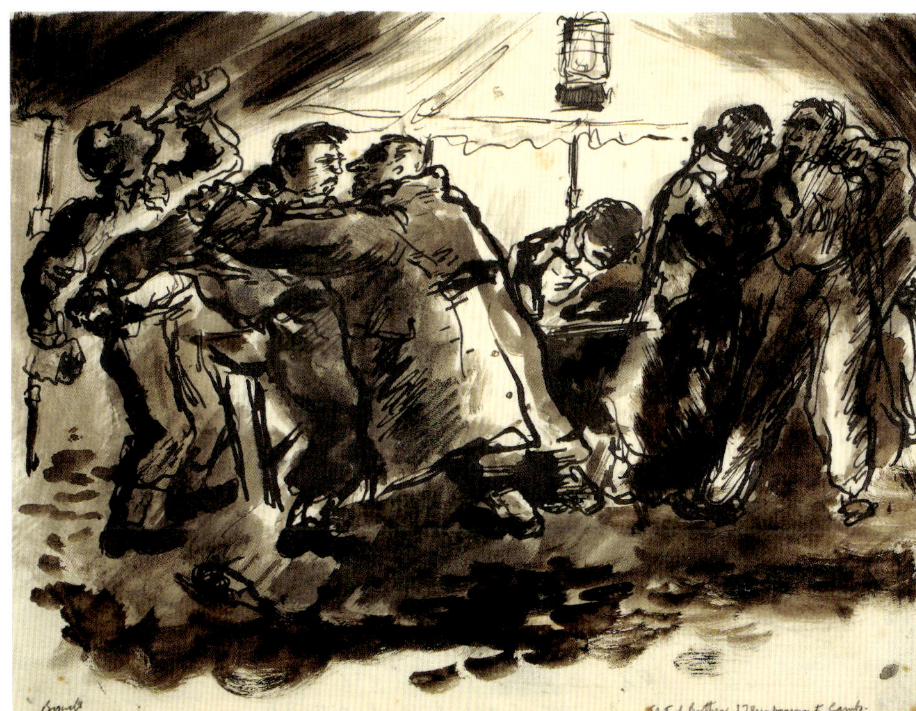

Top **Fight in Barrack Room II**

Bottom **Spot of Bother**

Left **Bringing in a Casualty**

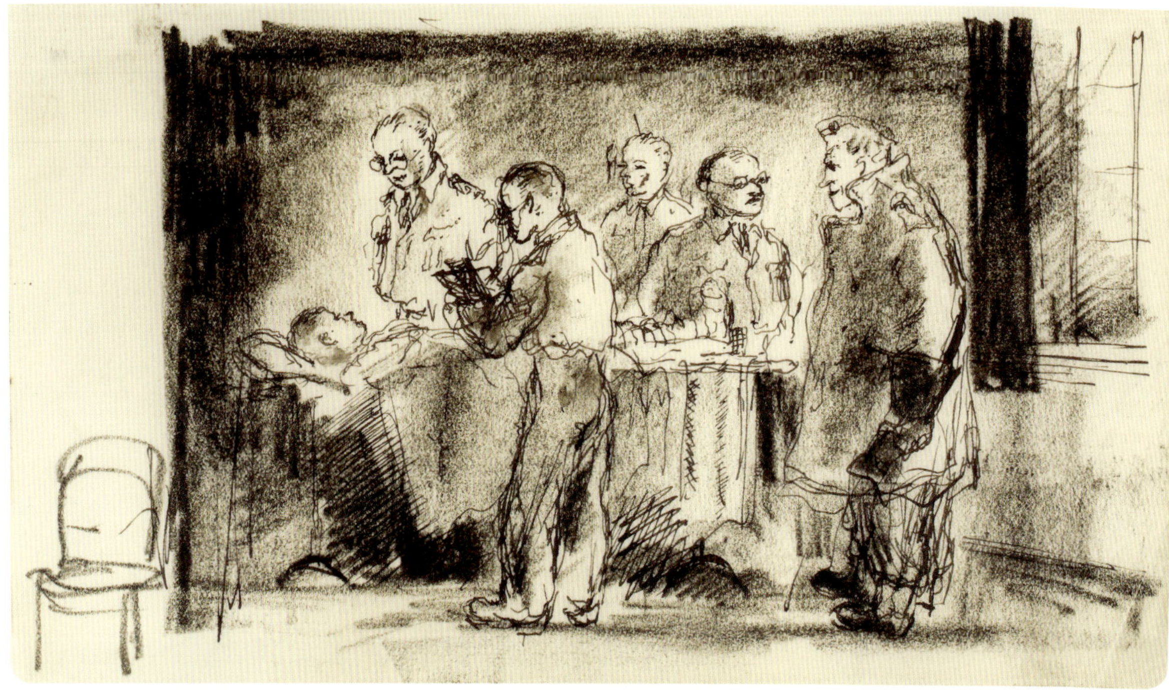

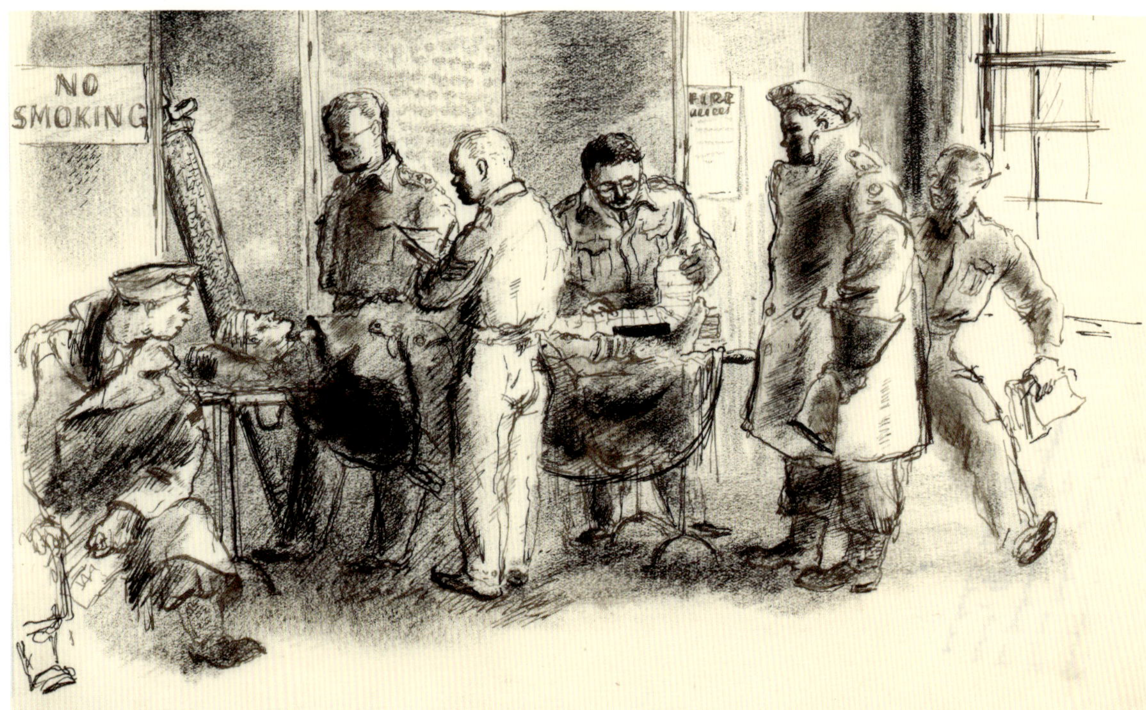

Top The Wounded Soldier
Bottom Bringing in a Casualty

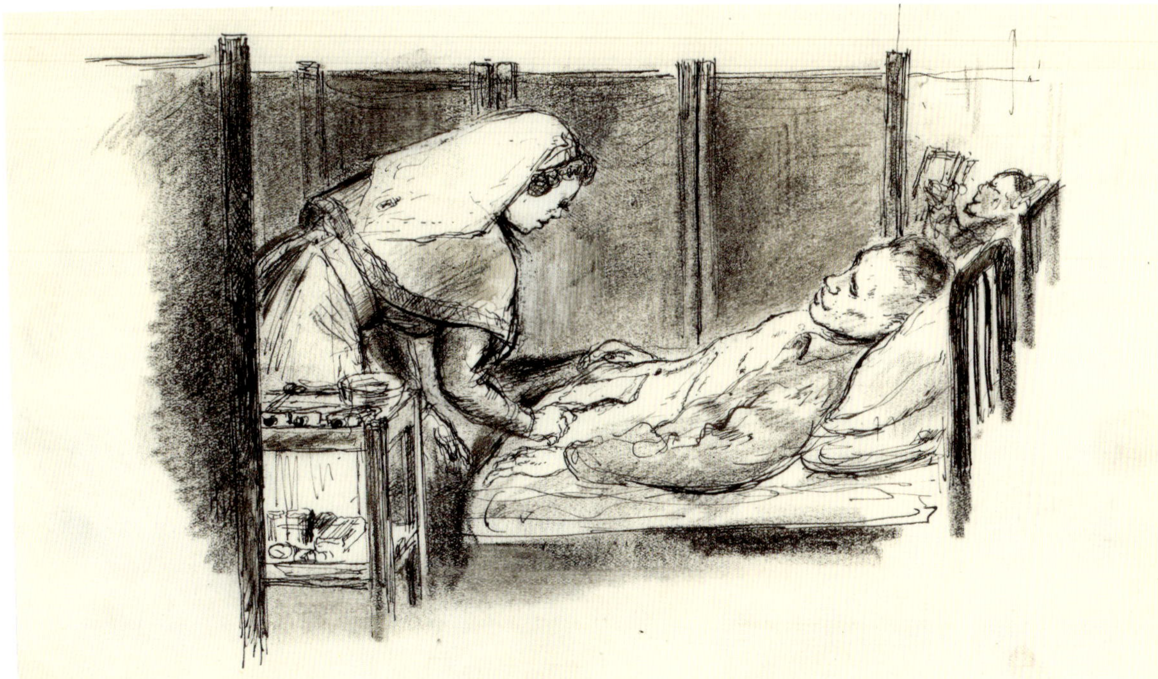

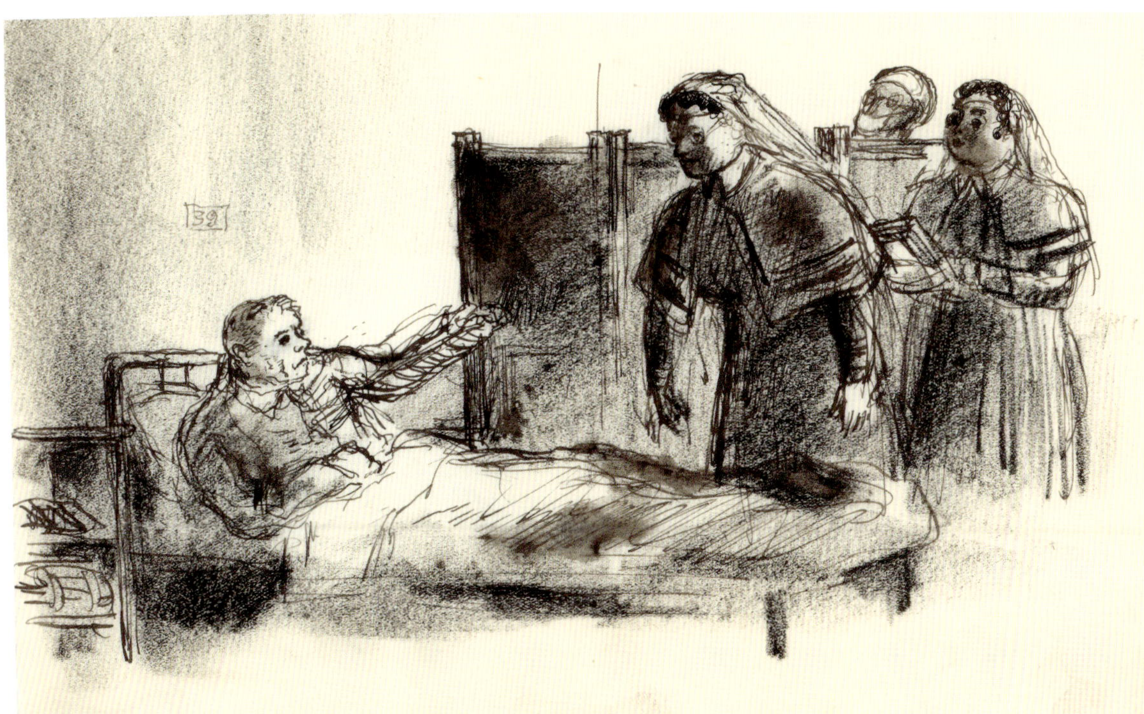

Top Physiotherapy Department a Sister doing a Dressing in the Wards.

Bottom Matron's Round

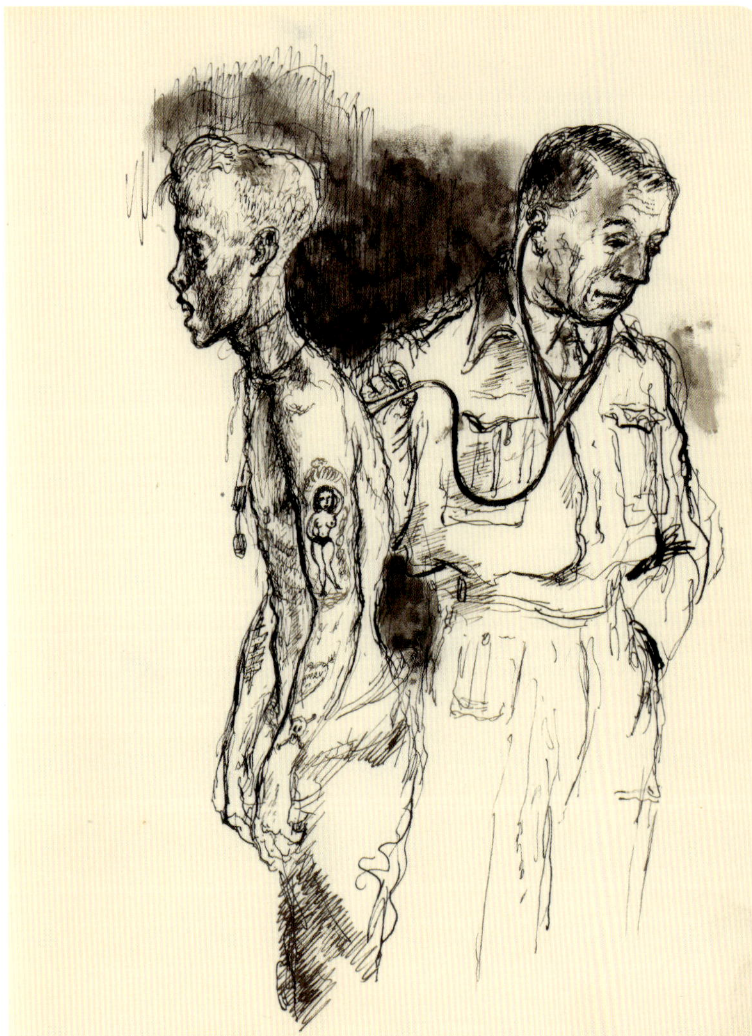

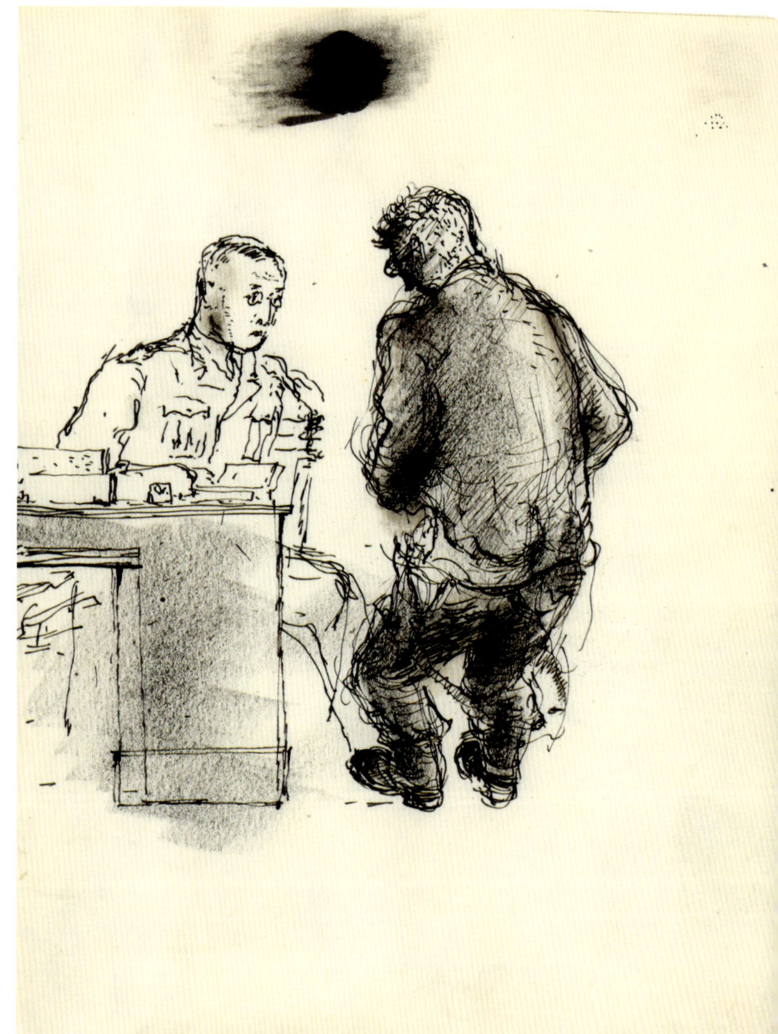

Right **Breathe In**

Far right **Oh!**

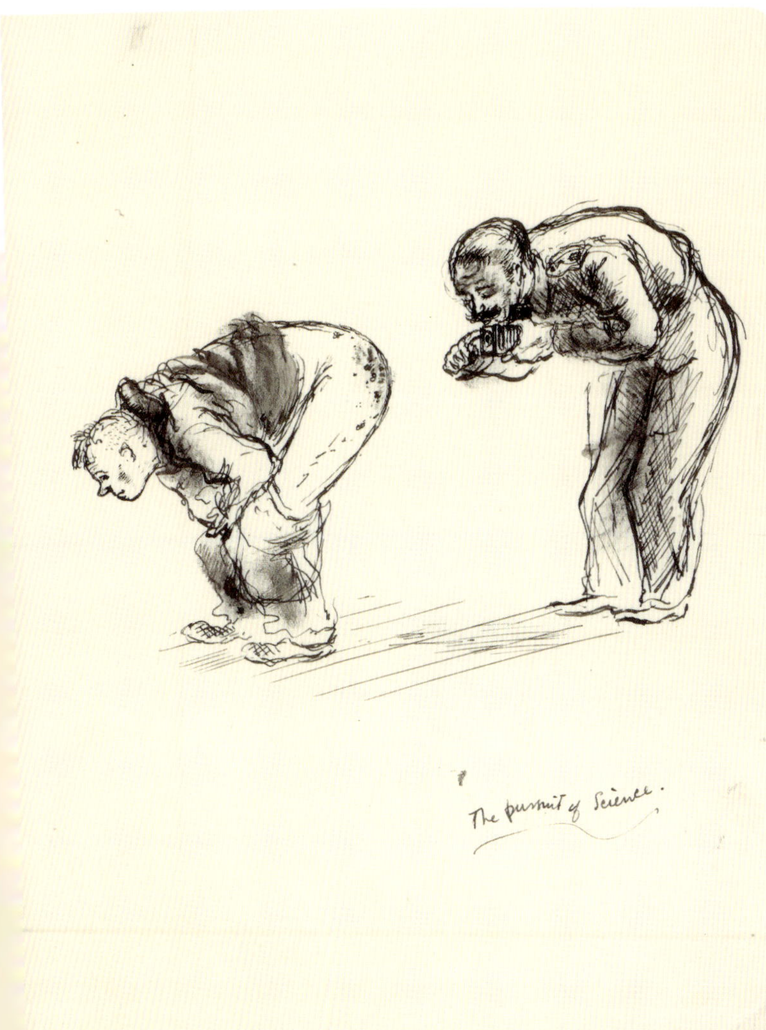

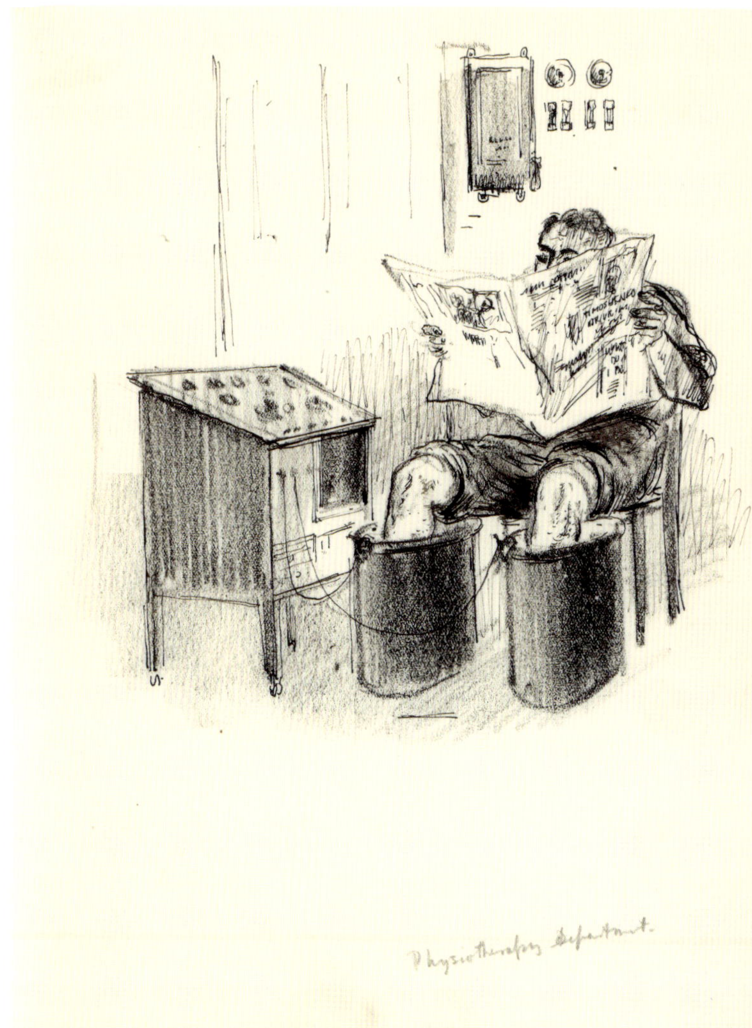

Far left **The Pursuit of Science**

Left **Physiotherapy Department**

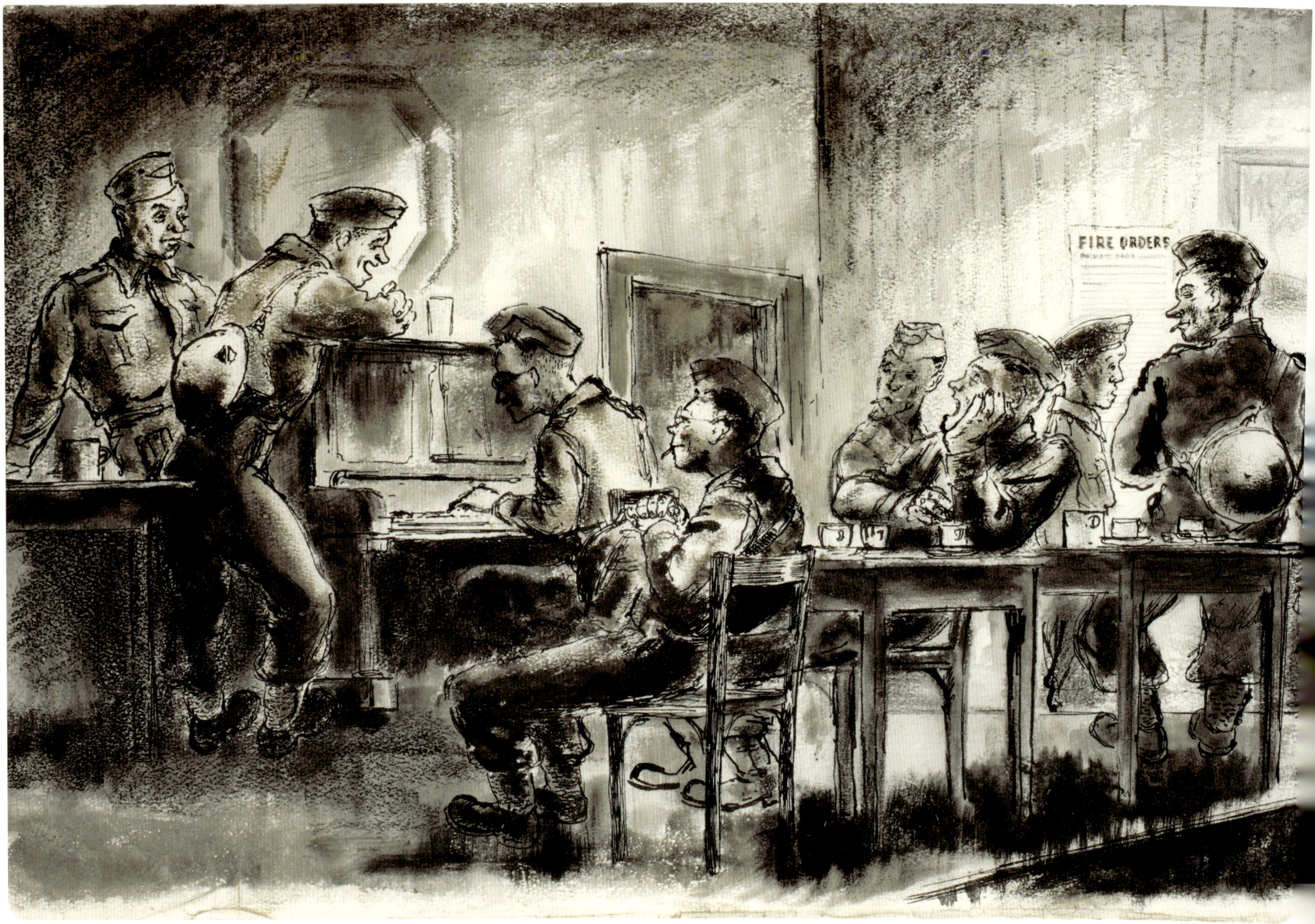
FIRE ORDERS

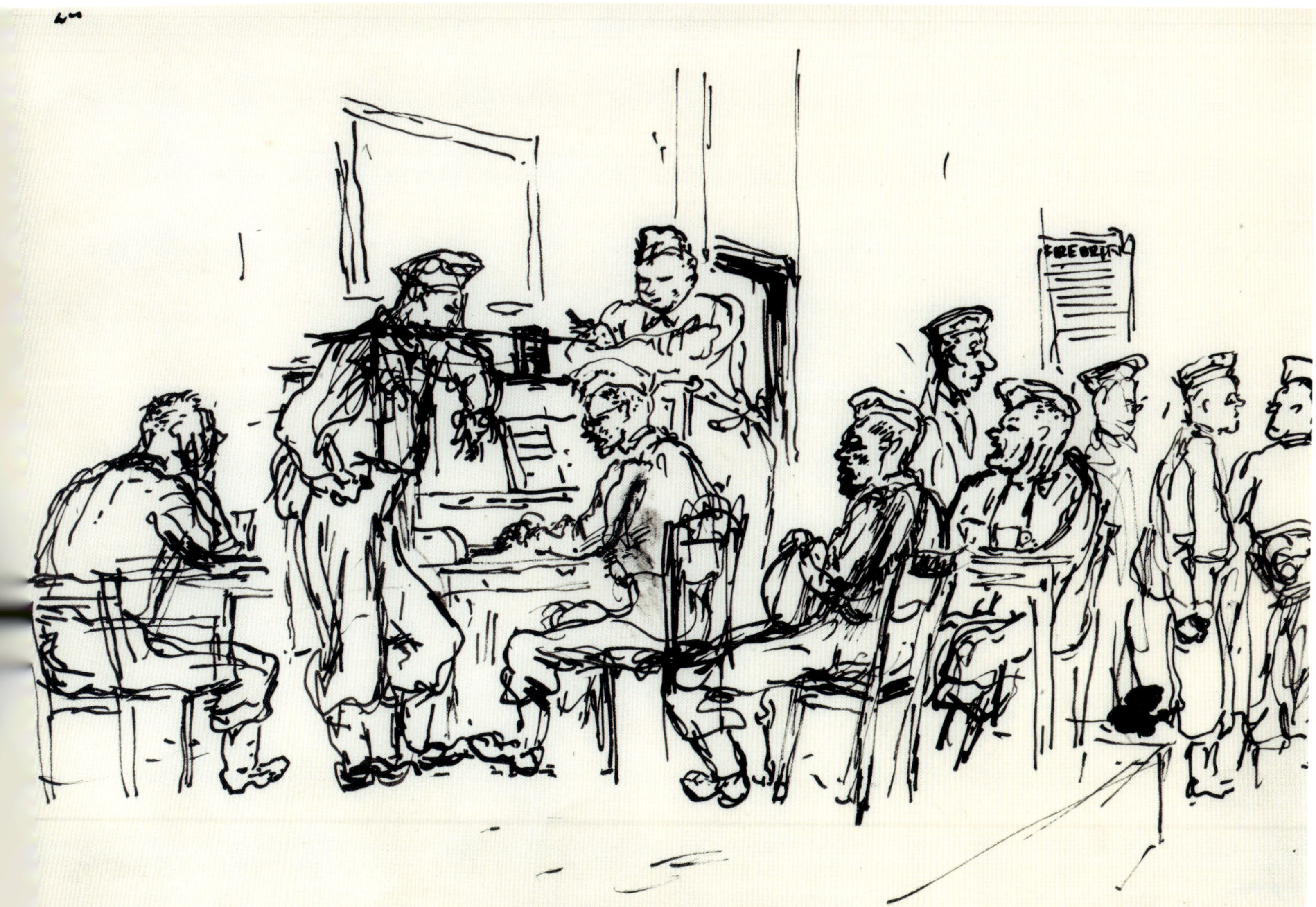

Opposite **Sing Song**

Left **Sketch for Sing Song**

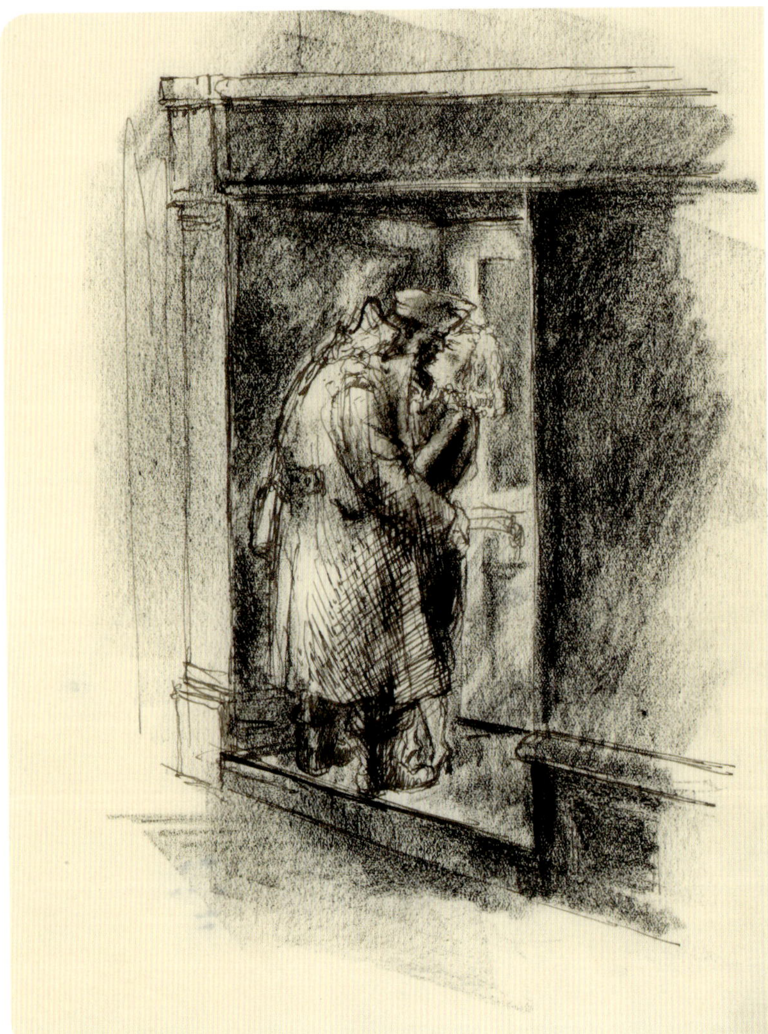

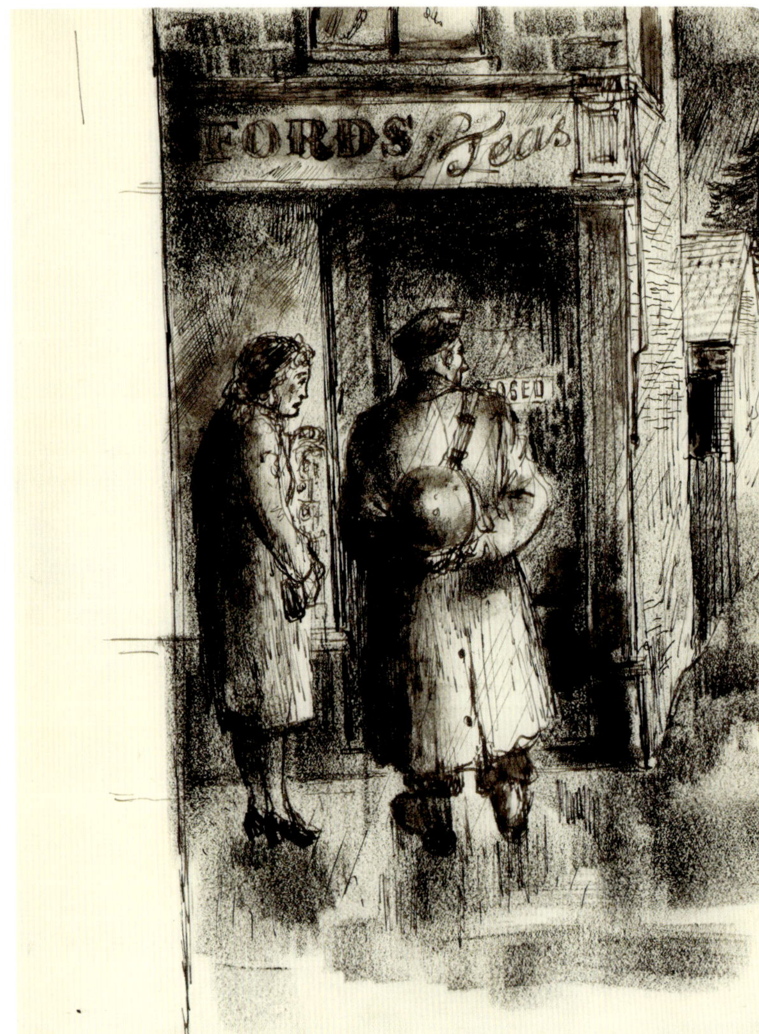

Far left and left **Off Duty**

Opposite **M.O.**

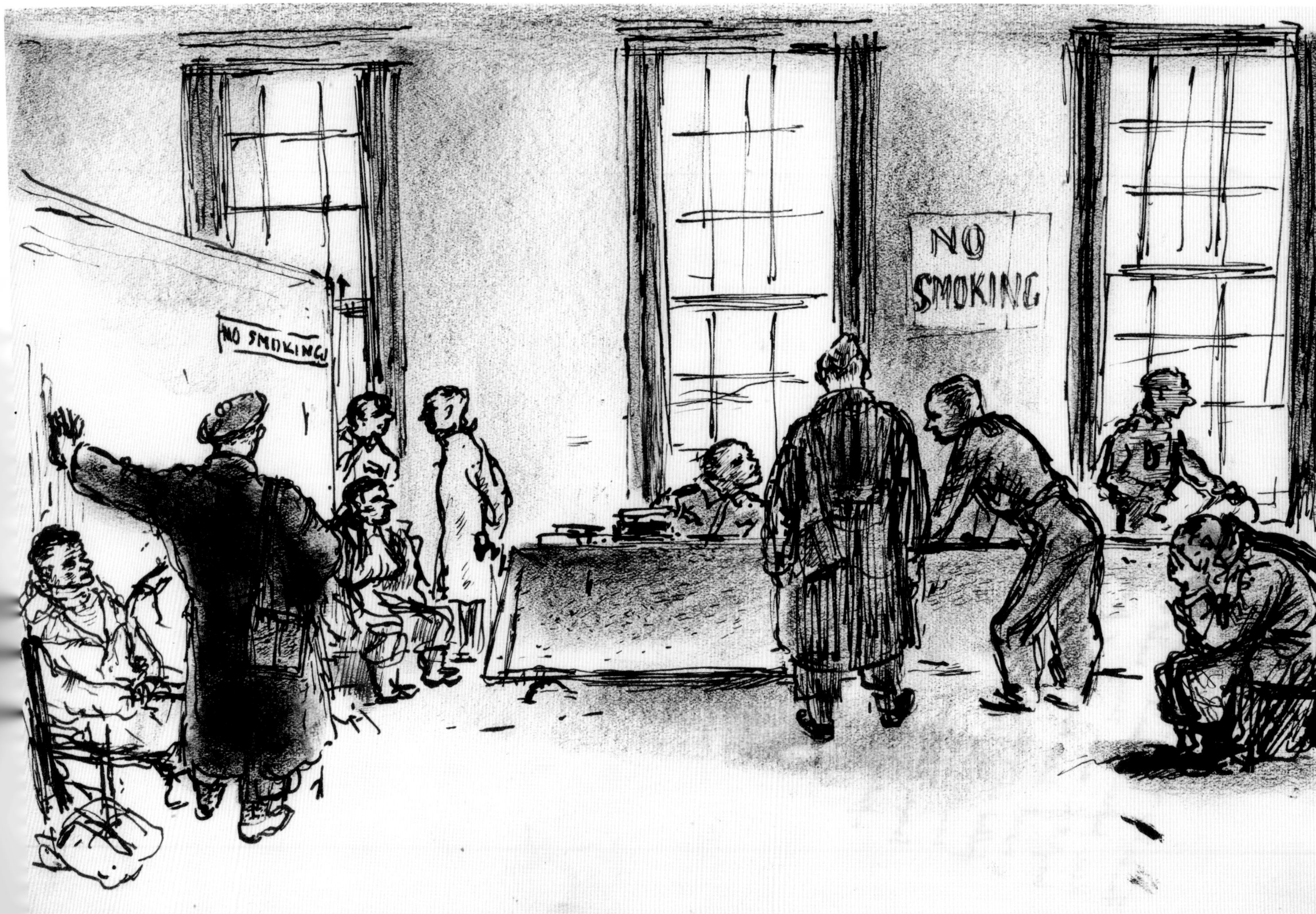
NO SMOKING
NO SMOKING

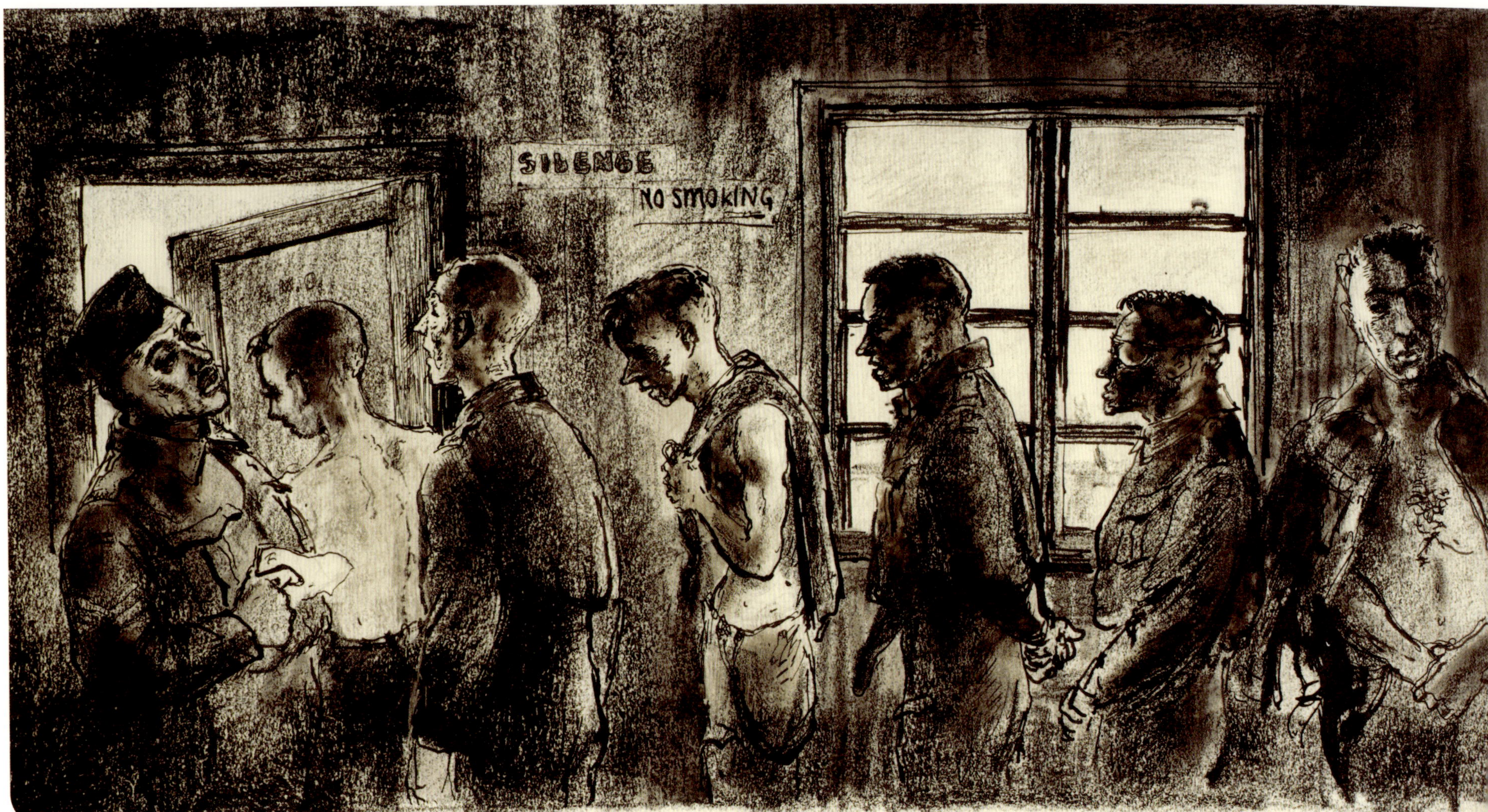
SILENCE
NO SMOKING

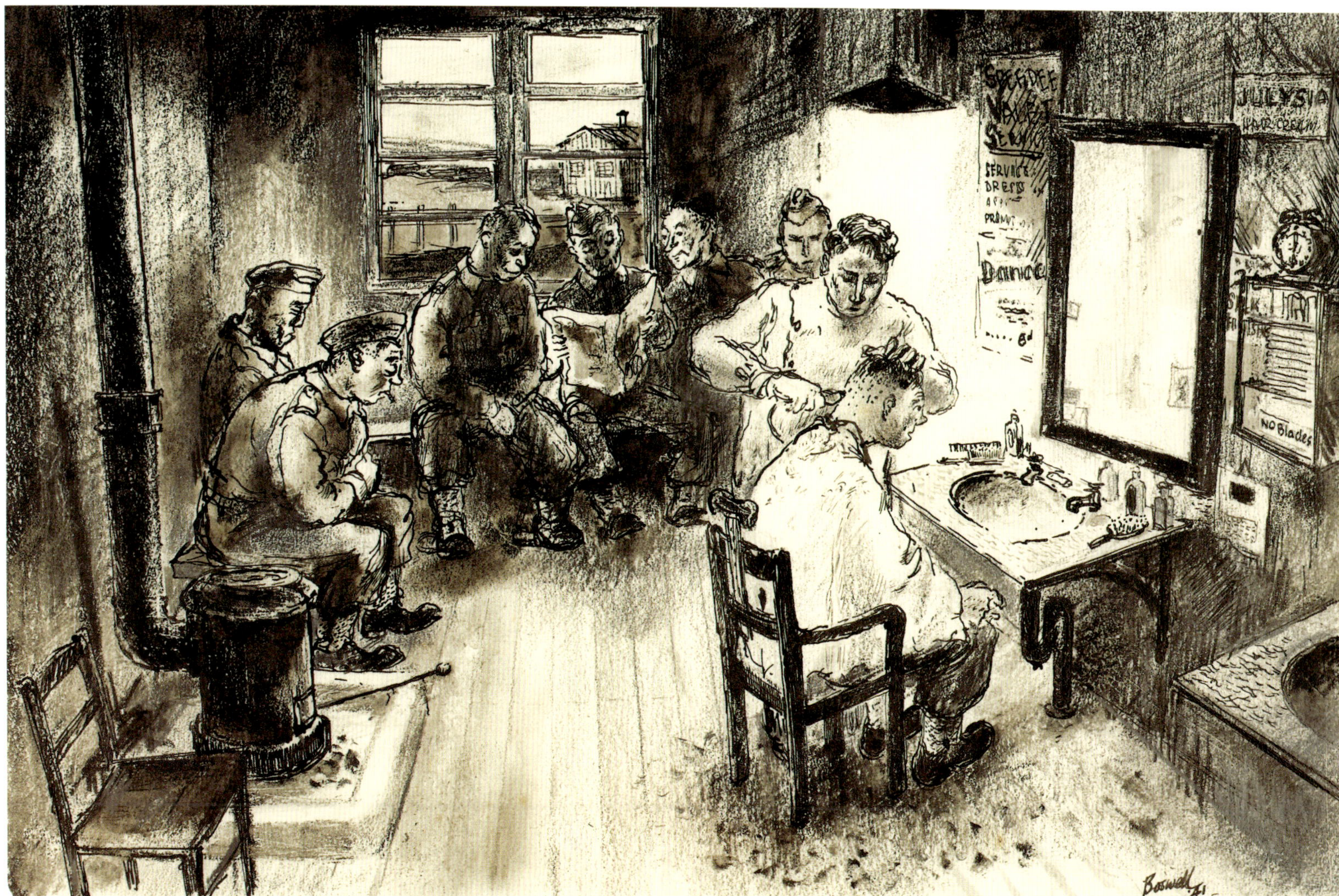

Opposite Queuing for the M.O.

Right The Haircut

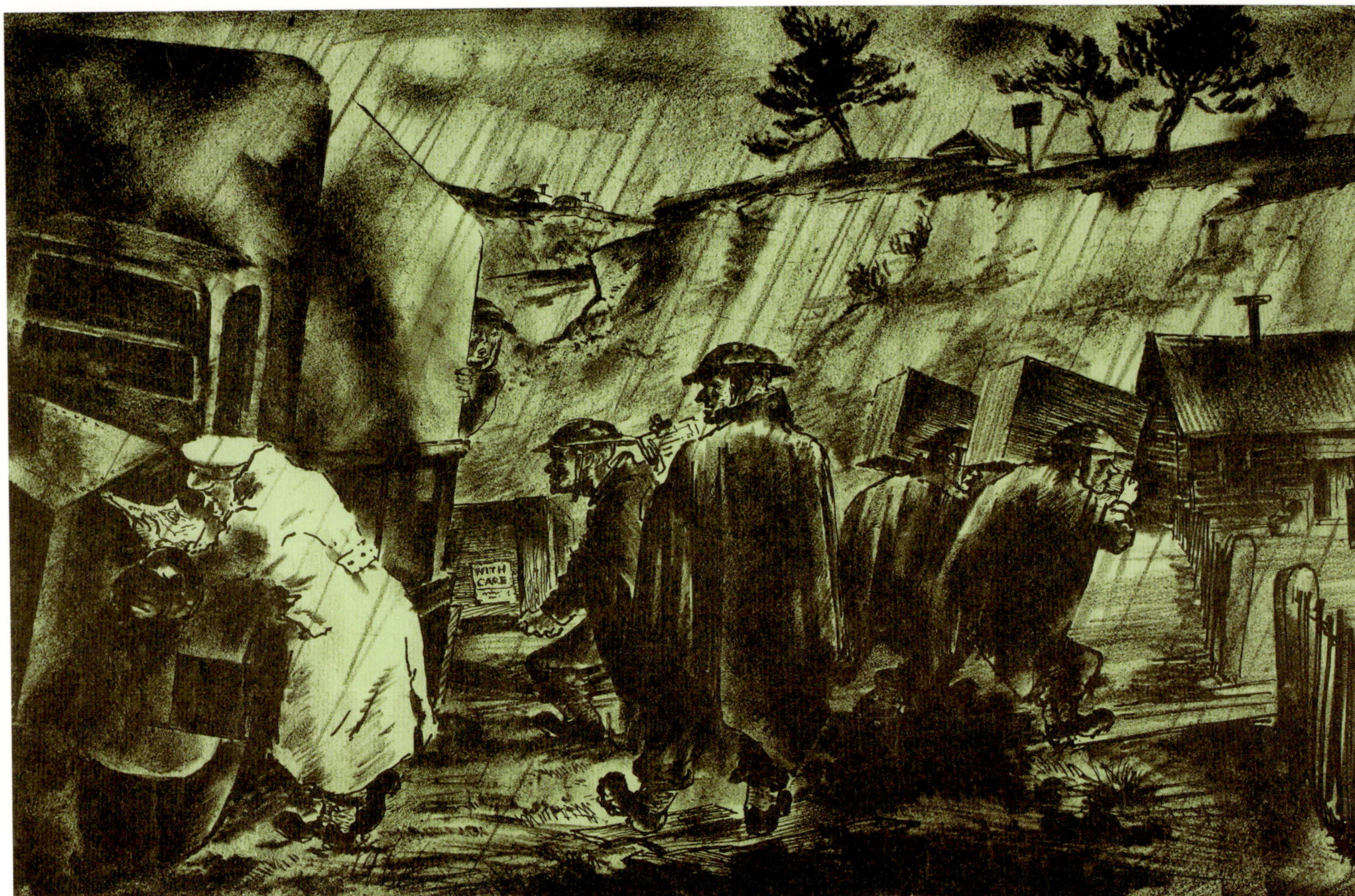

Left Fatigue Party. Unloading the Rations. Aldershot 1941

Opposite Fatigue Party, Aldershot

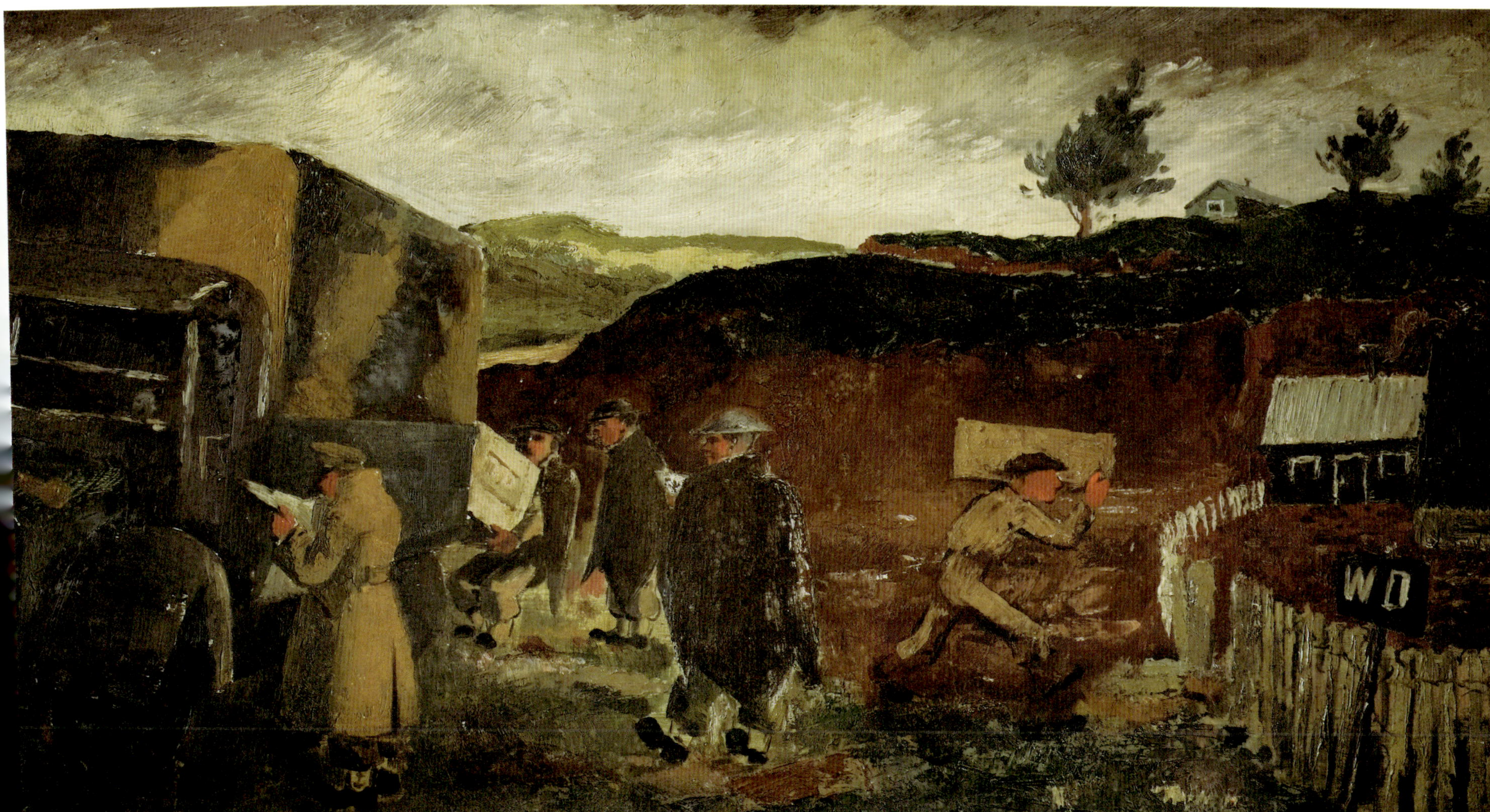
WD

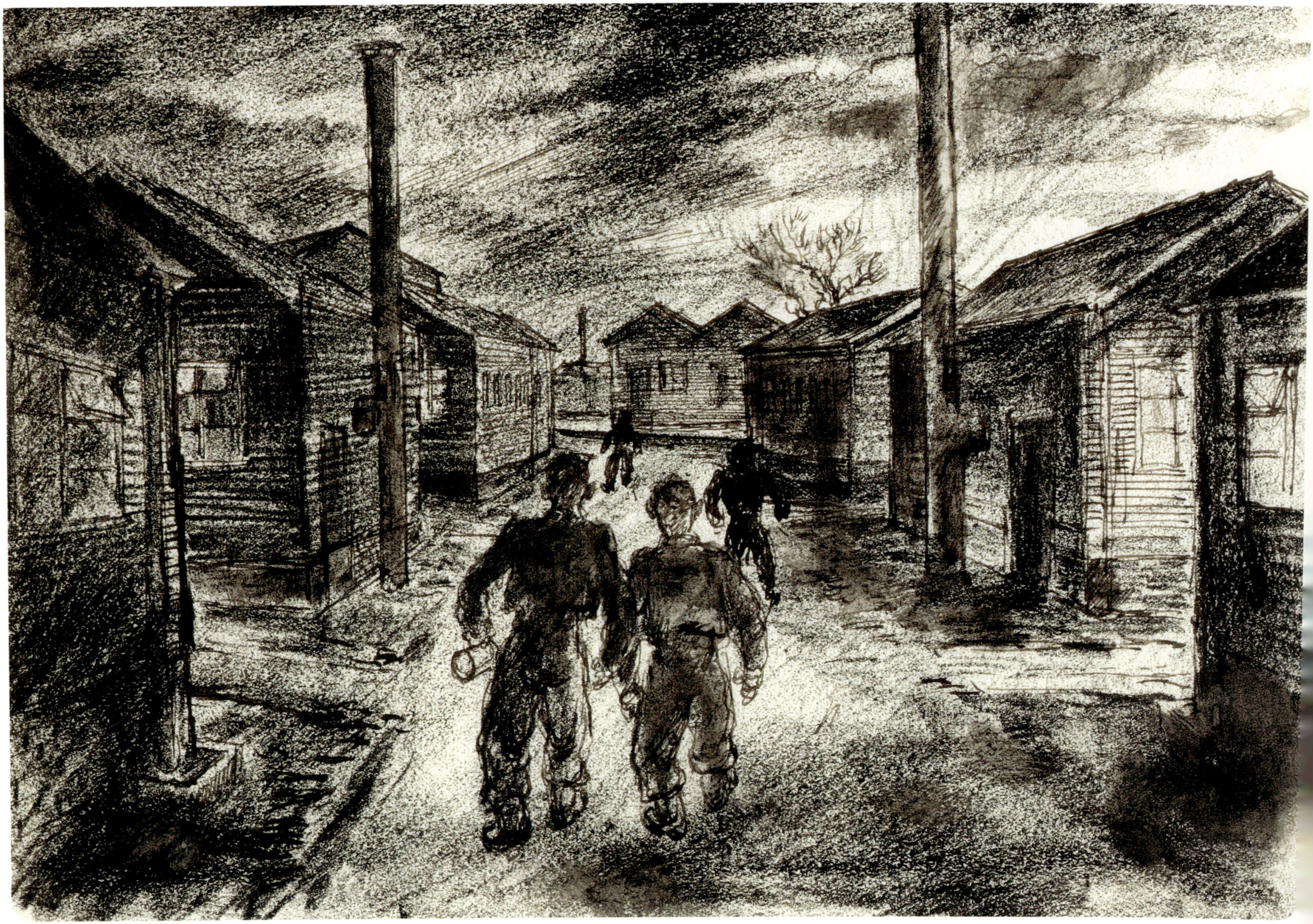

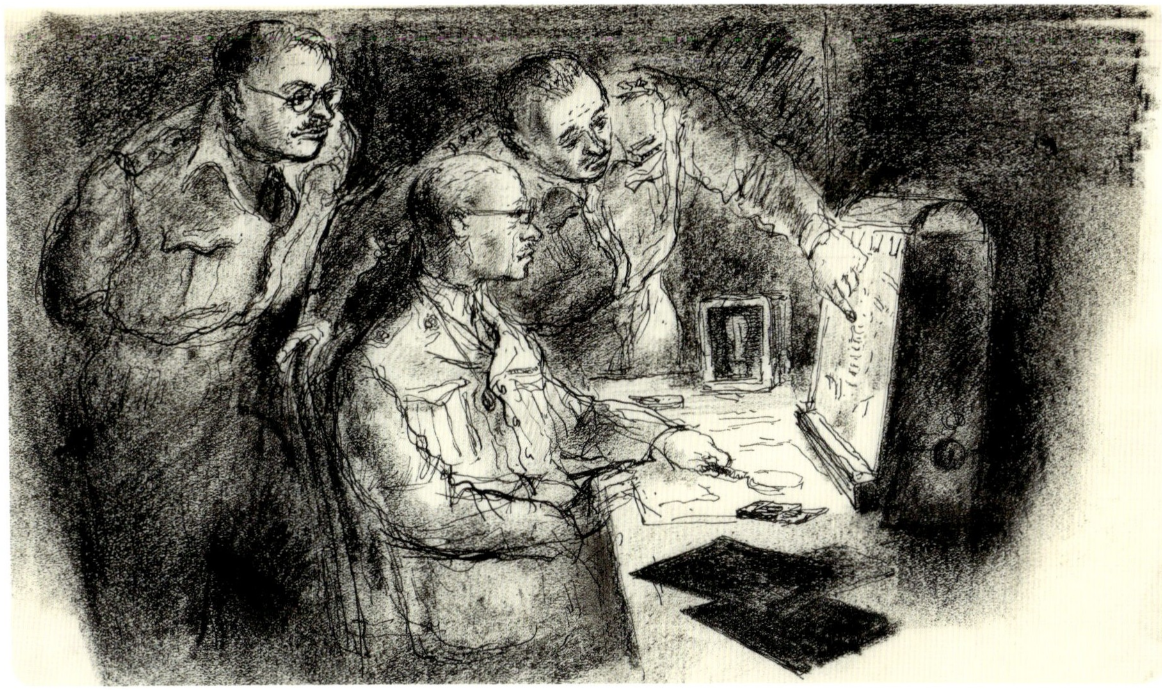

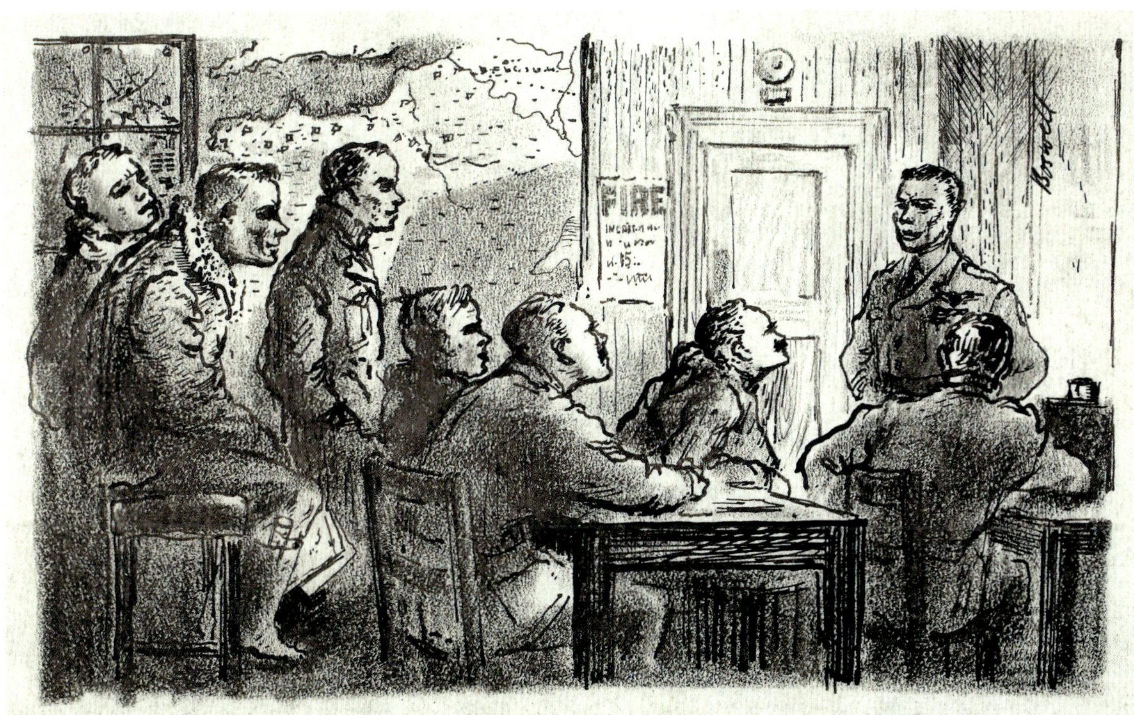

Top **M.O.s discussing a Radiograph**

Bottom **The Briefing**

Opposite **NAAFI Break**

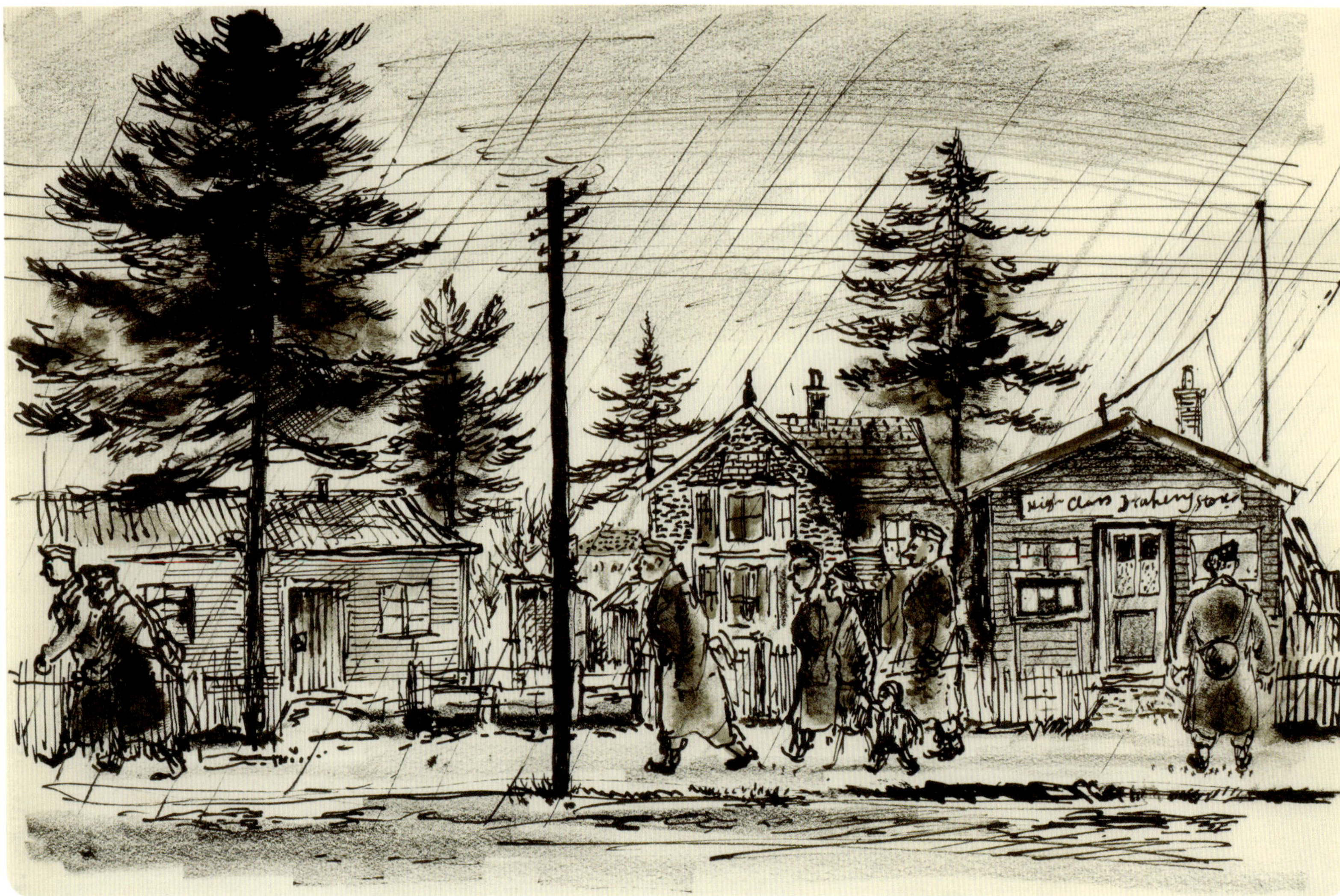

Left **Wet Sunday**

Opposite **Skin Wards at 33 General Hospital, Peebles, Scotland.**

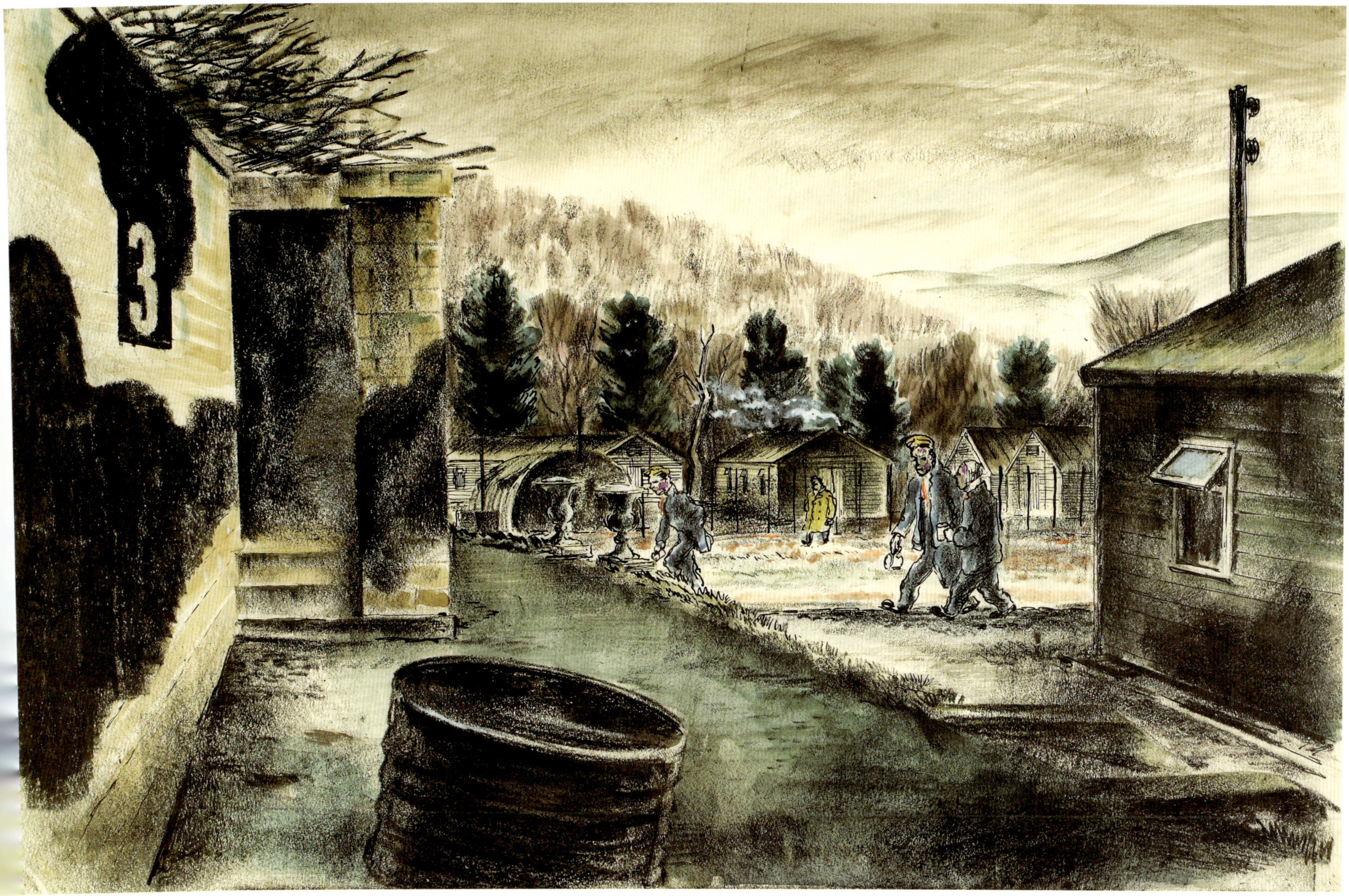
3

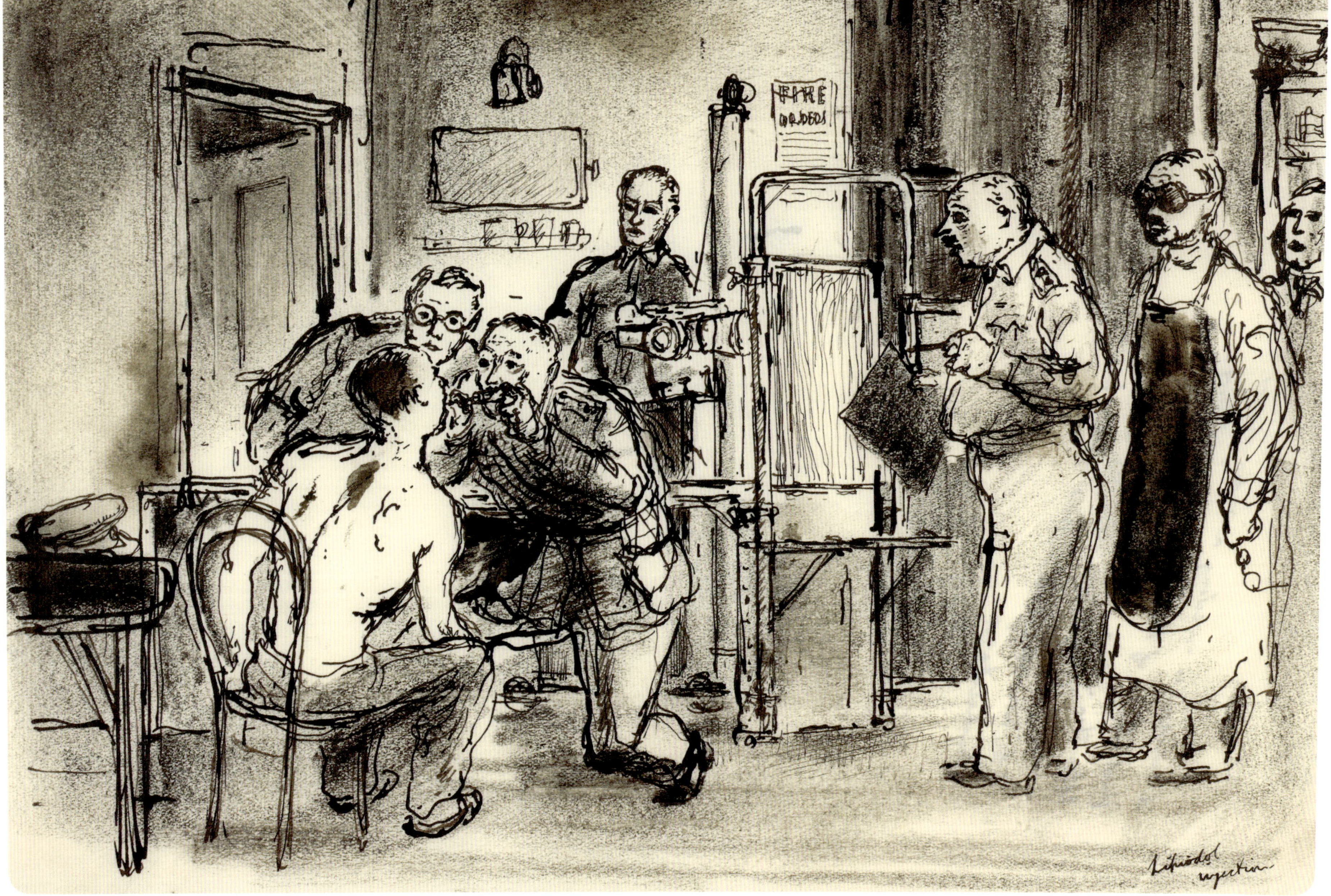
FIRE ORDERS
Lipiodol injection

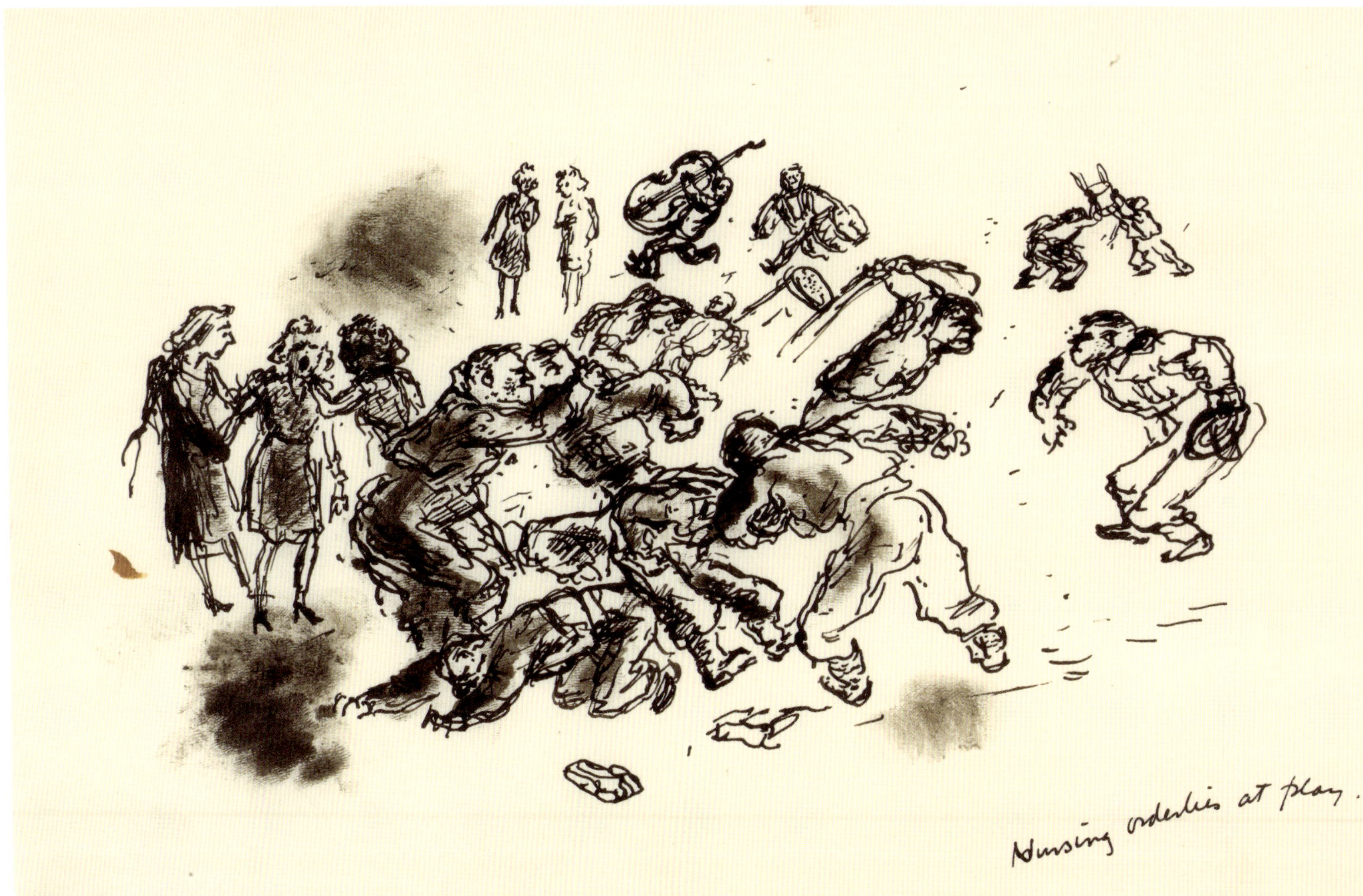

Opposite Liprodol Inspection

Right Nursing Orderlies at Play

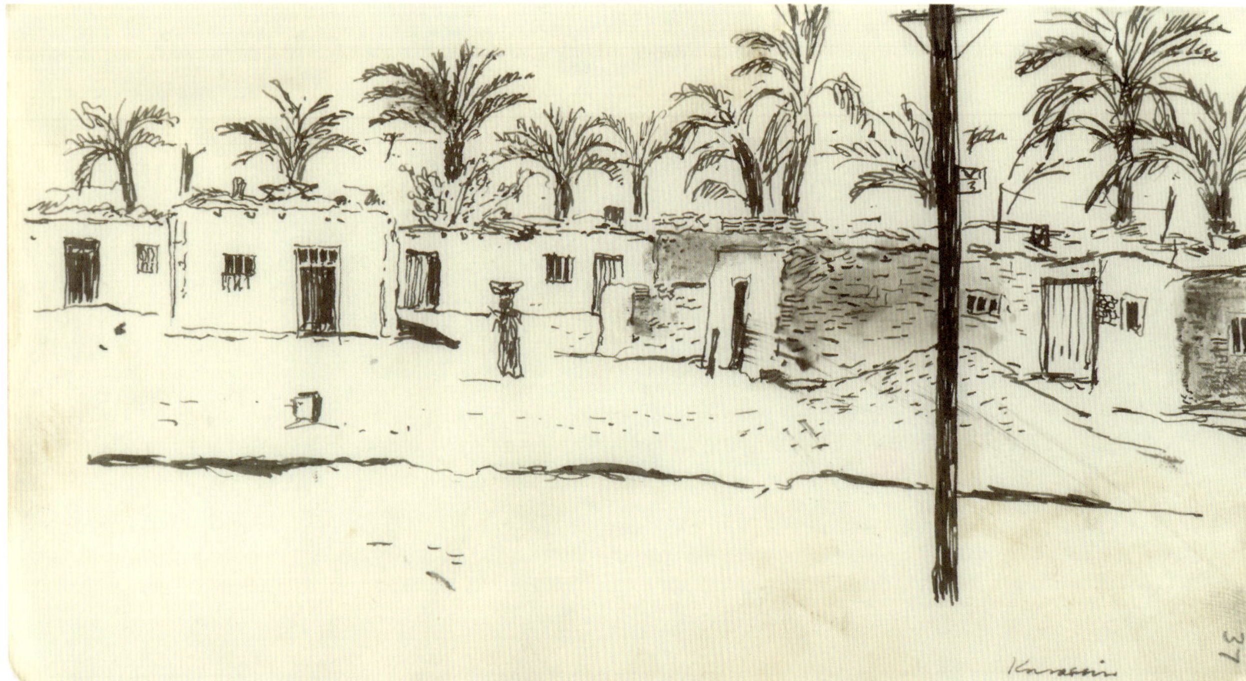

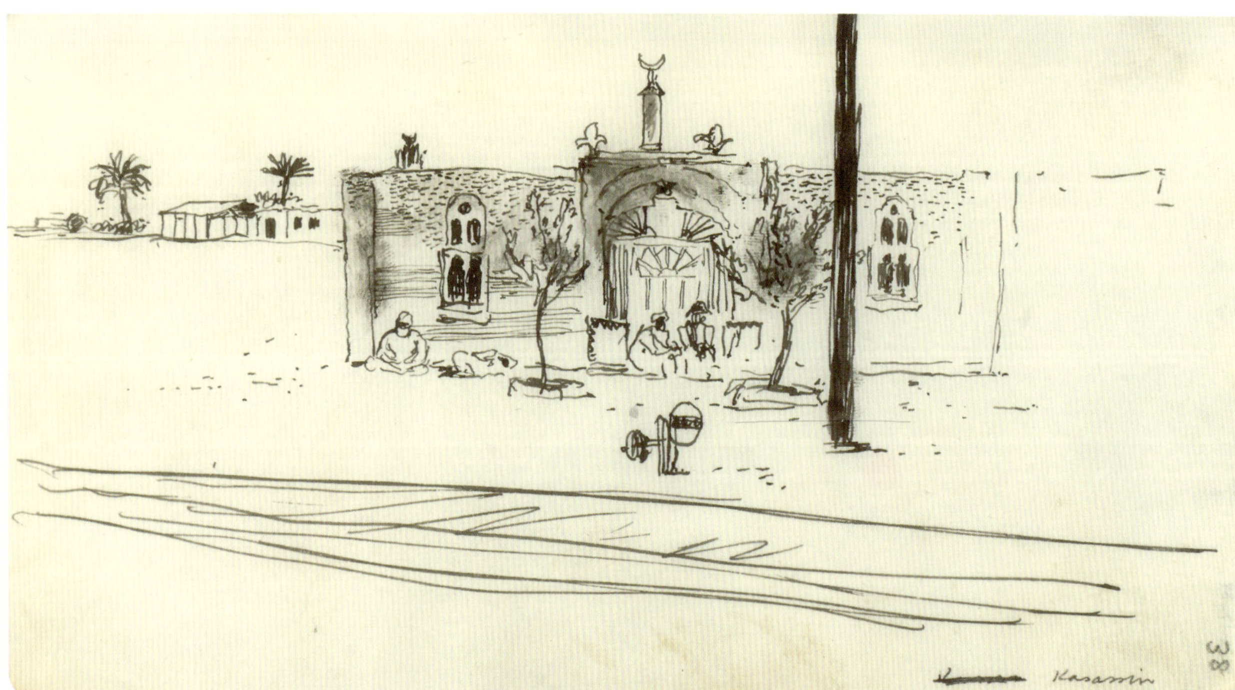

Top **Kavassin**

Bottom **Kavassin**

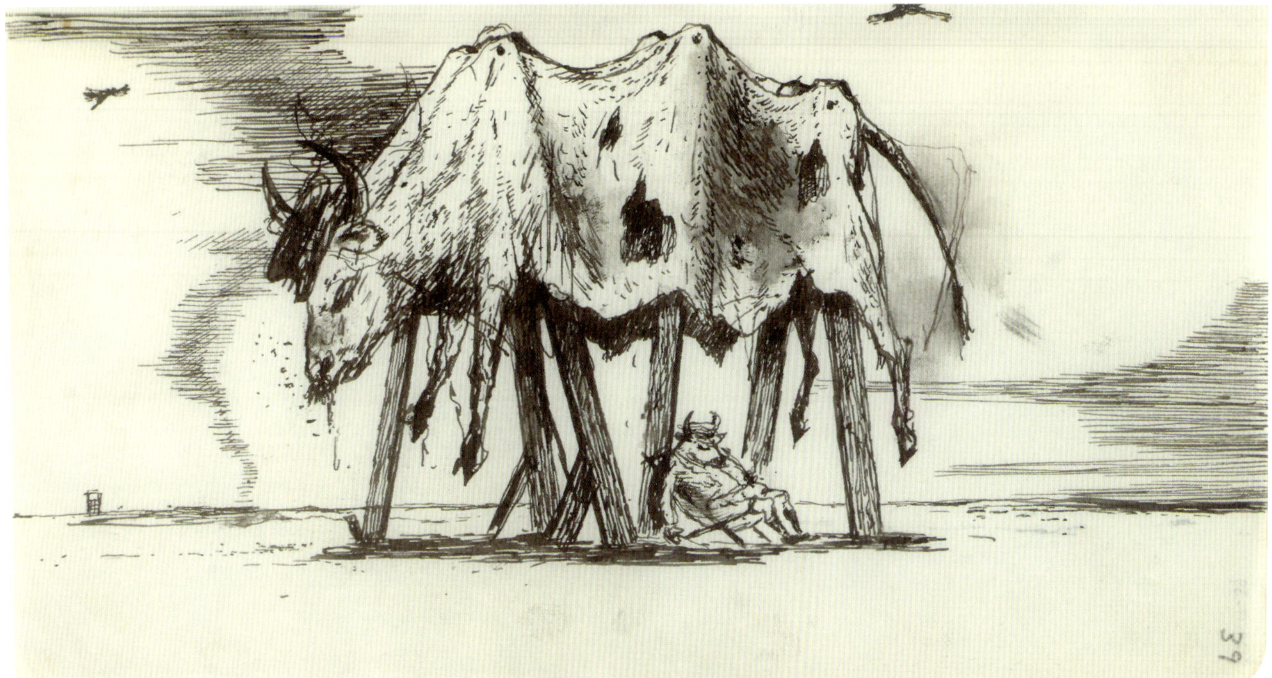

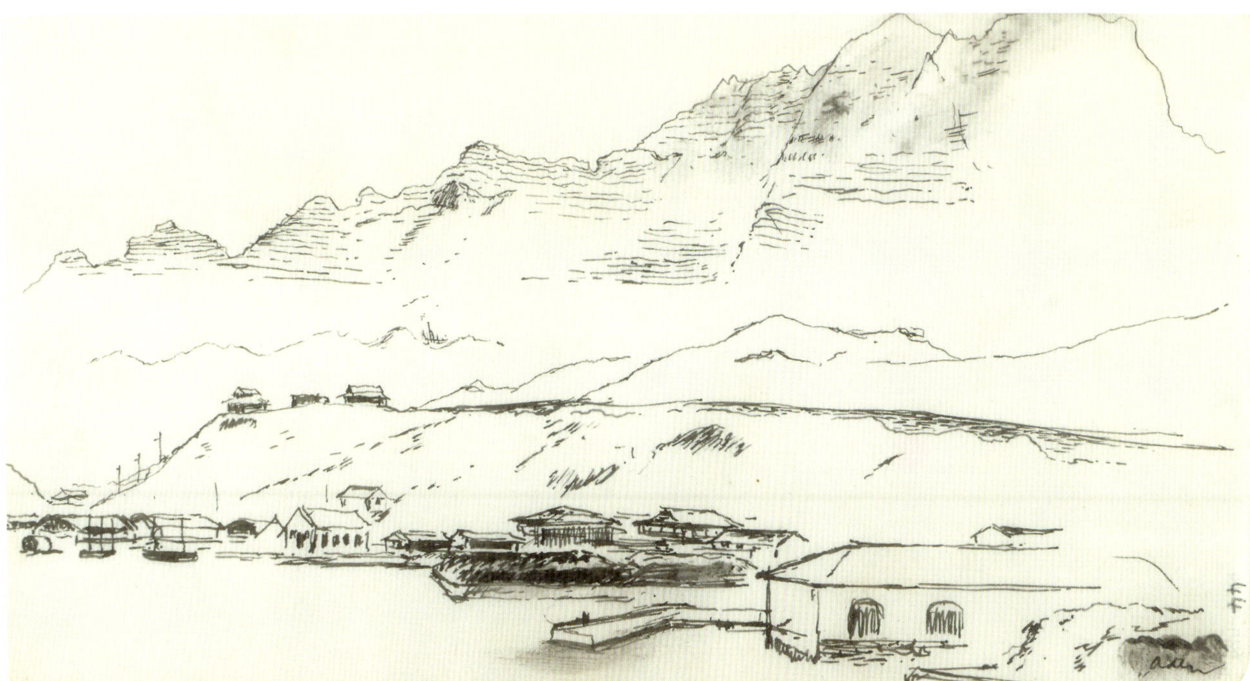

Bottom **Aden**

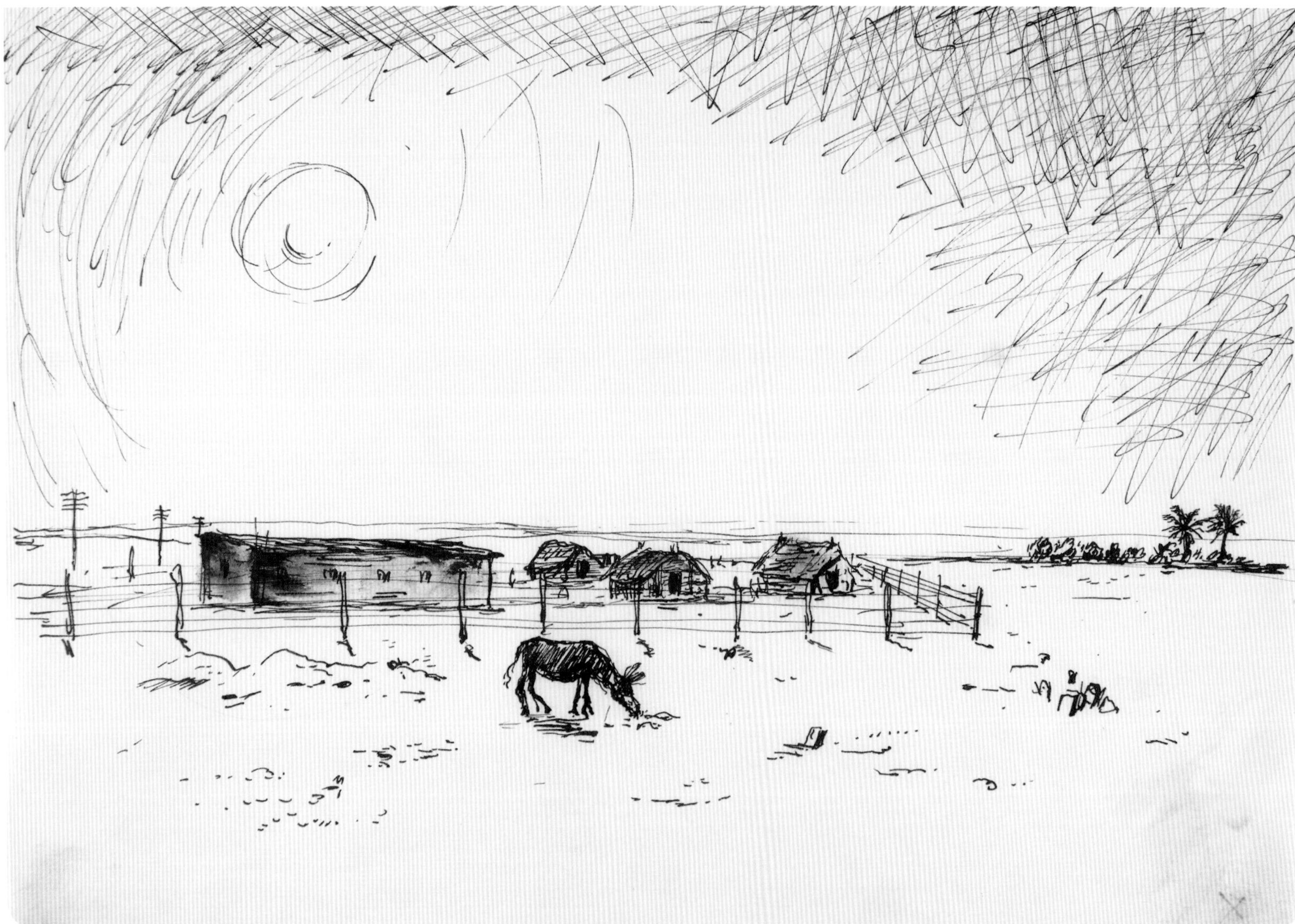

Left and opposite **Shaiba**

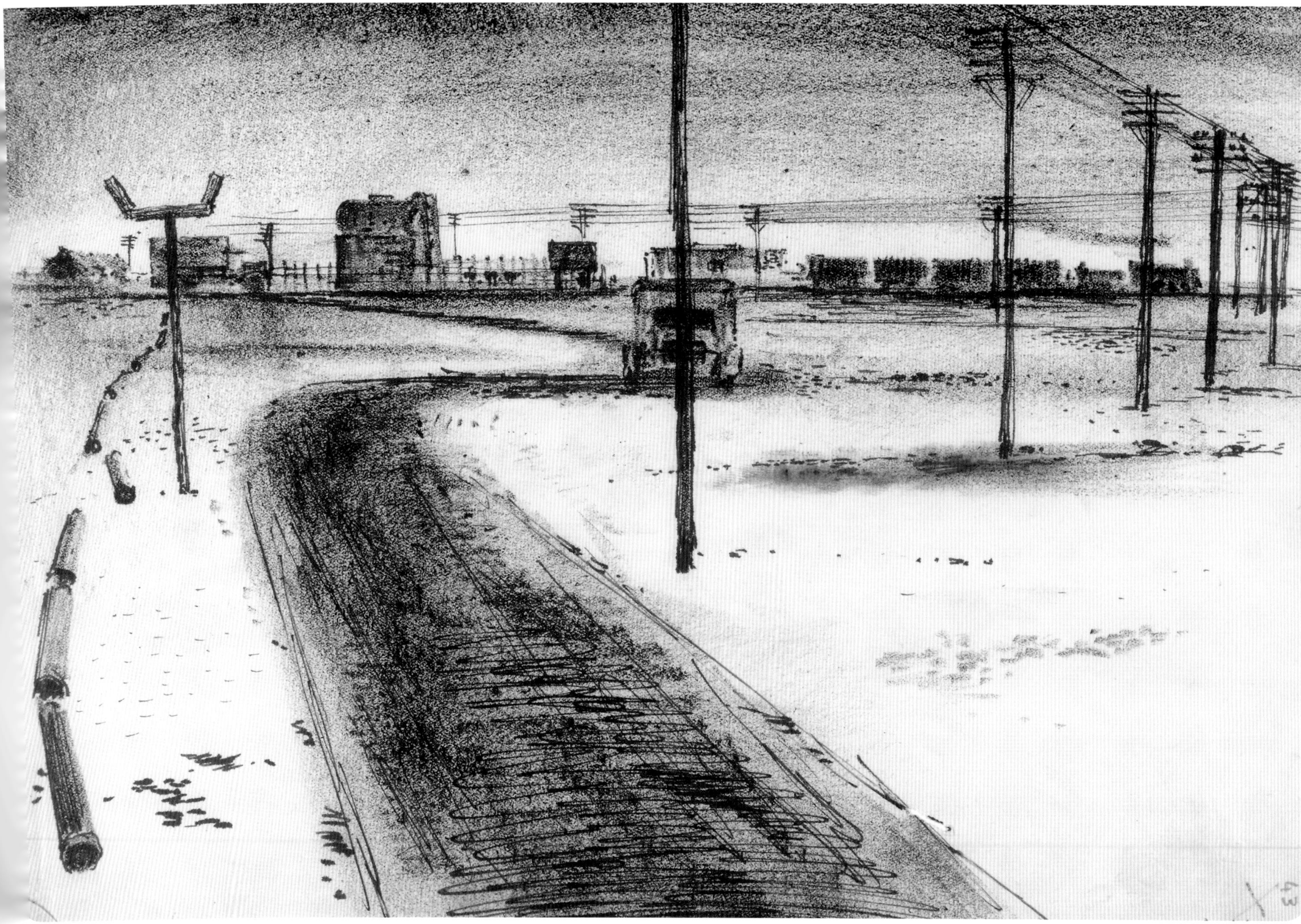

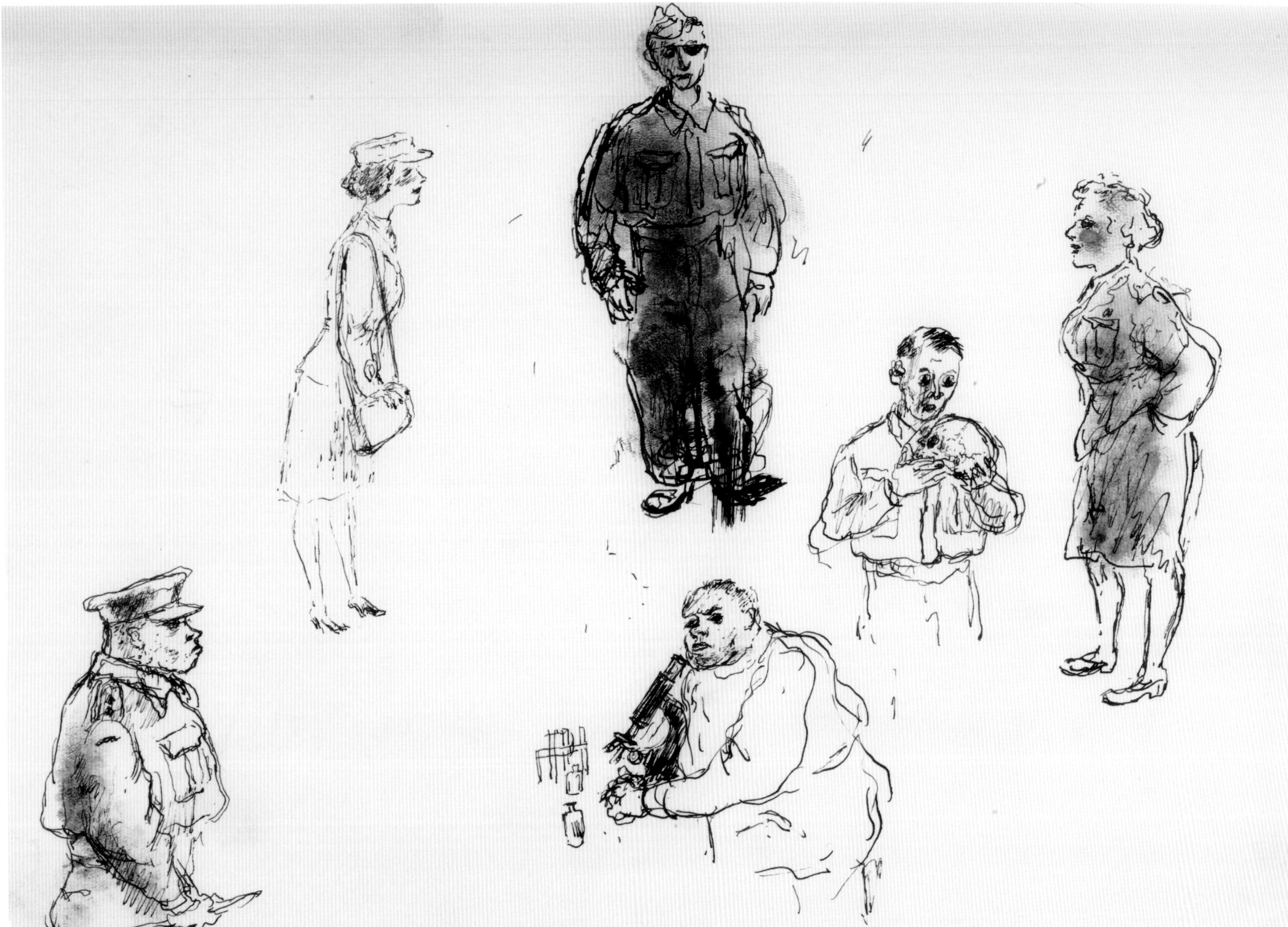

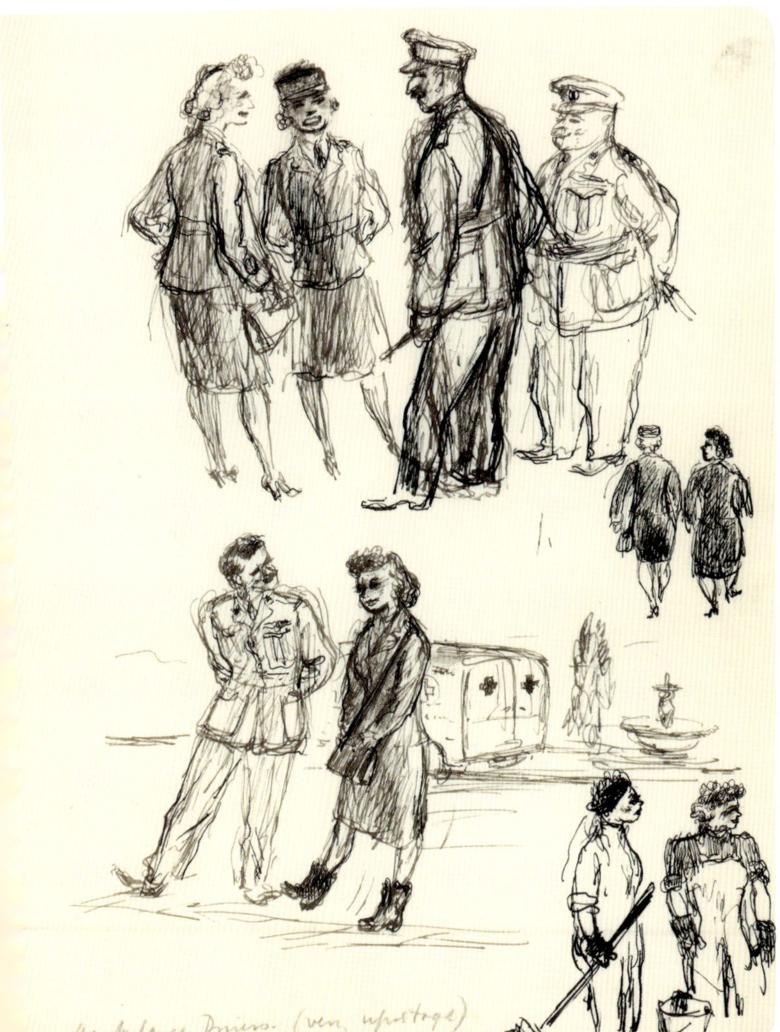

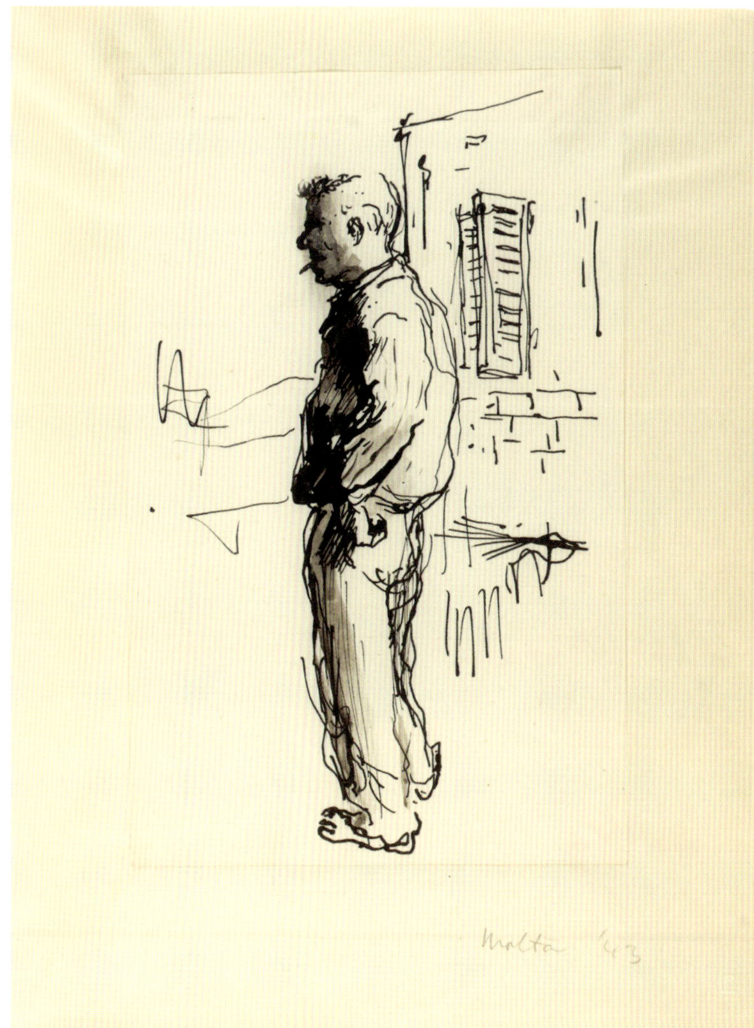

Opposite **Army Personnel**

Far left **Ambulance Drivers (Very Up-stage)**
Left **Malta**

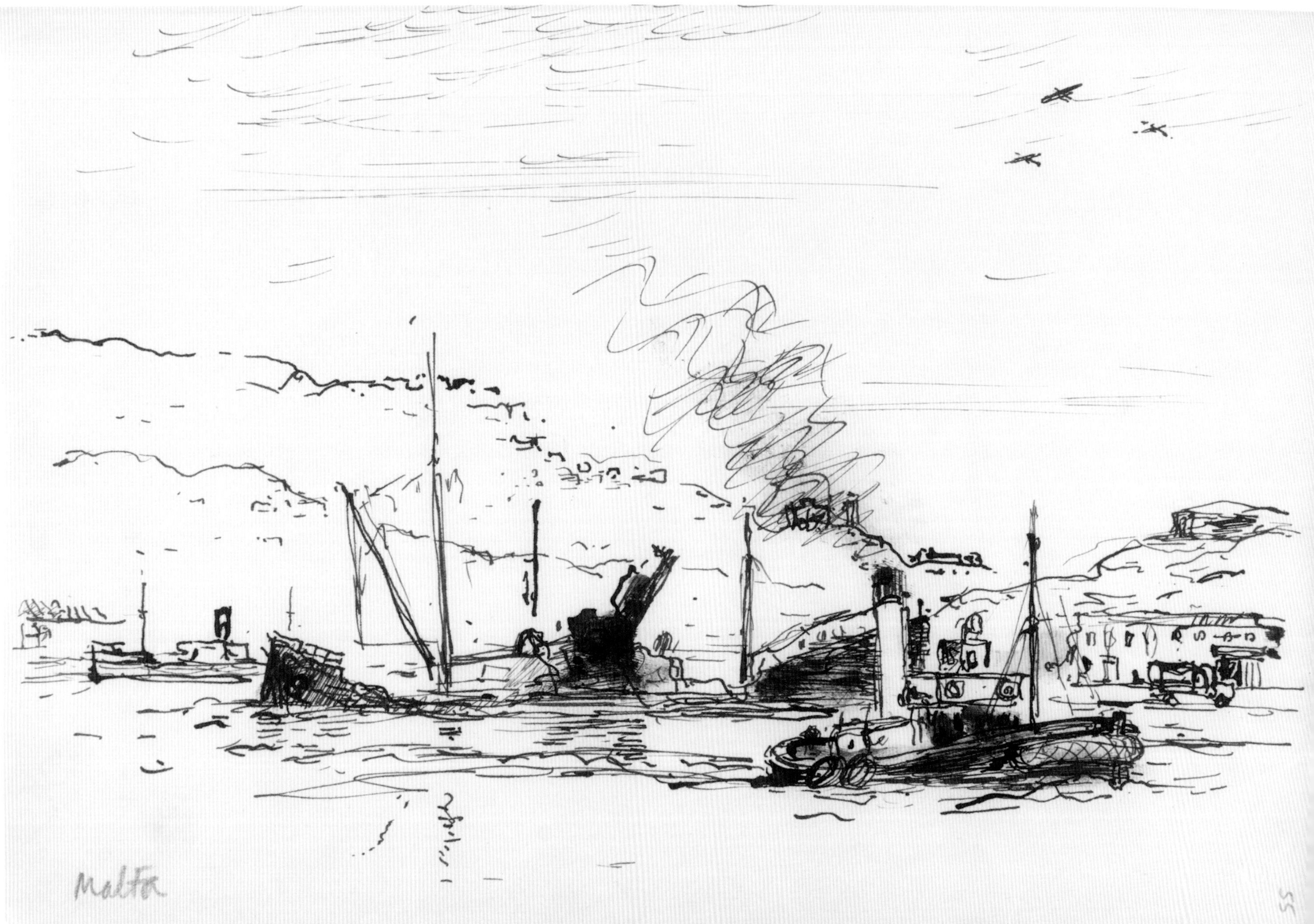
Malta

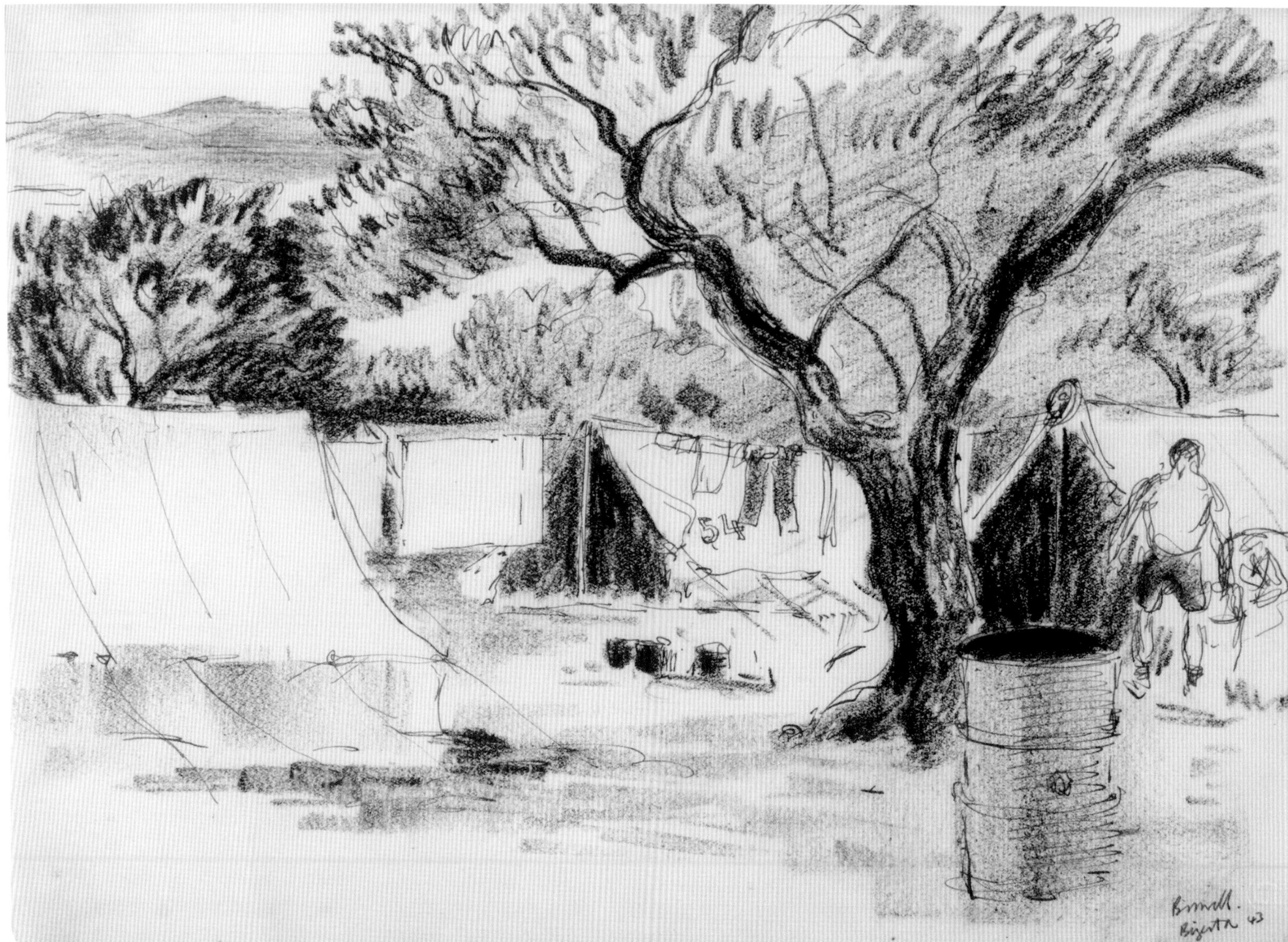

Opposite Malta

Right Bizerta, Tunisia

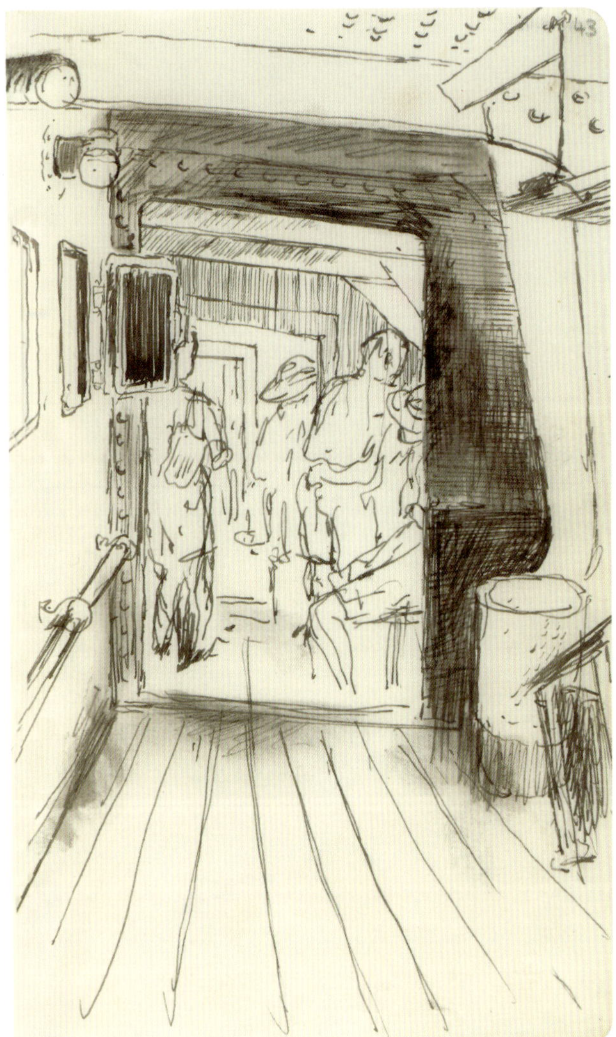

Our Mess Deck

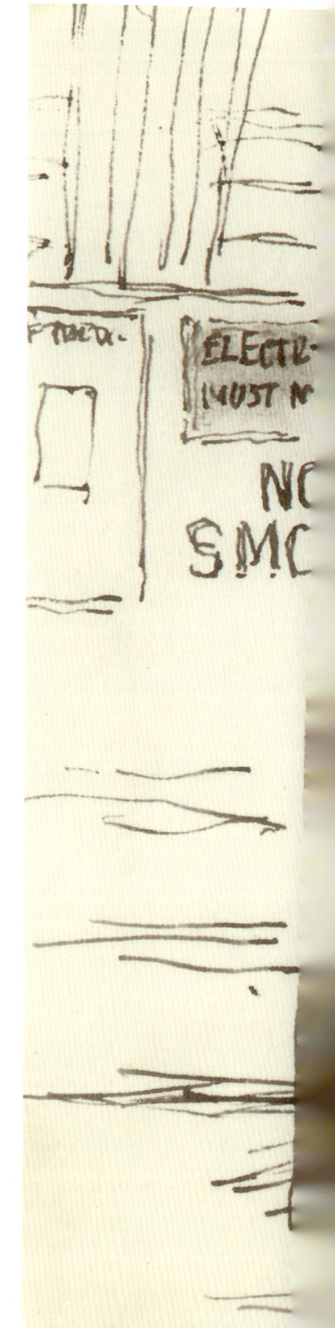

On Board Ship

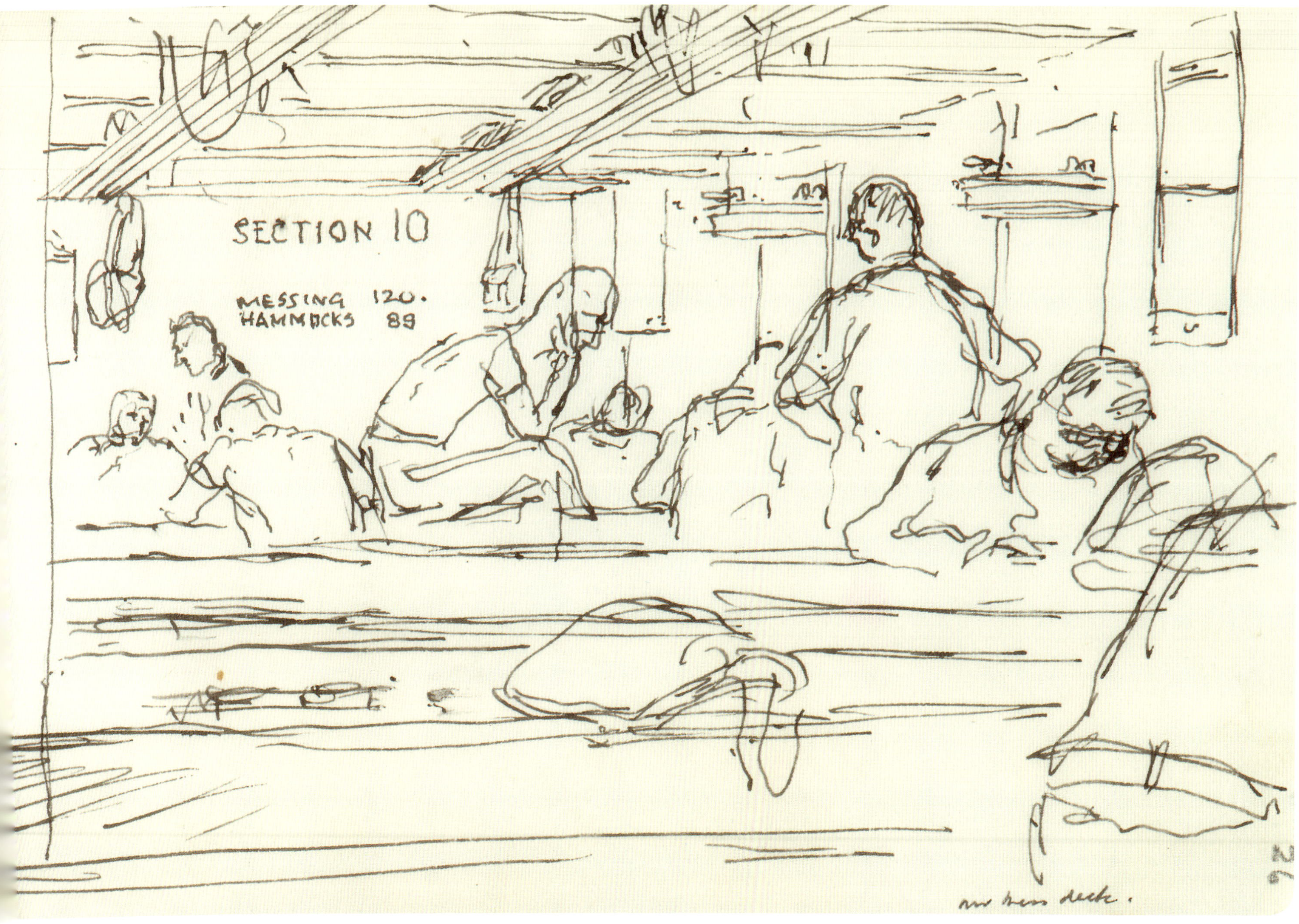
SECTION 10
MESSING 120.
HAMMOCKS 89
our mess deck.

IRAQ 1943

'Palestine is the Clapham Junction of the Empire,' it was asserted in *How is the Empire?*, a Communist Party penny pamphlet for which Boswell had provided illustrations and an armorial cover design of lion and unicorn replaced by Chamberlain and Baldwin, rampant, guarding gas mask, bomb, money-bags and truncheon. 'Millions of gallons of oil are brought from Mosul across the desert to Palestine to feed the tanks and battleships of British militarism. We cannot afford unrest here so we suppress it with brutal force.' That was in 1937. A Ministry of Information publication, *What Britain has done, 1939–1943*, had a different slant: 'The successful campaigns in Syria, Iraq and Iran consolidated the very important Middle Eastern area against Axis designs and secured the supply lines by way of the Persian Gulf to Russia.'

A Giles cartoon in *Reynolds News* summarily encapsulated the situation in early 1941. Two German soldiers are discovered drilling holes in the pipeline across a Beau Geste type desert. Four burly allied soldiers – British and Anzac – approach, rolling up their sleeves, and one of them says 'Well, well, well. Whatever will they be up to next?'

'They' had been trying to effect an anti-British coup in Iraq, a state created within the British 'sphere of influence' after the break up of the Ottoman Empire following the First World War. A treaty of 'alliance' between Britain and Iraq had been signed in 1930 and two years later Iraq became the first Arab nation in the League of Nations. The country's strategic importance to Britain however for the defence of Suez, the Anglo-Iranian Oil Company fields and the Basra to Palestine air route and pipeline, meant that when the Germans invaded Greece in April 1941 and their protégé Rashid Ali tried to seize power in Baghdad, the British had to react promptly. In May pro-German Iraqi troops opened fire on British forces round Habbaniyah, an RAF base 60 miles west of Baghdad. Retaliation was swift; Rashid Ali appealed to Hitler for assistance, failed to get it and fled to Germany. The Australian journalist Alan Moorehead, arriving soon afterwards at Habbaniyah, reported 'nothing here to be greatly excited about, nothing, apart from the technical smoothness of the operation, to be very proud of.'

Moorehead went on south to Basra, now occupied by British forces, and was not impressed. 'It festers along the banks of the Shatt-el-Arab river and the prevailing colour of this flat unlovely landscape is lifeless grey.' It was here that Boswell arrived nine months later

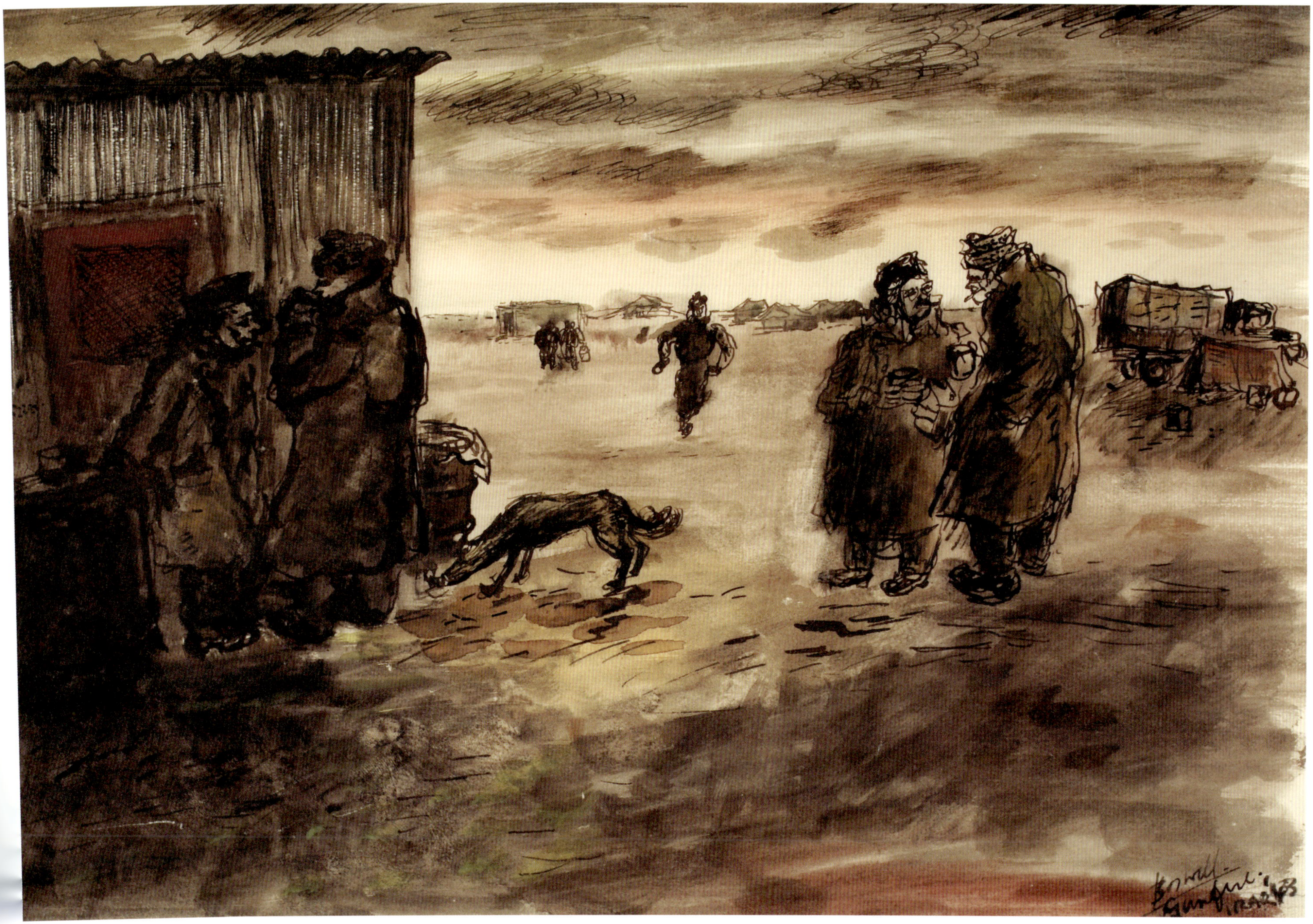

via Aden, by which time, following victory at El Alamein in the Western Desert, Iraq was less of a strategic worry. Allied HQ had been established in Baghdad and a road route had been developed through to Iran for American supplies to Russia. The troops stationed there, many of them Indian, were expected not to see action but to discourage further unrest.

In 1942 Cecil Beaton flew in to photograph Shah Faisal II (*Life Calls on Boy King of Iraq*), but he did so as an Air Ministry photographer, not an artist, for Iraq was of no great interest to those issuing instructions to the official war artists, though Edward Bawden included it on his itinerary, working in North Africa and the Middle East in two long tours interrupted by a torpedoing in the South Atlantic. In Iraq, in 1943 and 1944, he mainly drew Sheikhs and their surroundings.

Boswell's Iraq was very different. Not for him the land of Shahs or Sheikhs, let alone ancient Sumerians and Chaldeans. Spending over a year in army camps, initially near Basra at Shaiba, a field hospital and detention centre on the RAF base, later in the Khasail region near Baghdad, he worked as a radiographer for the sick (dysentery and heatstroke mainly), there being few if any wounded in the field hospitals, and he filled sketchbooks in off-duty hours with scenes of uneventful, unprivileged, service life.

Here in the middle of nowhere with barbed wire perimeters and ruler-straight roads leading to vanishing points on featureless horizons, he drew the constant unloading and loading, the business of cookhouse and latrine, tents pitched during storms, swill sloshed into oil drums and the sun threatening to melt corrugated iron roofs. The military with their telegraph wires, their hubristic or sarcastic signboards (*Victory Canteen*) and their will to turn small areas of desert into nether Aldershots, created an orderliness banal enough to be reassuring. Shimmering heat gave way to dour cold; hands in pockets, cigarette permanently on the lip, men stood around, watching for stuff to scrounge. Earth removed for roadbuilding and brickmaking left rectangular roadside craters like conveniently placed graves.

The setting provoked Boswell to full-on surreality: deserts filled with Daliesque hallucinations, skeletal structures dripping cultural fragments, a coffin-size cage of barbed wire in which a poor dumb private stands helpless. A hide stretched over a wooden framework gives shade to a bully-general sound asleep, dreaming of peerages and victory parades. These compare to the wartime work of

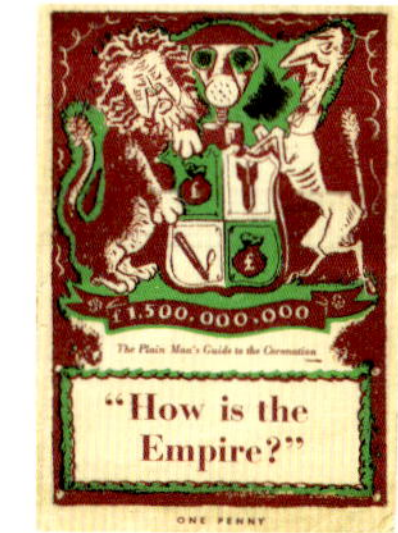

Communist Party Pamphlet 1937

Julian Trevelyan, the AIA painter and wearer of a Chamberlain mask in the May Day parade of ’38, who found that drawing ‘quasi-Surrealist satires on the Army’ helped preserve his sanity. (One of his efforts, he remembered, was ‘a monster, half myself no doubt with grand piano legs, weeping flowers and poetry into a steel helmet.’) Trevelyan devised camouflage schemes and at one stage toured the Western Desert checking the construction of dummy railheads made up of oil drums and planks to fool the enemy. Boswell’s kitbag Surrealism was similarly bizarre and equally a distraction: an excursion into the symbolical. His ordinary drawings, by contrast, have humour, atmosphere and attentive qualities; prosaic as they are, recording the minutiae of army life in alien territory, they complement the ghostly images that Private Boswell (radiographer) was responsible for producing.

‘Second Stag’: middle watch and outside a tent where a sergeant writes home by the yellow light of a hurricane lamp an overcoated figure stands (the artist himself maybe) marvelling at the stars.

Boswell set down his thoughts on such a night:

‘Here in the Euphrates valley we work and play. We do all the things that soldiers have always done – drink, gossip, gamble, fight, sleep as much as we can and carry on a guerrilla war against the ennui that descends on an idle army…Fifty miles out here is as good as fifty years.

‘Stalingrad has begun to strike back. To the west the Eighth have begun their drive from Alamein. But here there is quiet and news is scarce and sometimes when the rain cuts us off for days, our world shrinks to a tiny island… No steady stream of casualties fills our hospital to remind us that we are part of the war. For us there is only the tedious everyday struggle against malaria, dysentery and boredom.

‘The dust floats evocative of human suffering and vanity in the impersonal glare of a savage sun and we are caught in a web of circumstance that stretches into past and future in an infinite series of repeated patterns…It’s all a badly done stage setting – characterless and obvious. The yellow sand, the date palm, the inevitable camel and the shameless vulgarity of it the sunsets awake no other memories than the *Desert Song* and the Woolworths calendar.

‘In dreams, waking, suddenly in the night and in daylight moments of evocation that

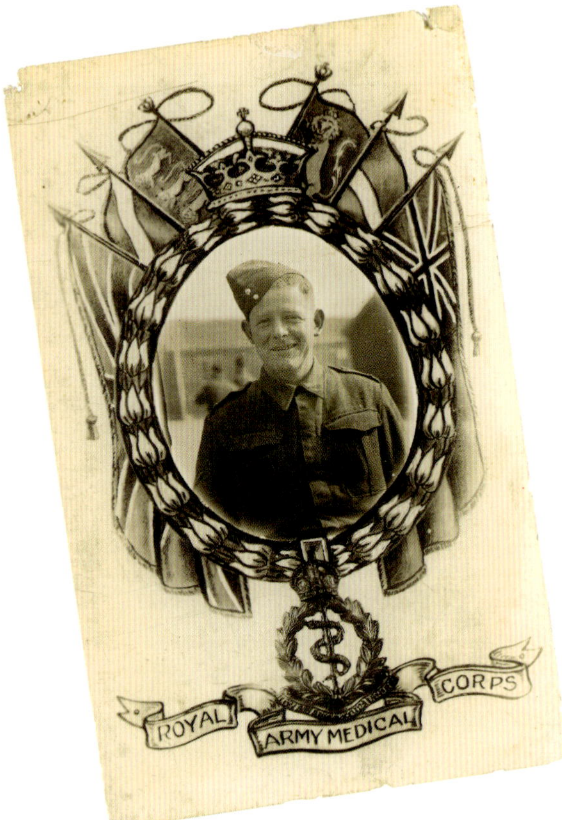

Chapter opener **Gunfire**

Above **7392959 Private Boswell J.**

Opposite **Private Boswell**

say what to paint. The lorry lights along the palings, the shadows and cords of the hammocks at night in the belly of the ship, the faces in the hurricane lamplight and the blue crude letters on the ration boxes. And the worn wooden floors of trucks and railway wagons – all that is worn and used until it has grown a patina of humanity like the dining tables scrubbed yellow in the sun or the mallets and spades and the tents whose textures ensnare soldiers' dreams. The comforting look of a petrol tin grey with soap and the bridal colour of the nets. And a hundred things.

'So to eliminate the incidental. To extract the dream reality, to evoke the unreality of the soldier's life. In the world that lives in dreams are the pictures that say what we love and how we feel. False worlds, we create to hide our past from us. Reality glows through only that true world of dream and love and terror.

'Man is lost among the uncountable grains of sand and here above all if he had no God would he find it necessary to invent one. And here above all would belief be unassailable… In the comfort and comradeship of cities the stark framework of which man has built his world can be concealed in the social sense of communication. These comfortable rationalisations have no validity in the desert world.'

At Kavassin ('Kav'), 17 Reinforcement Camp, on the railway line near Baghdad, the encampment was permanent, with Nissen huts and a proper brick building for the Roman Catholic canteen. Boswell concentrated for a while on detailed description: stores stocked with boxes of Service Biscuits, Australian beef sausages, sweetened condensed milk and M&V (Meat & Veg) rations. He also drew, as though memorising the set-up, *One of our Rooms (the one we lived in)*. Bed, sink, towels, radiography equipment and the procedures followed when each new case was stretchered in, X-rayed, diagnosed over the light box and operated upon.

Men as specimens: the Tommy sweltering beneath his pinup calendar, the laundry squad prodding a tub of soaked clothing (*Cheese Pie*), then off for the evening or perhaps a spot of leave. (*Eric goes to town with stardust! Oh boy.*) Transported into Baghdad by Passion Wagon, there to get drunk and loiter in River Street, outside the Babylon Hotel, assessing the temptresses. (There were further drawings of women undressing and performing blow jobs.)

At Baghdad West station Boswell tried sketching the locals but obviously felt excessively detached as they sat inscrutably or scurried past: remote creatures, as picturesque as extras in *The Thief of Baghdad*. It was easier to draw inconspicuous native supernumeraries back at the base, washboys with water cans and service caps, a child begging and two soldiers (used to it by now) affecting incomprehension. Later on he elaborated some of these studies as magazine illustrations. Others he worked up into exhibition pictures, emphasising the backdrop look of scooped and hollowed ground, sunbaked orange and yellow, the dereliction of buildings and always a stray dog nosing about.

Iraq ceased to be a danger spot on the War Office maps. By the autumn the Allies pretty well controlled the Mediterranean and so when Boswell was shipped home he went by way of Egypt and Libya, making the odd drawing at ports of call, Benghazi and Bizerta (tents under olive trees), Malta (a wreck in Valetta harbour) and on to Gibraltar. He arrived in London just before Christmas 1943.

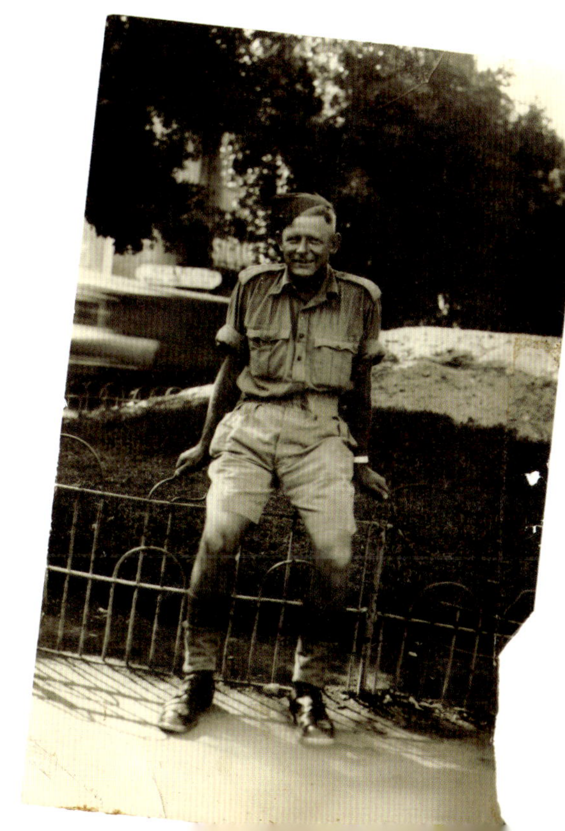

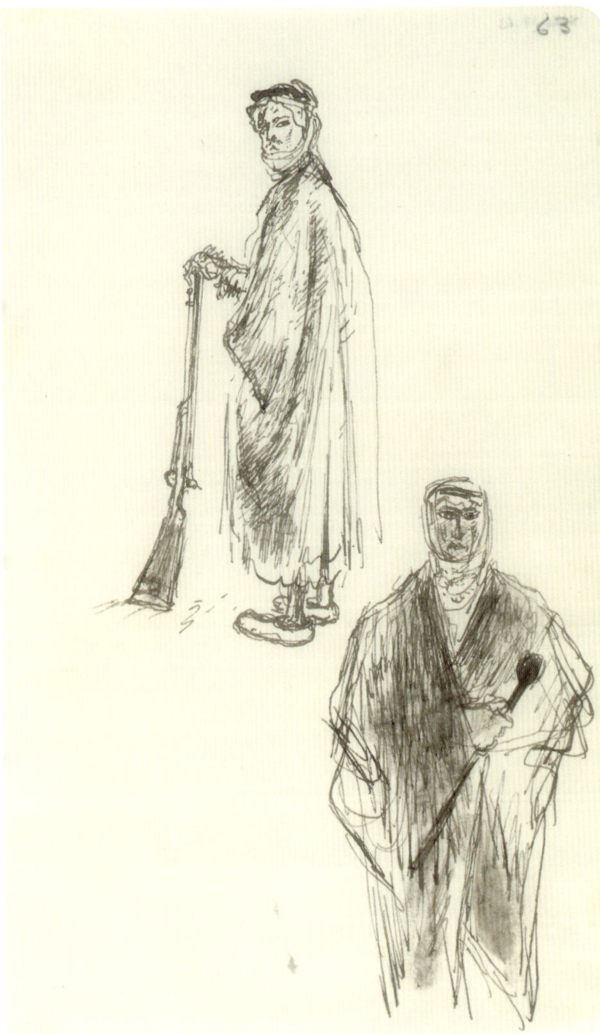
63

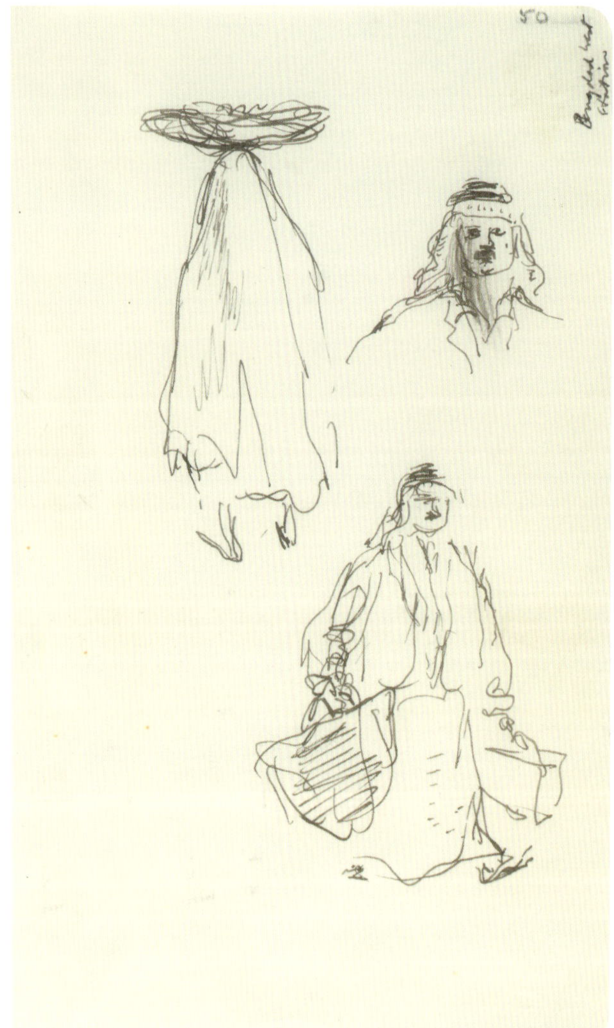
50

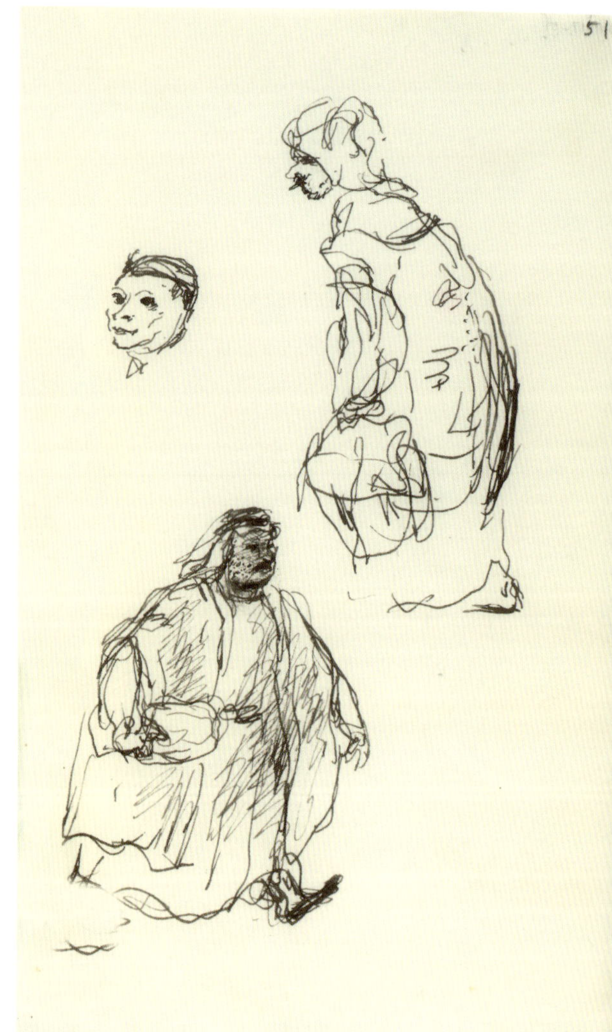
51

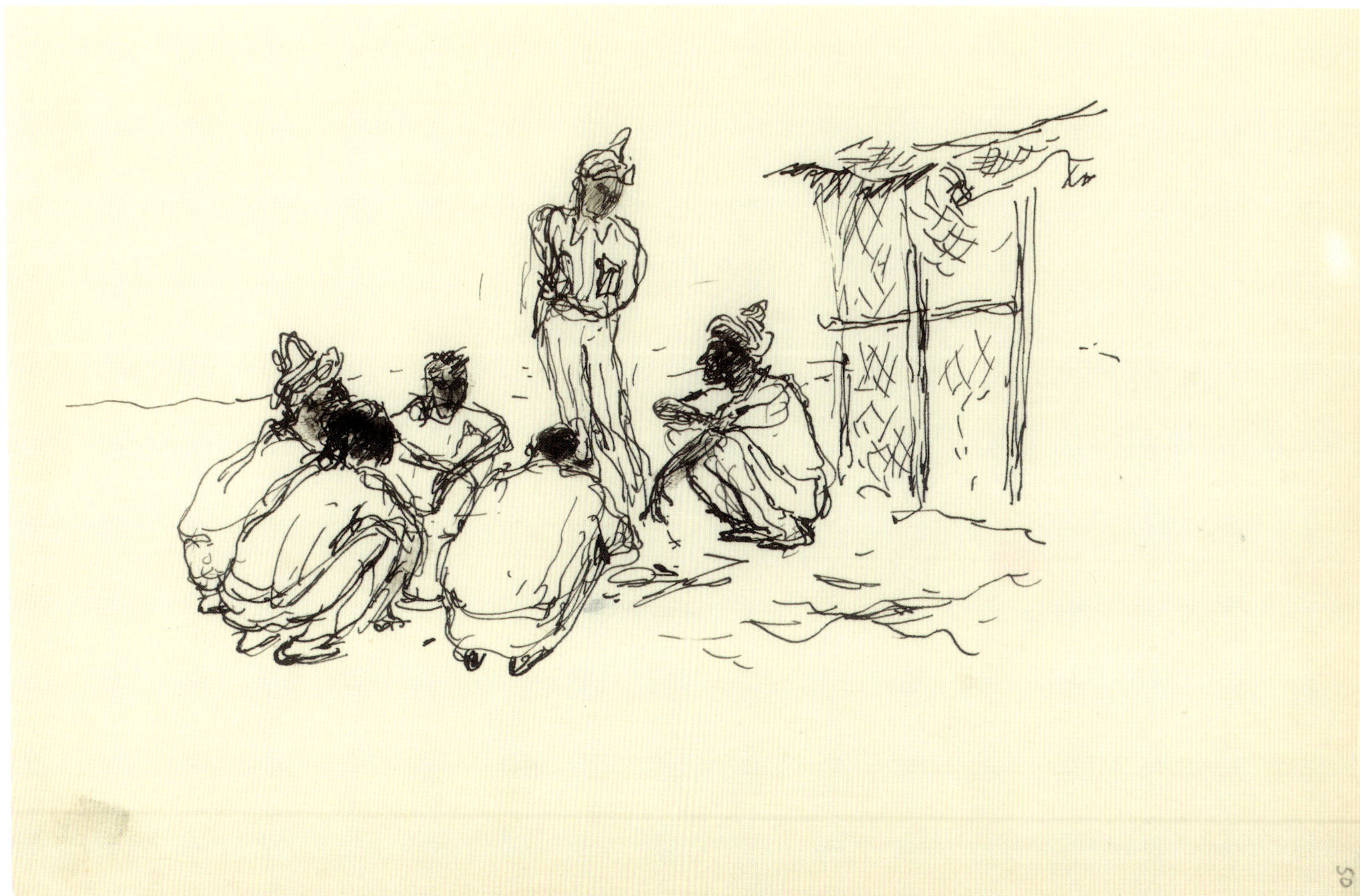

Opposite Baghdad 1-3

Right Baghdad 4

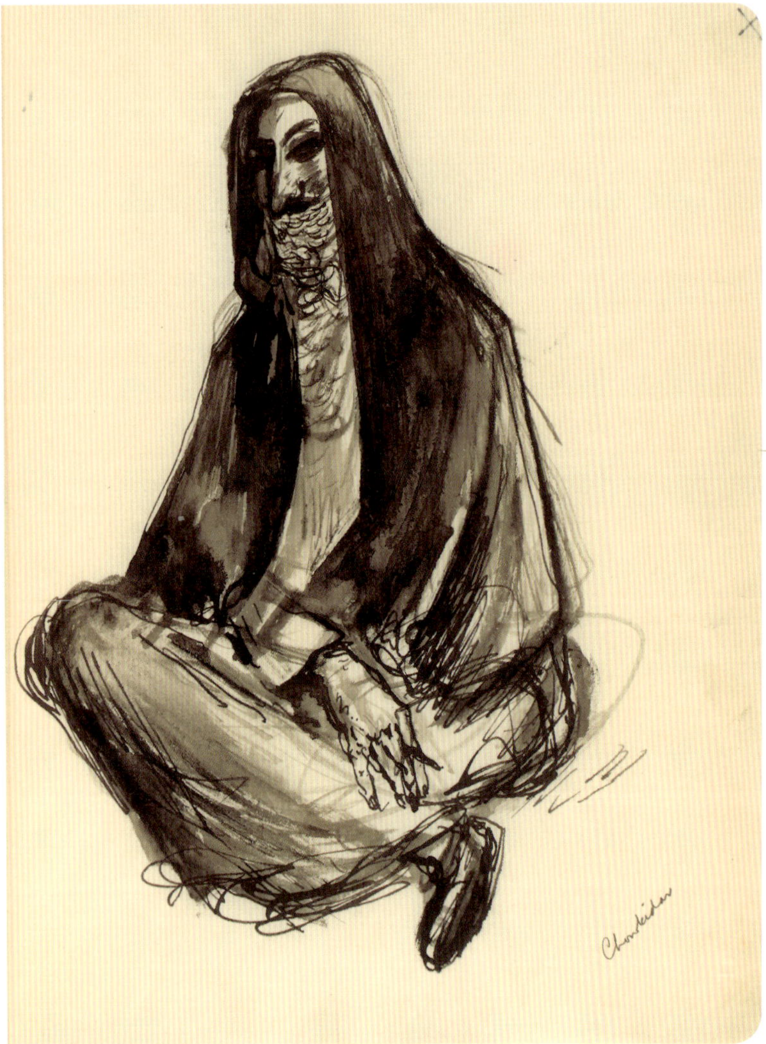

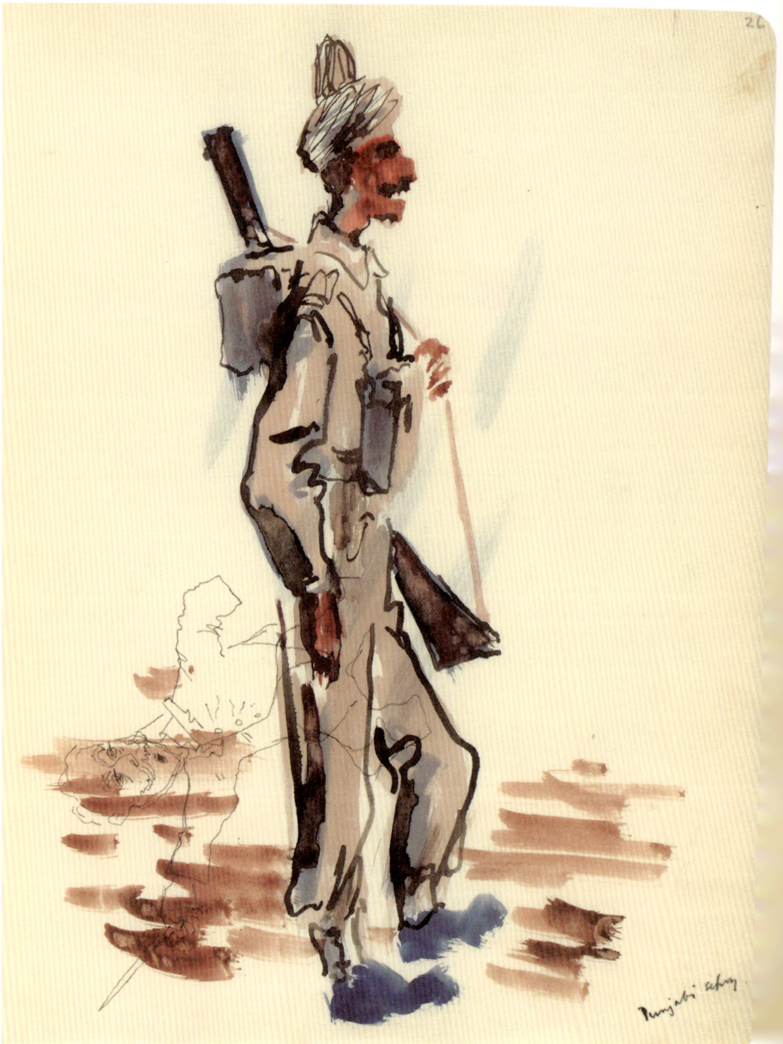

Far right **Chowkidar**
Right **Punjabi Sepoy**

Opposite **Break for Khama**

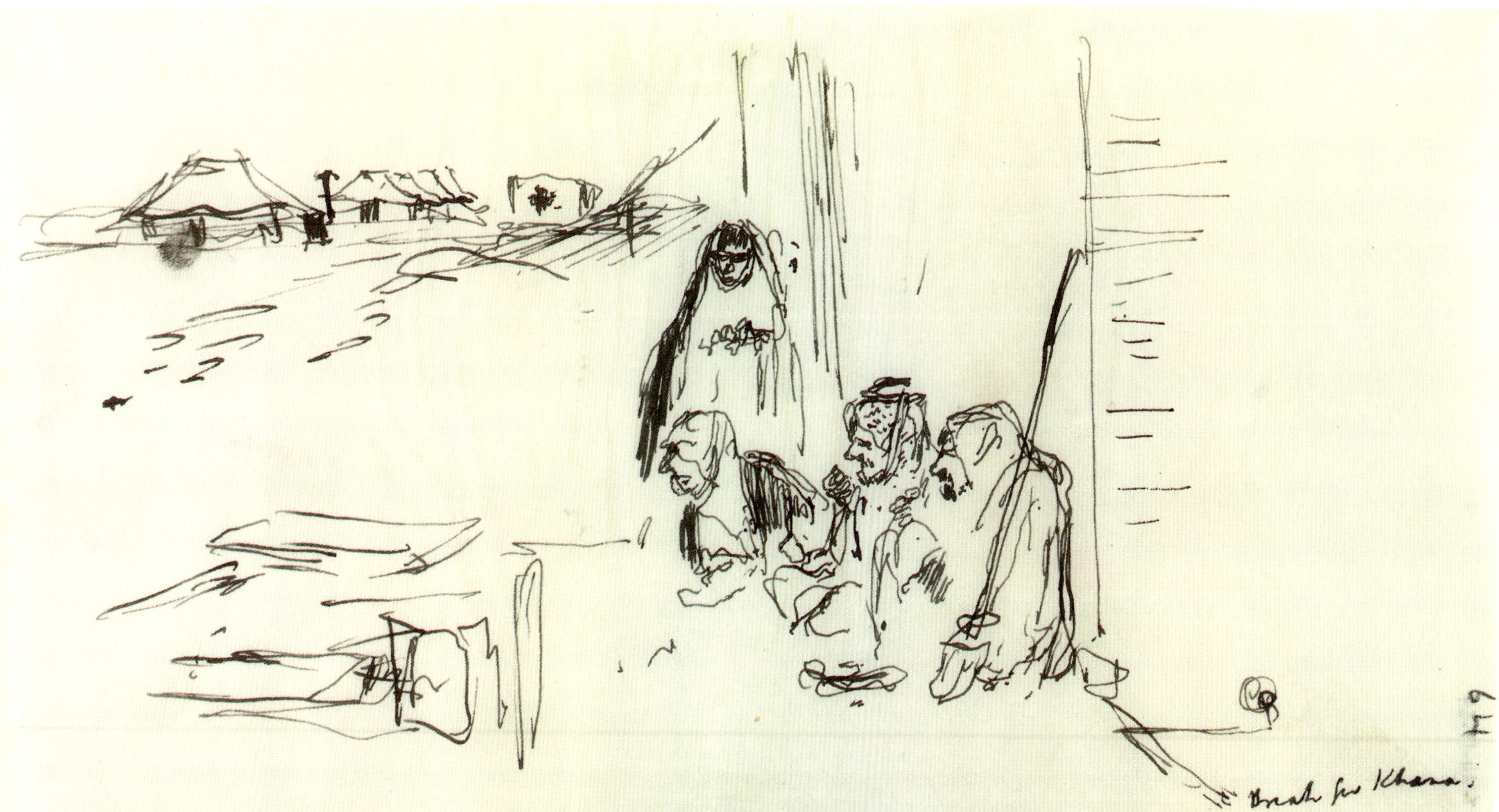
Break for Khana.

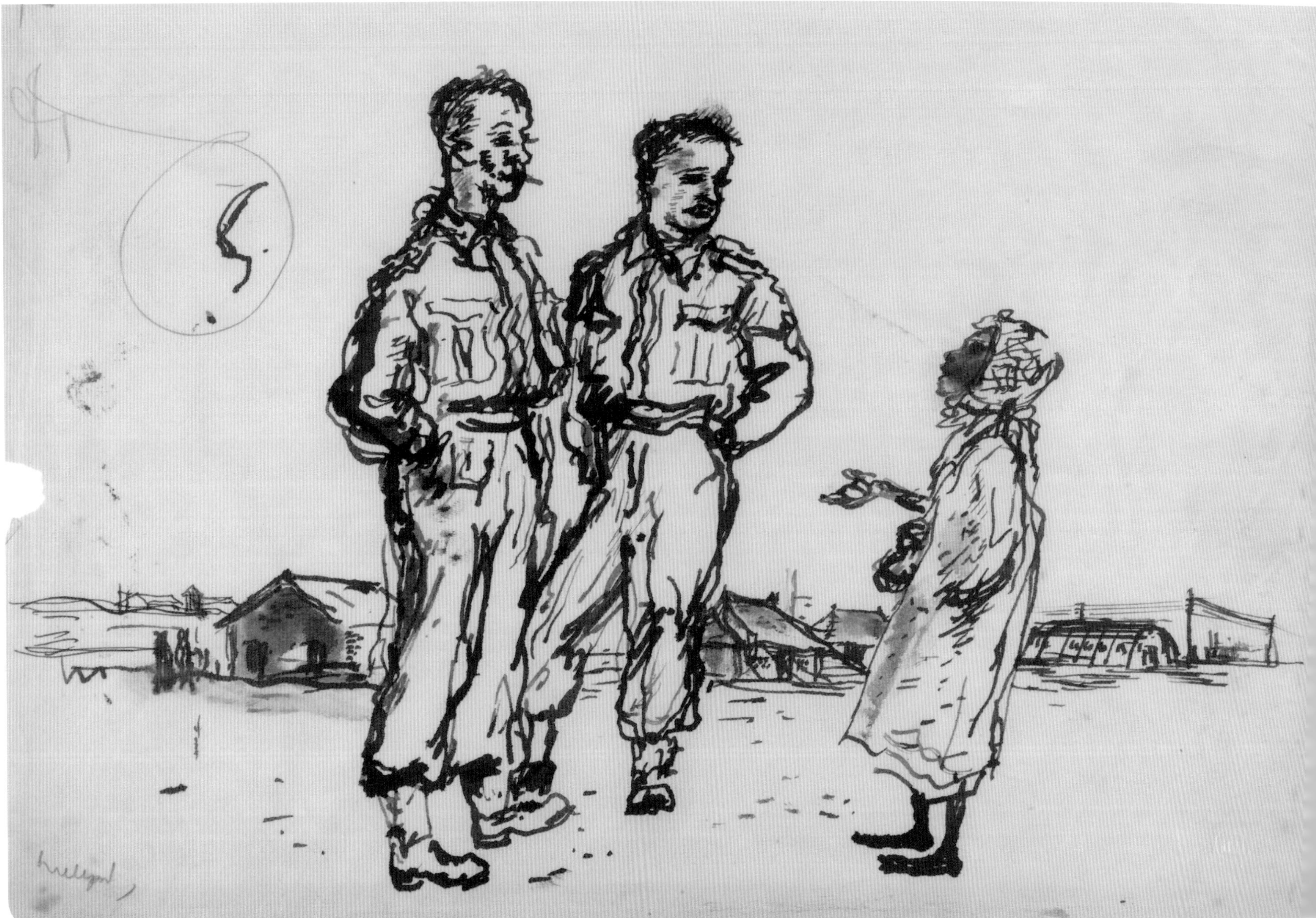

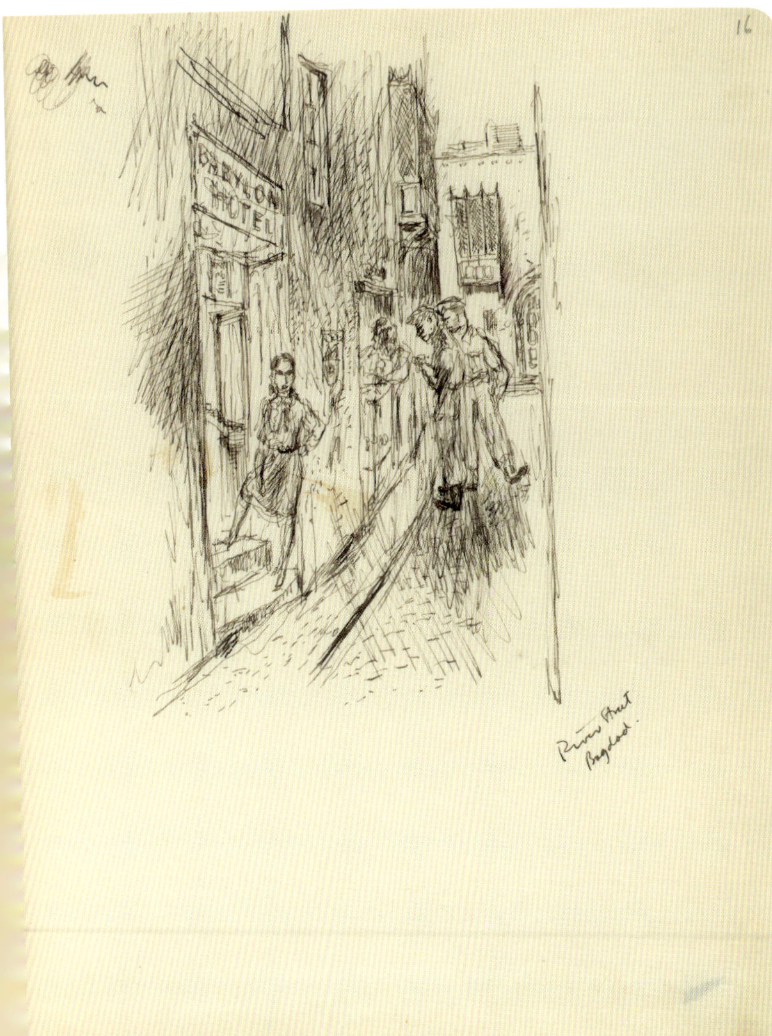

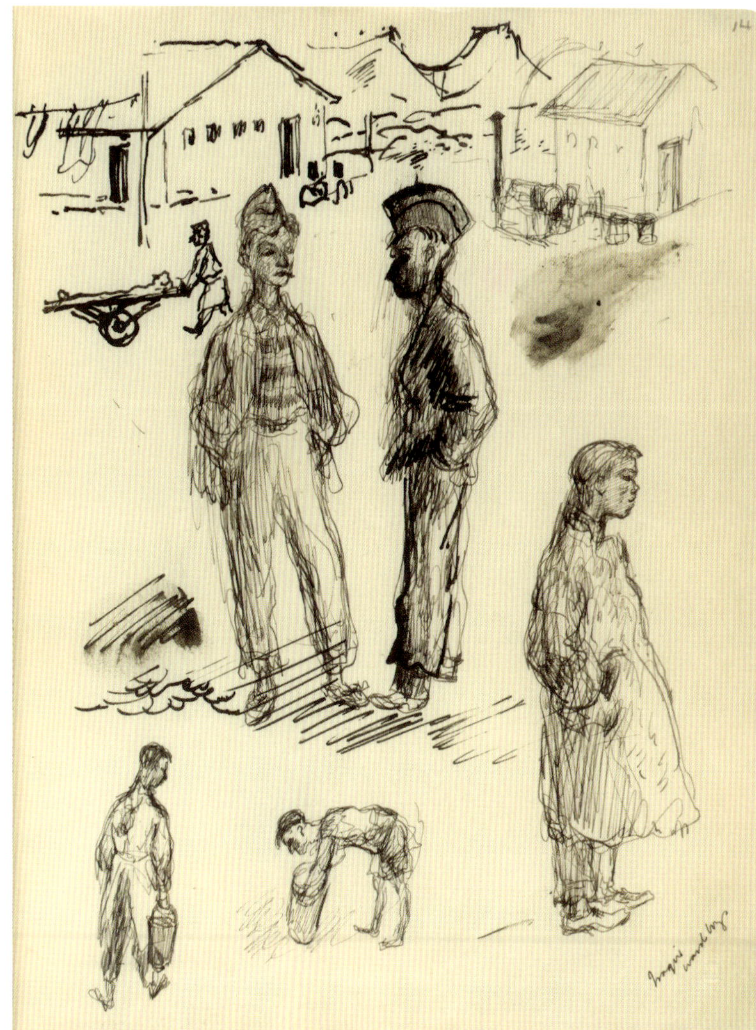

Opposite **Baksheesh**

Far left **River Street, Baghdad**

Left **Iraqi Washboys**

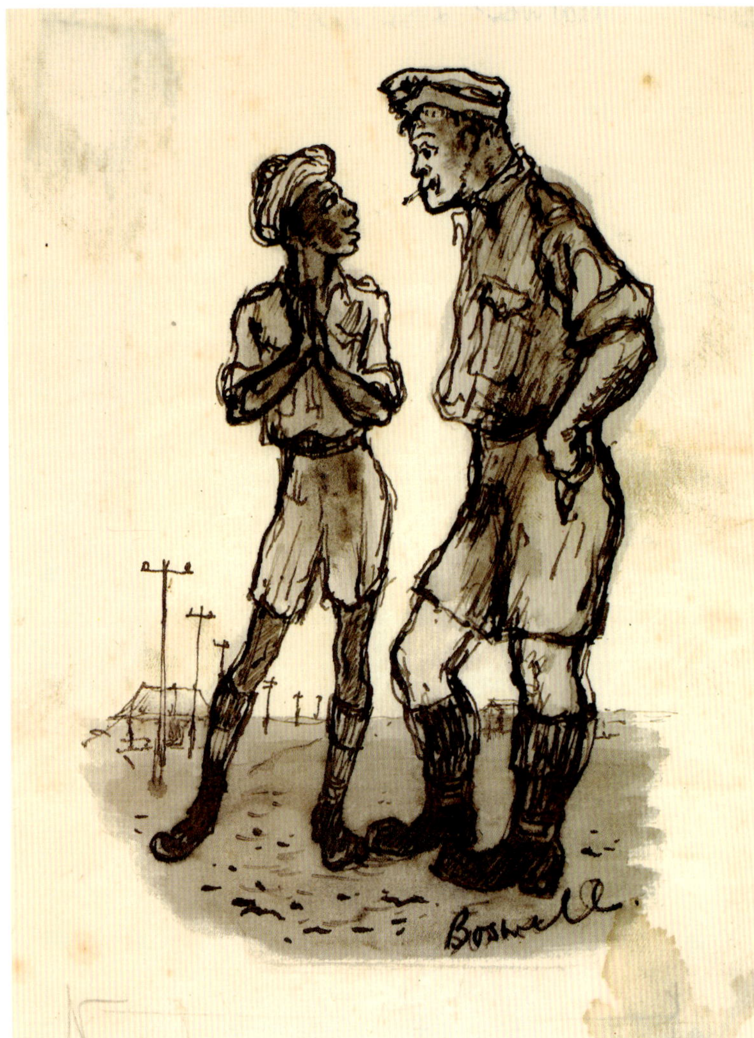

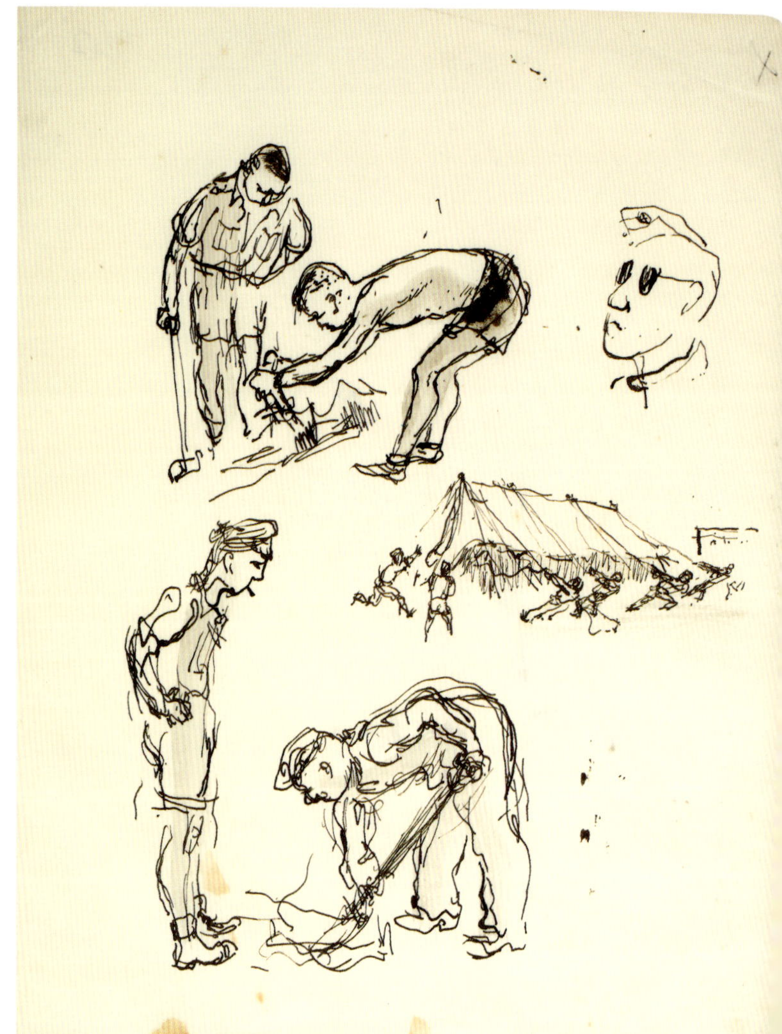

Right **Native and Soldier**

Far right **Setting up Camp**

Opposite **Cooking**

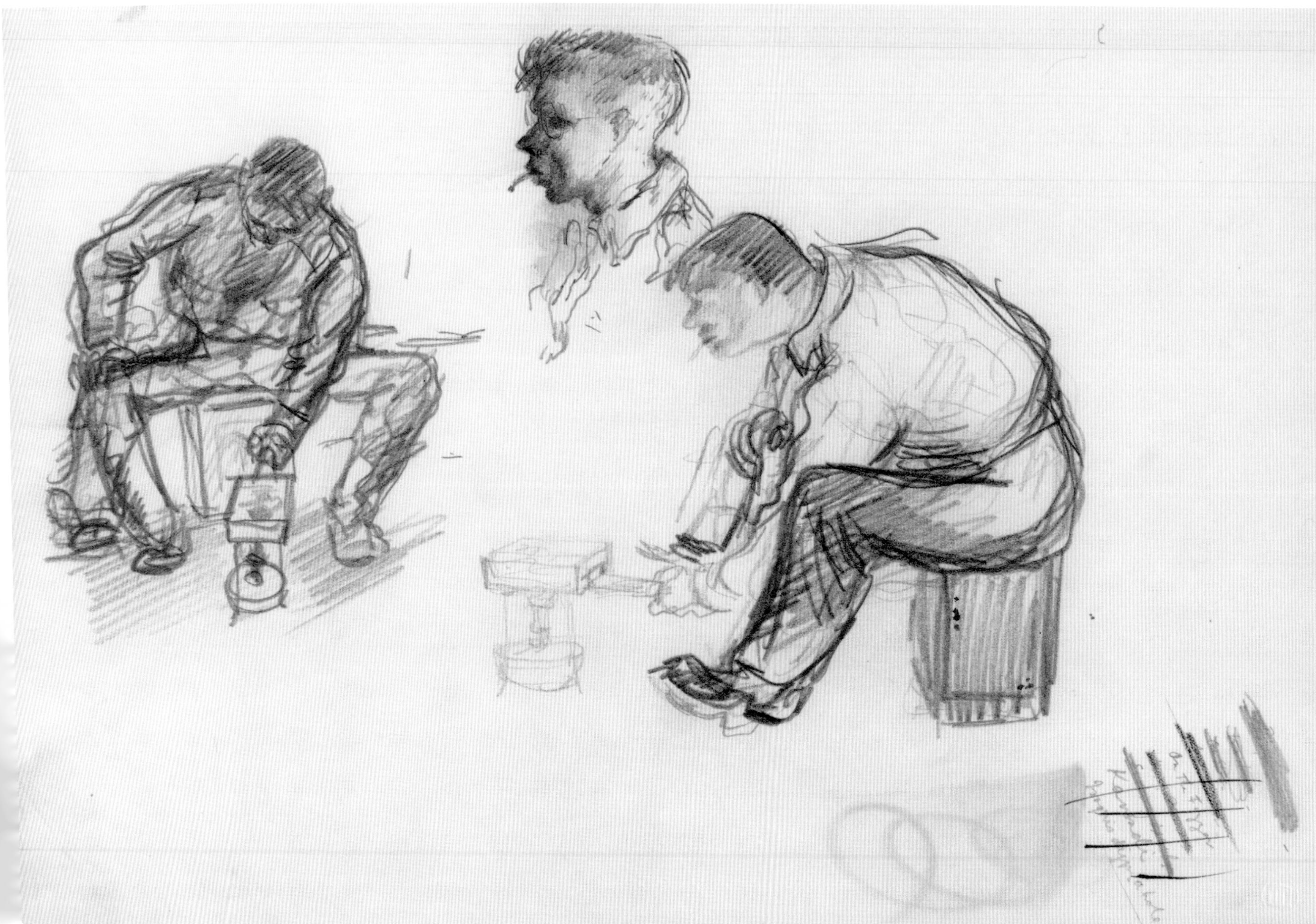

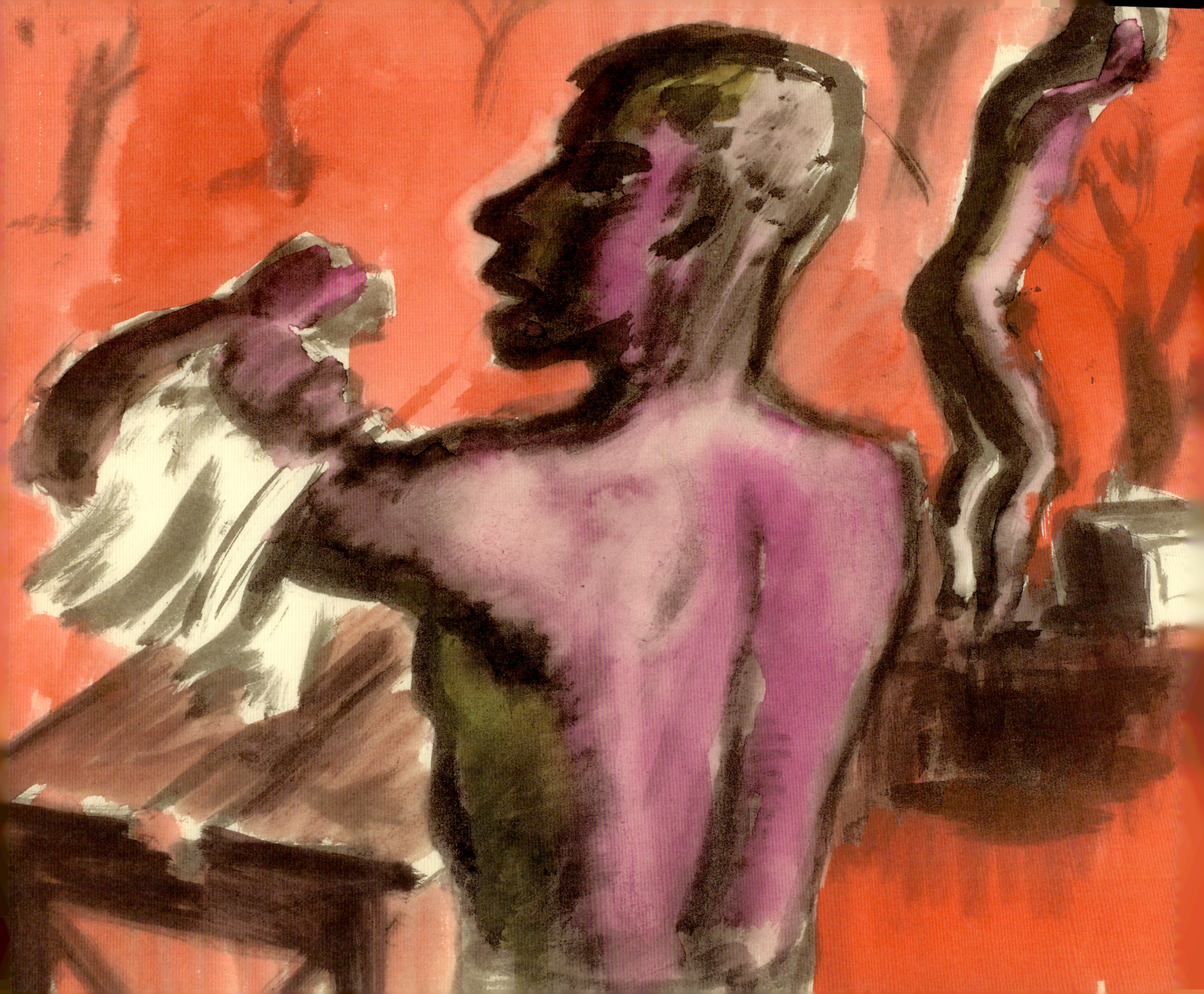

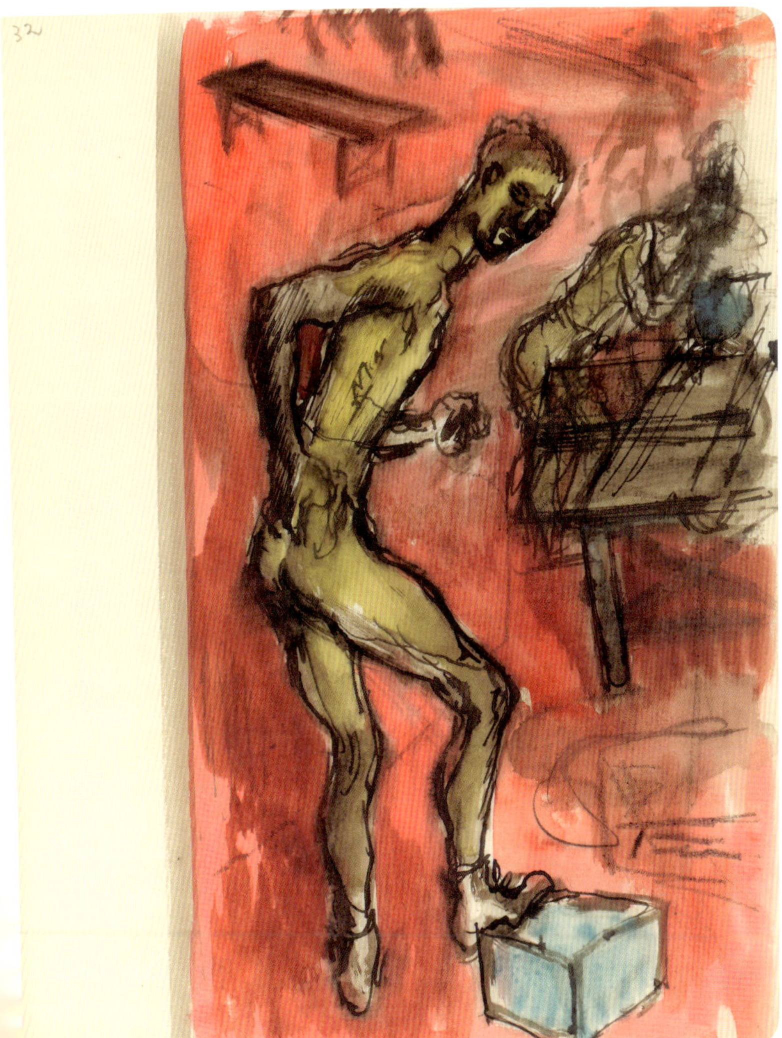

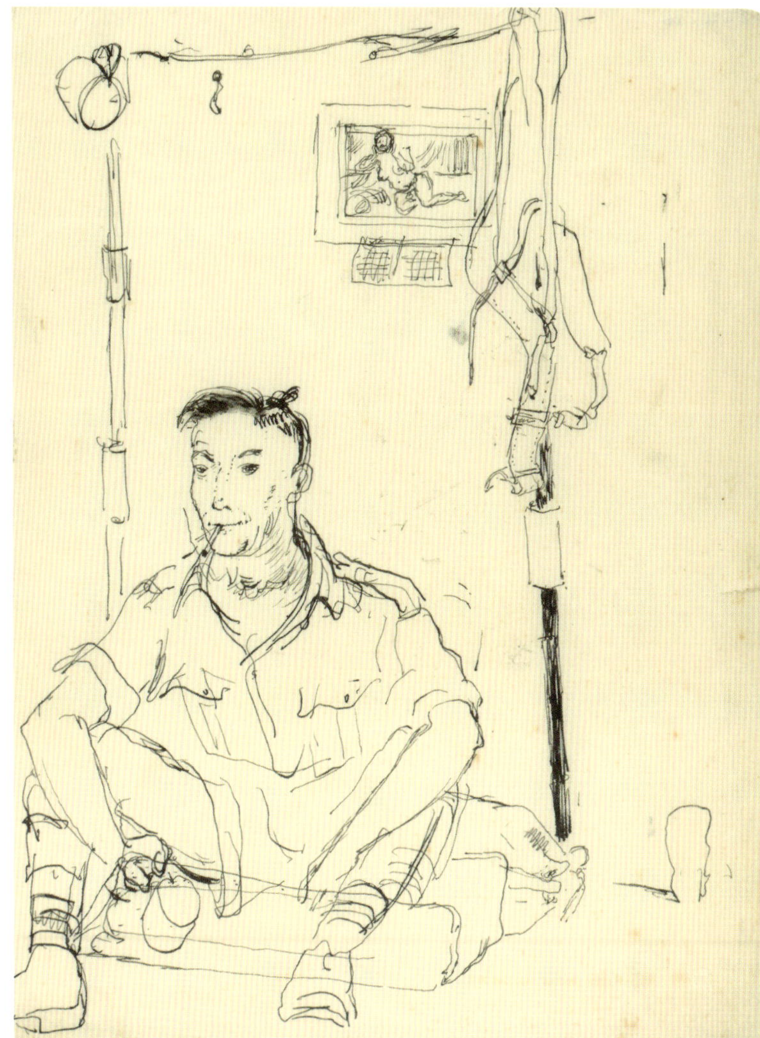

Opposite **Showers**

Far left **Showering**

Left **At Ease**

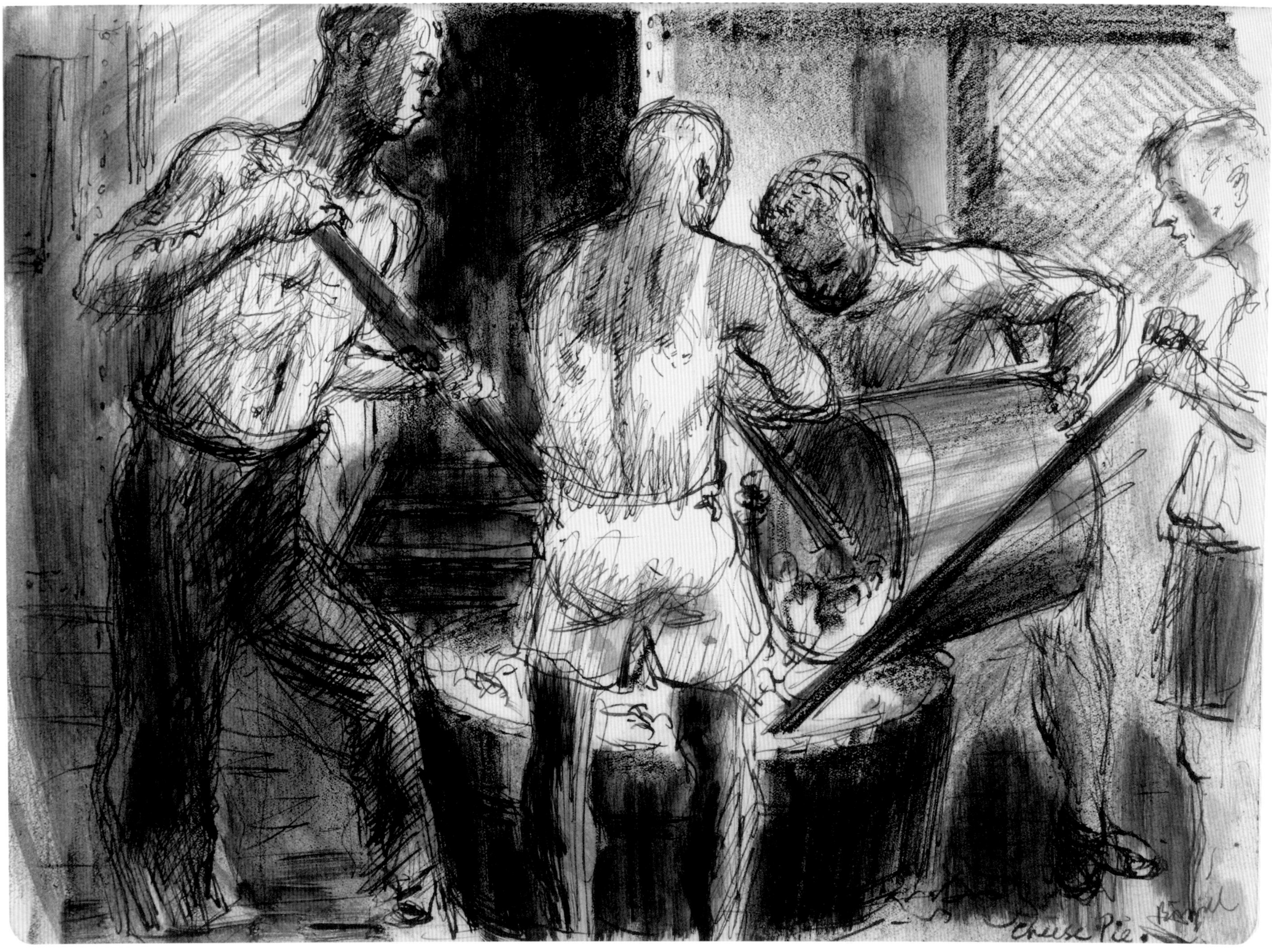
Cheese Pie.

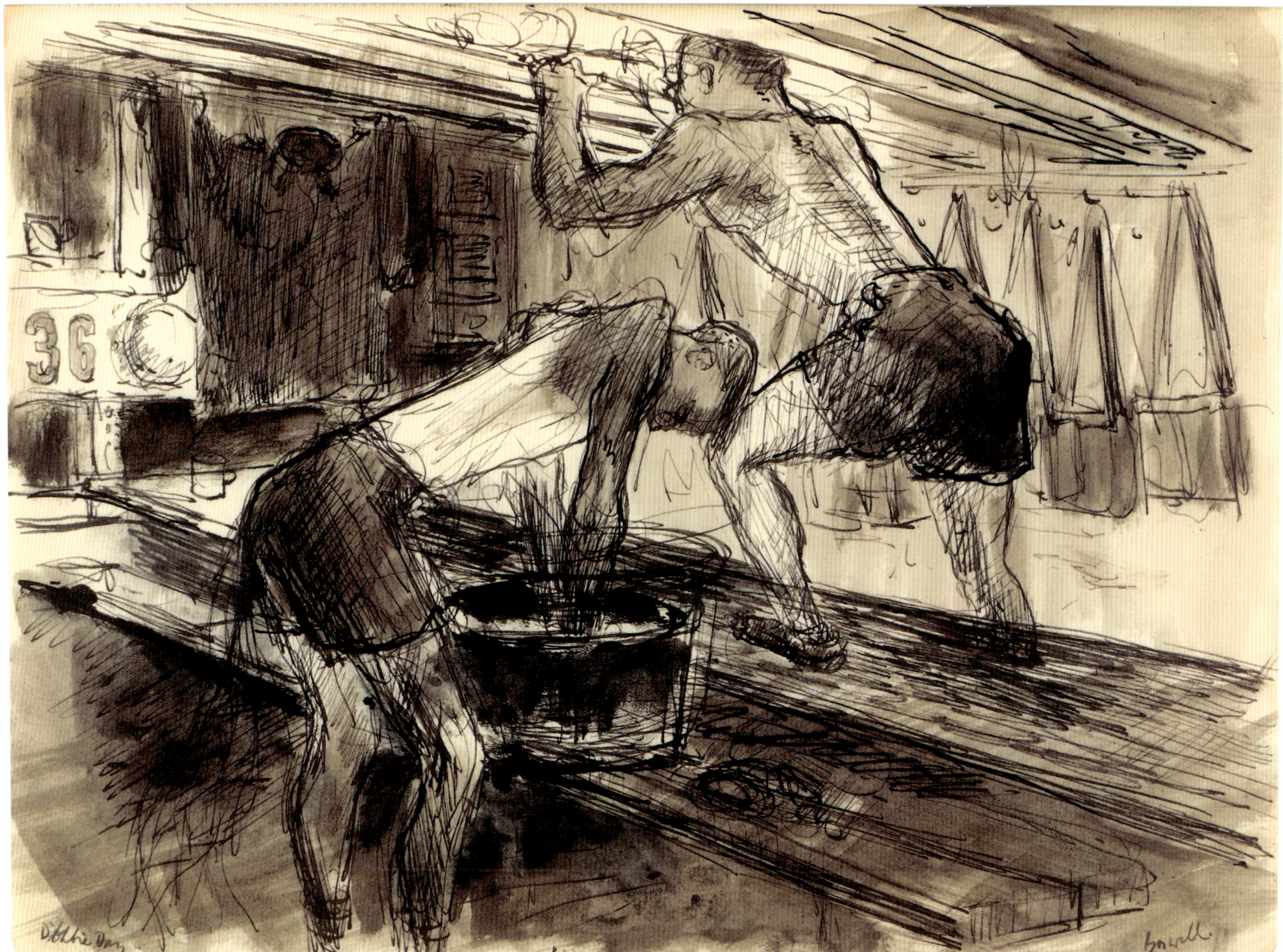

Opposite **Cheese Pie**

Right **Dhobi Day**

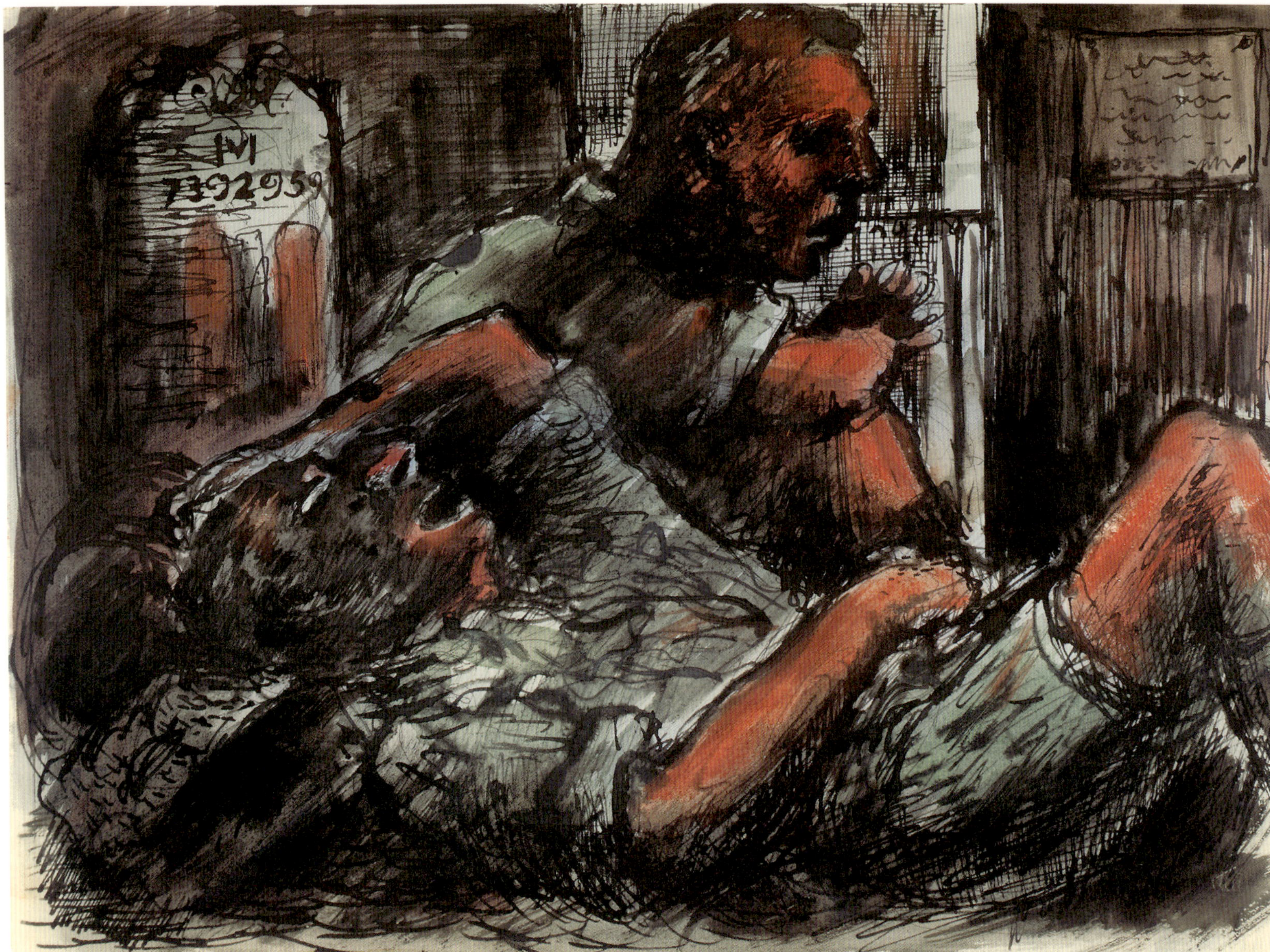

Left **Time to Go Home**

Opposite **Egypt**

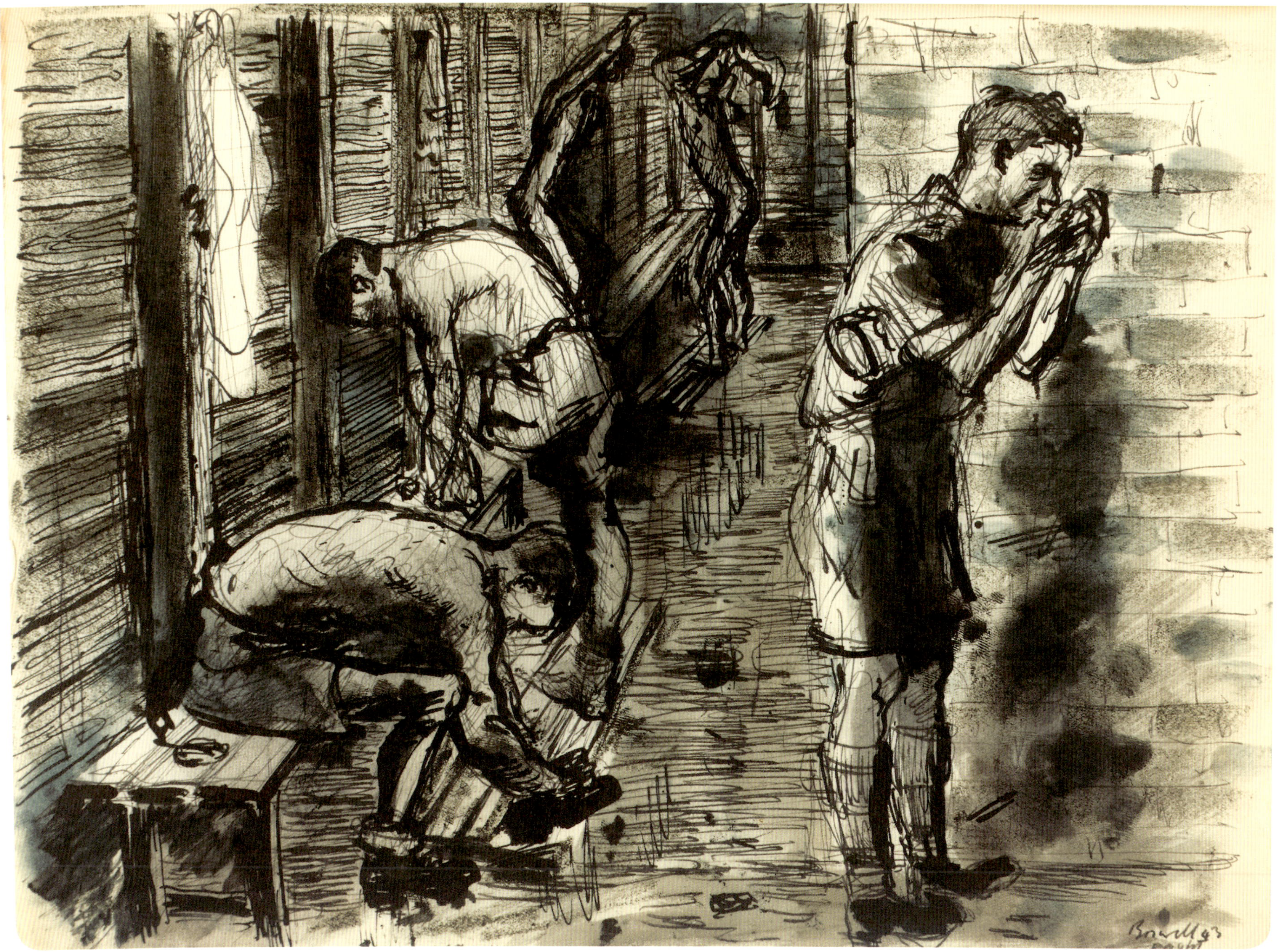

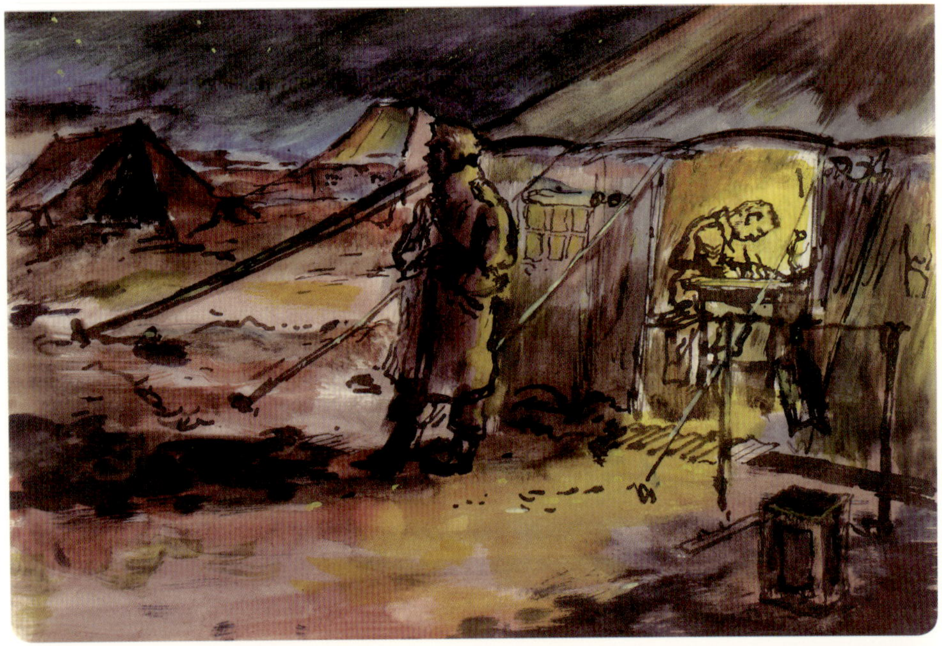

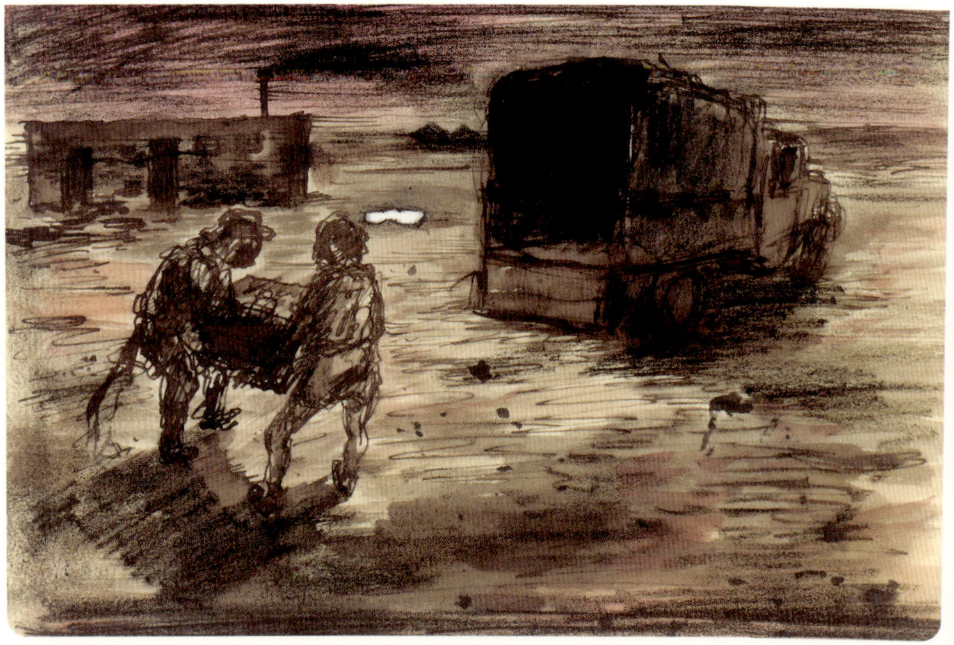

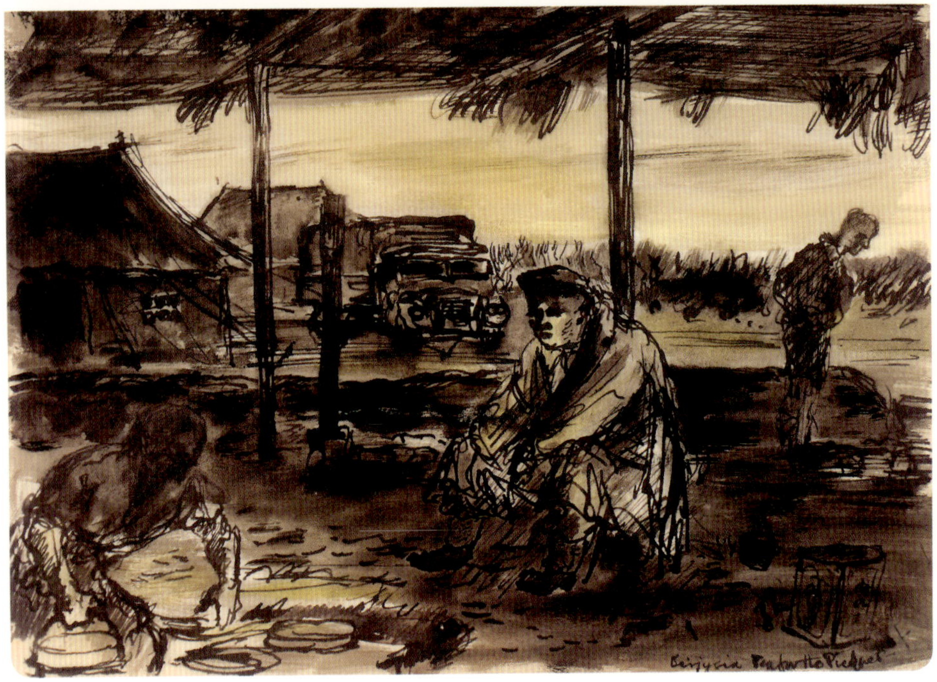

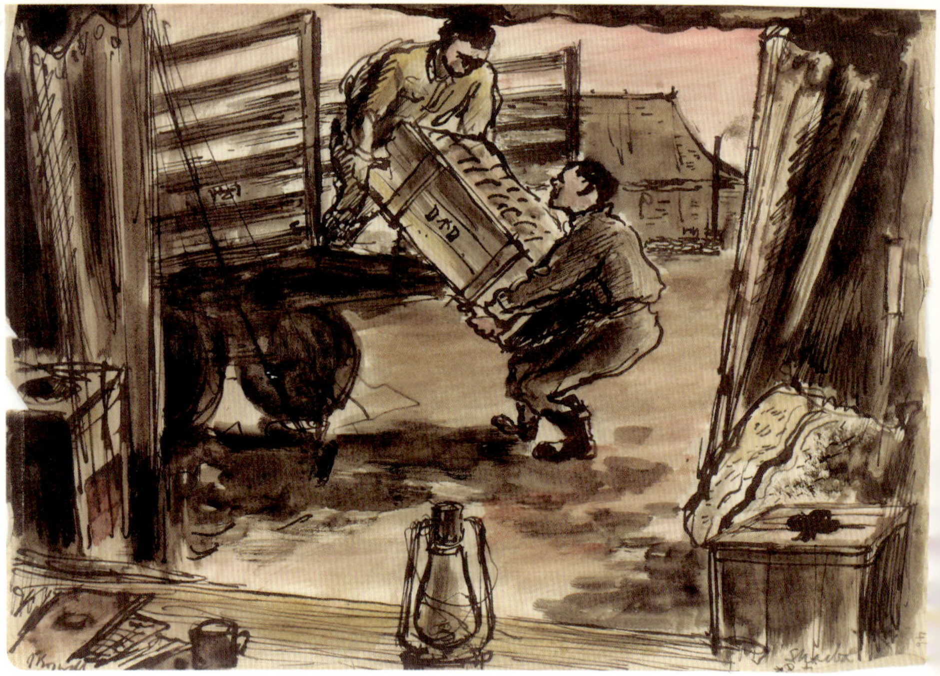

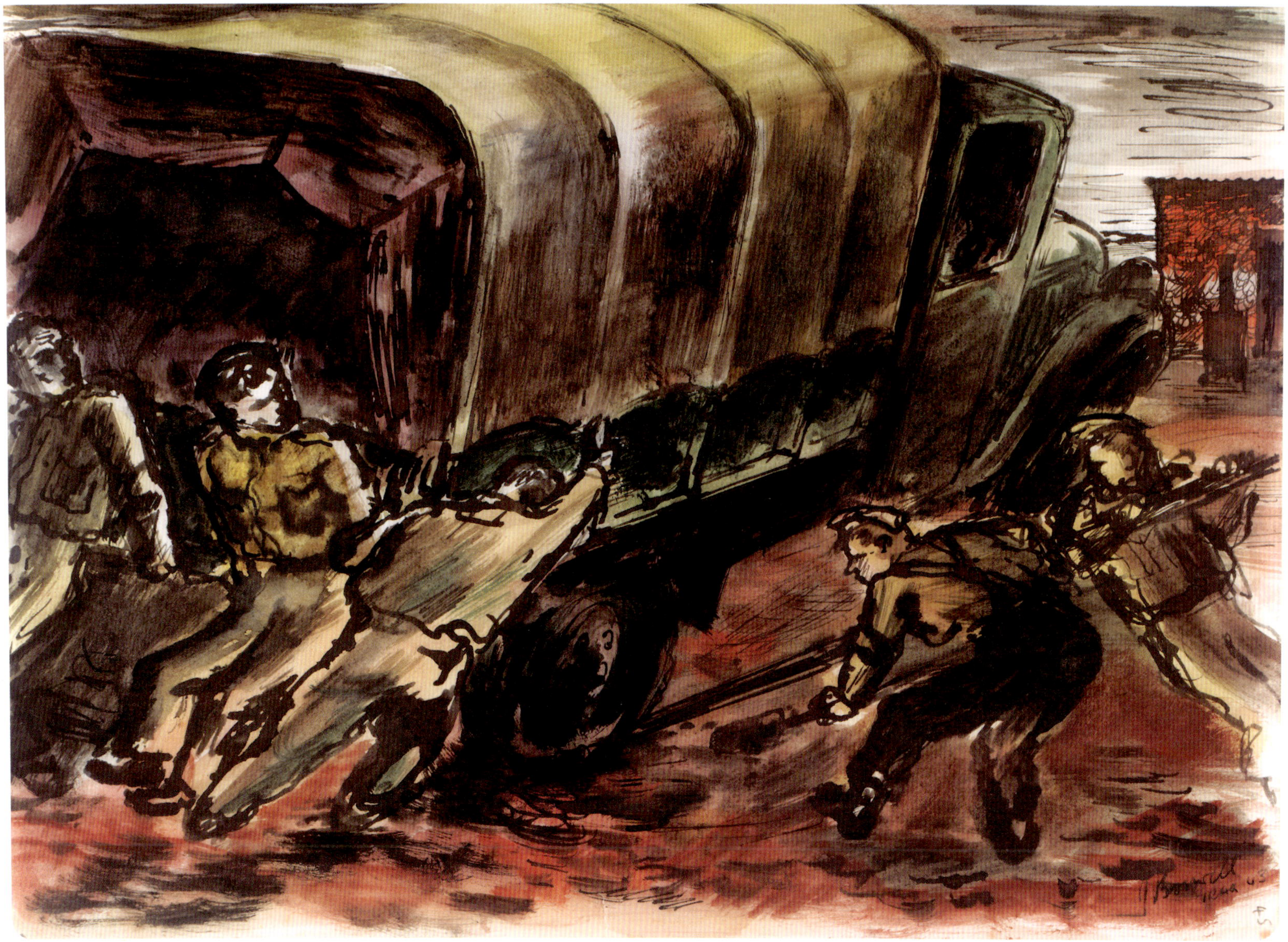

Opposite
Top left **Second Stag**
Bottom left **Banjysia. Tea for the Picket**
Top right **Carrying Stores**
Bottom right **Shaiba**

Right **Stuck in the Sand**

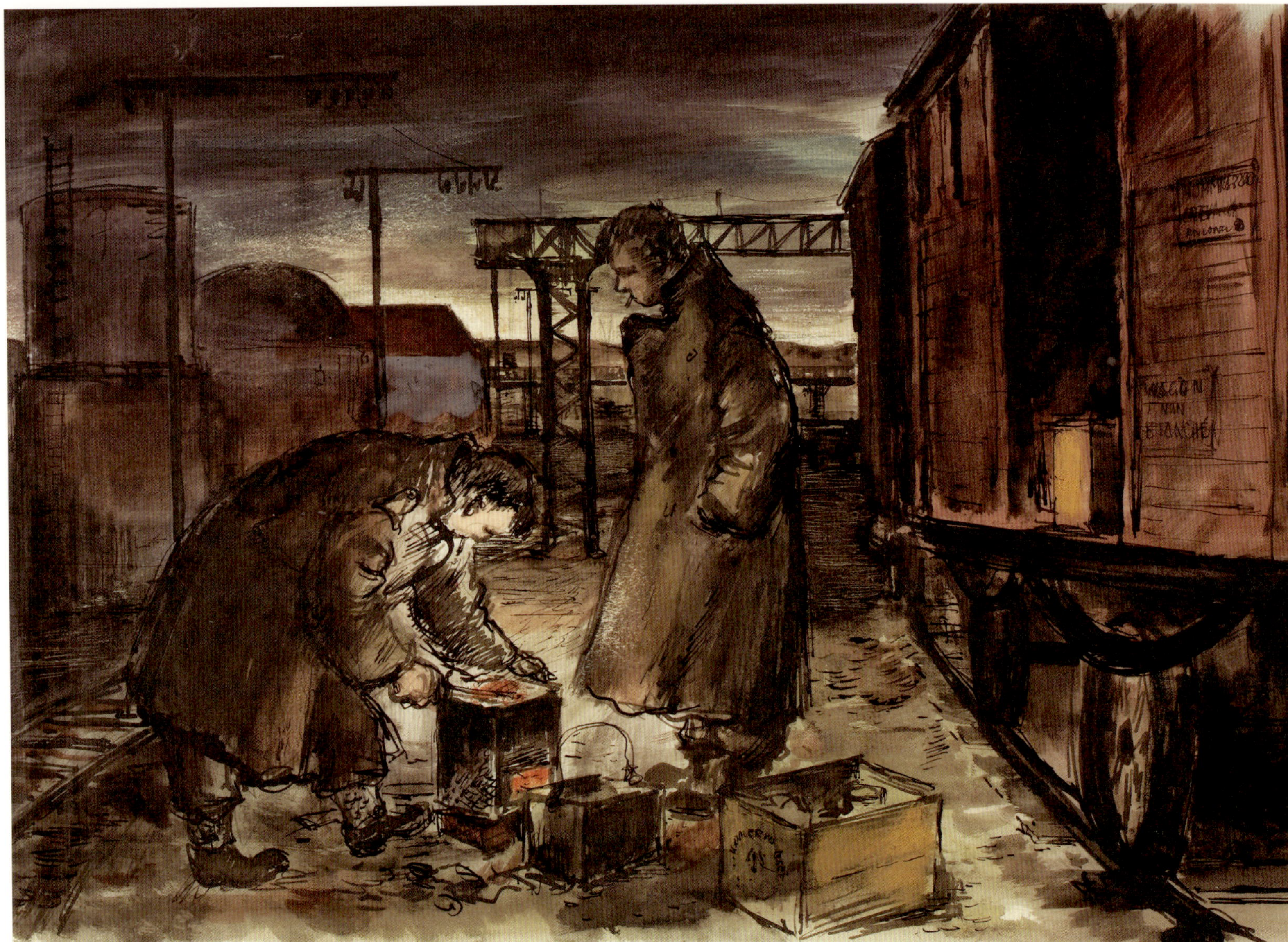

Left **En Route**

Opposite
Top left **The Watercart**
Bottom left **The Ration Store**
Top right **Company Kitchen**
Bottom right **The Canteen, Shaiba**

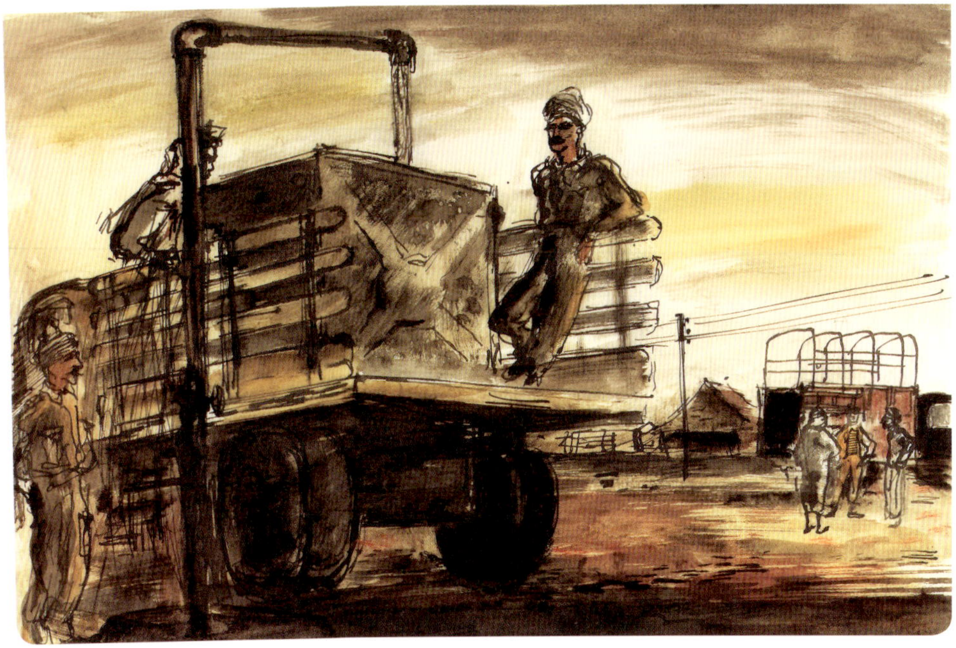

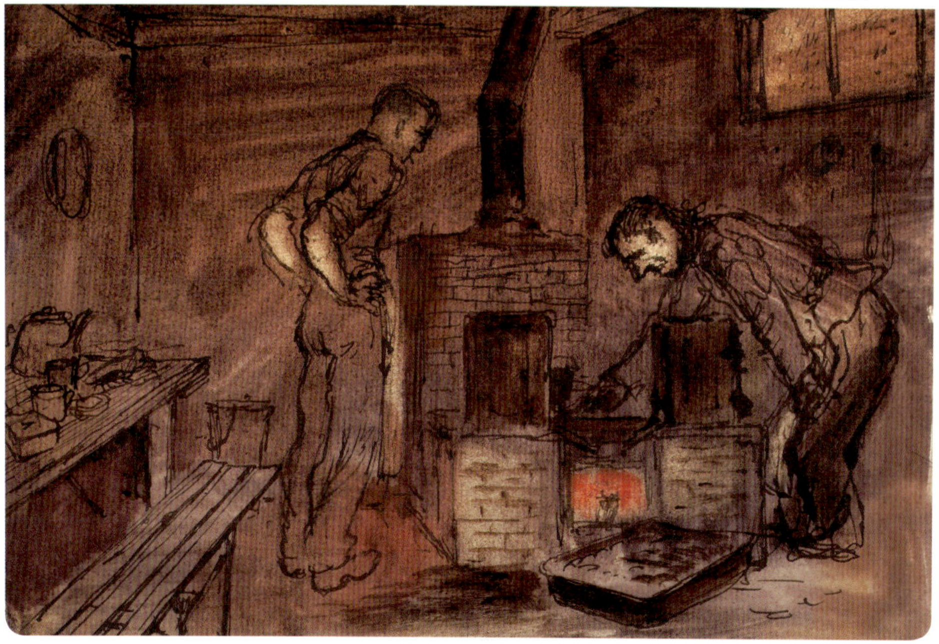

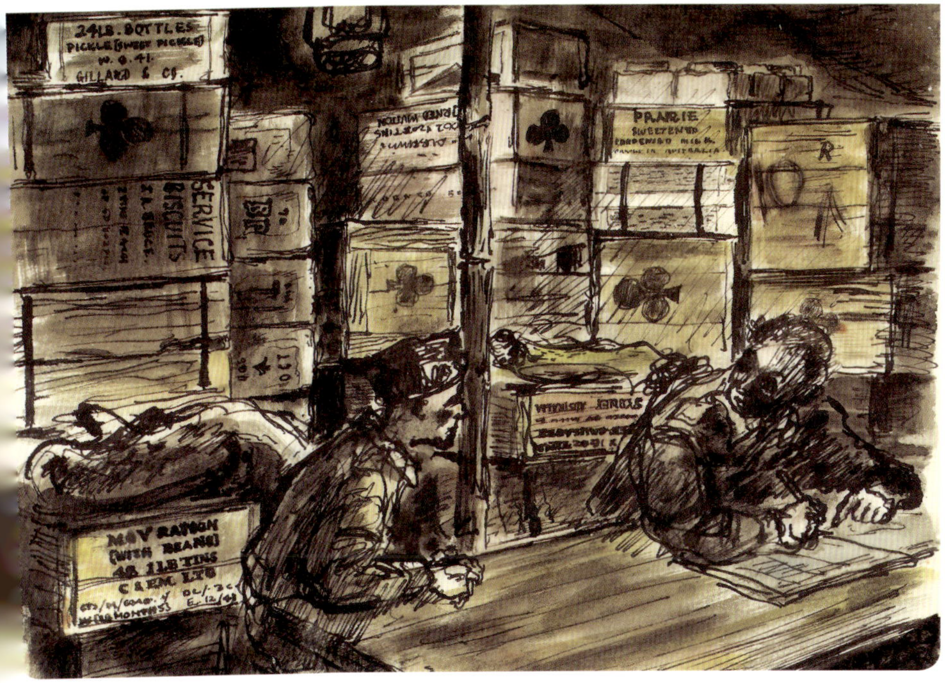
24LB. BOTTLES
PICKLE [SWEET PICKLE]
W. Q. 41.
GILLARD & Co.
SERVICE
BISCUITS
PRARIE
SWEETENED
M&V RATION
(WITH BEANS)
48 1LB TINS
C & E.M. LTD

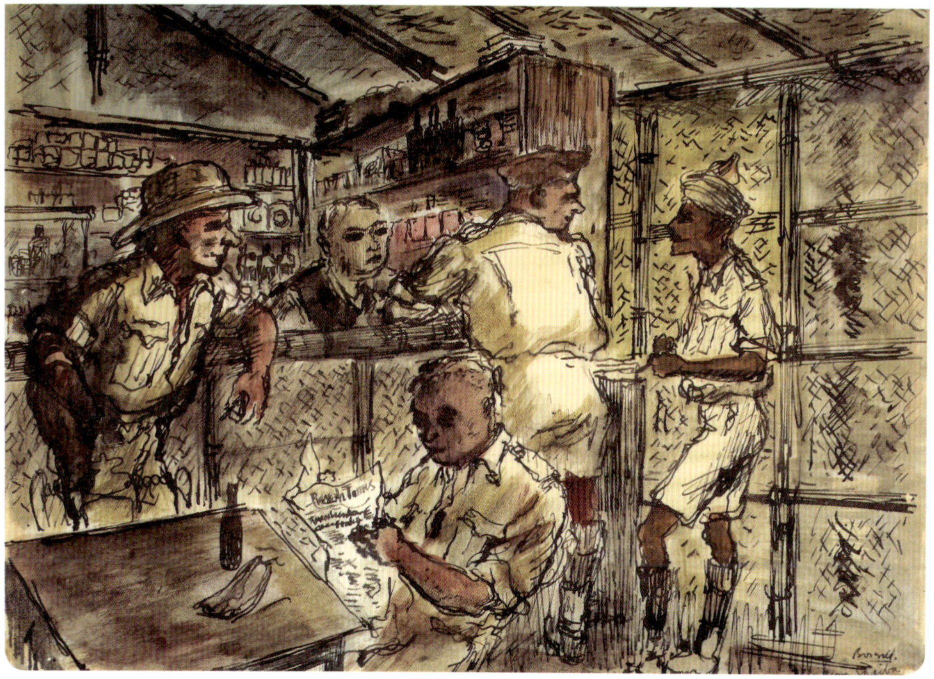

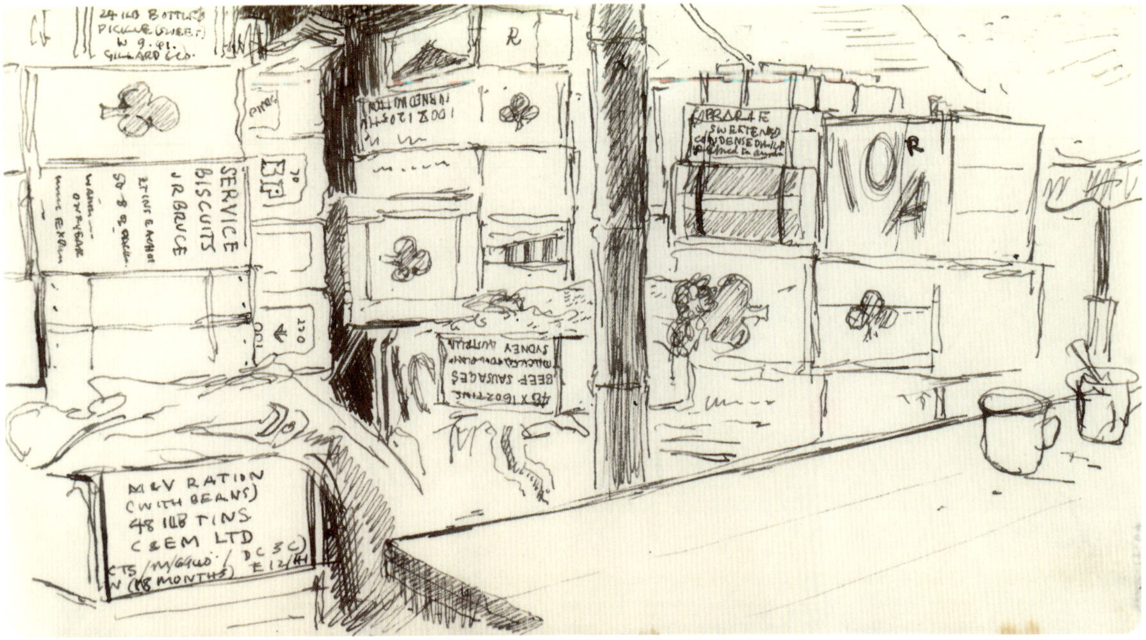

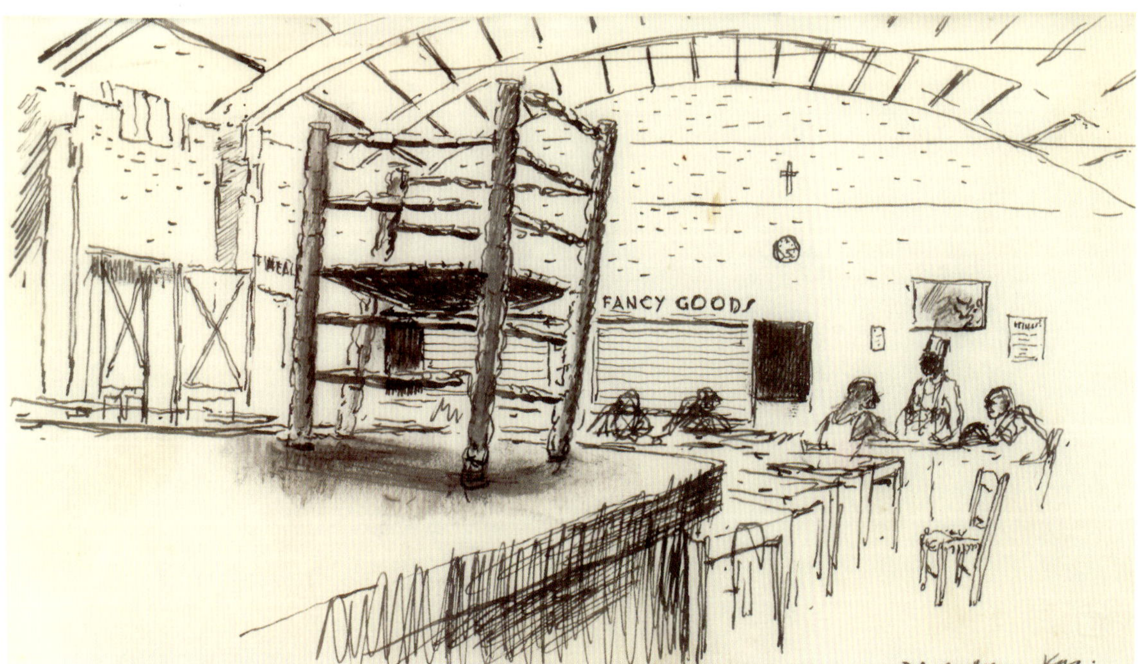

Top **Rations**

Bottom **RC Canteen, Kav.**

Opposite

Left **The Victory Canteen, Shaiba**

Right **One of our rooms, the one we lived in**

Overleaf **Some of 33rd Hospital Site, Iraq**

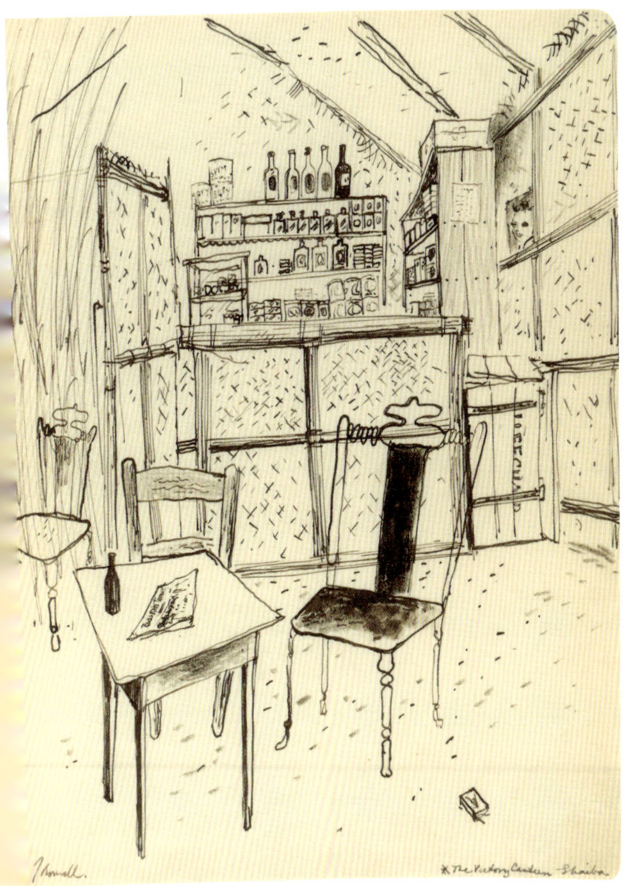
* The Victory Canteen - Shaiba

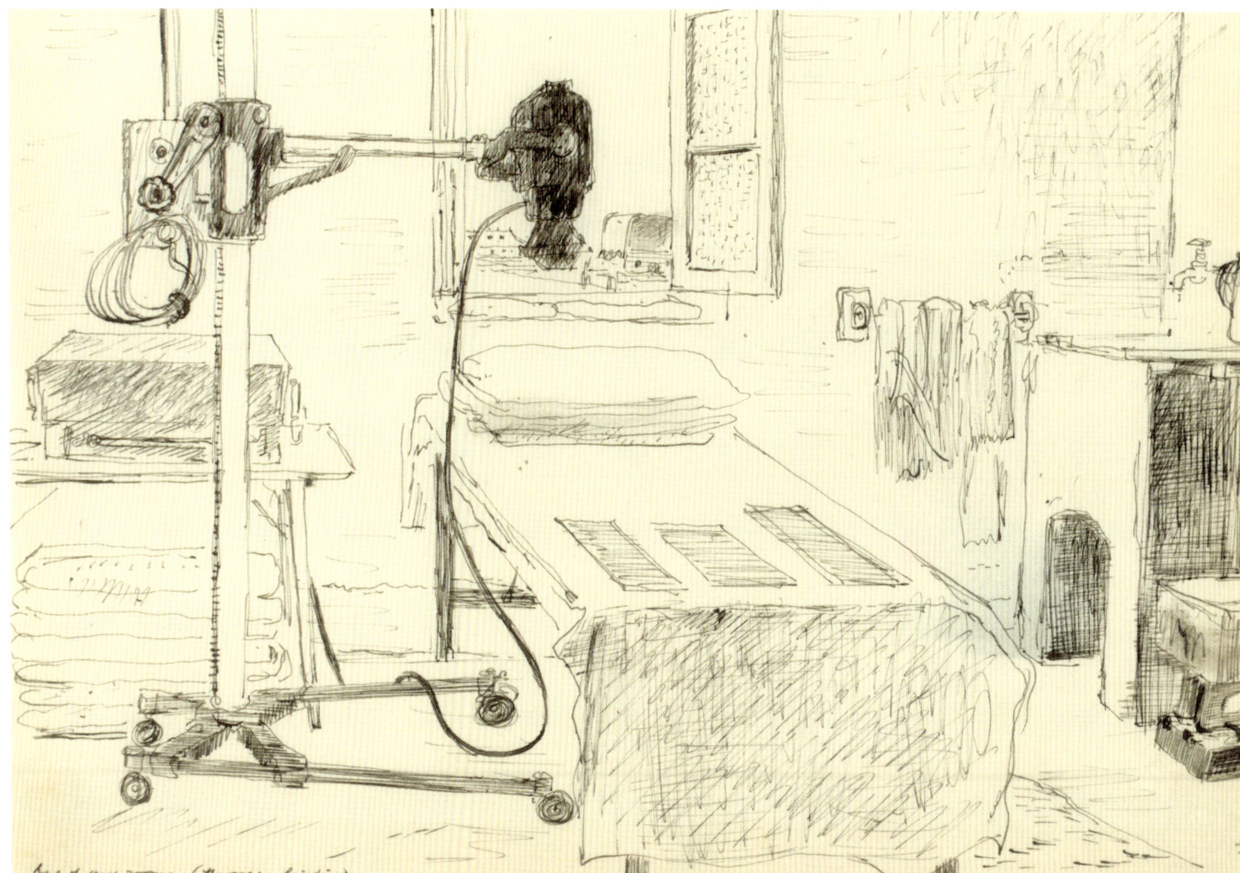
One of our rooms.

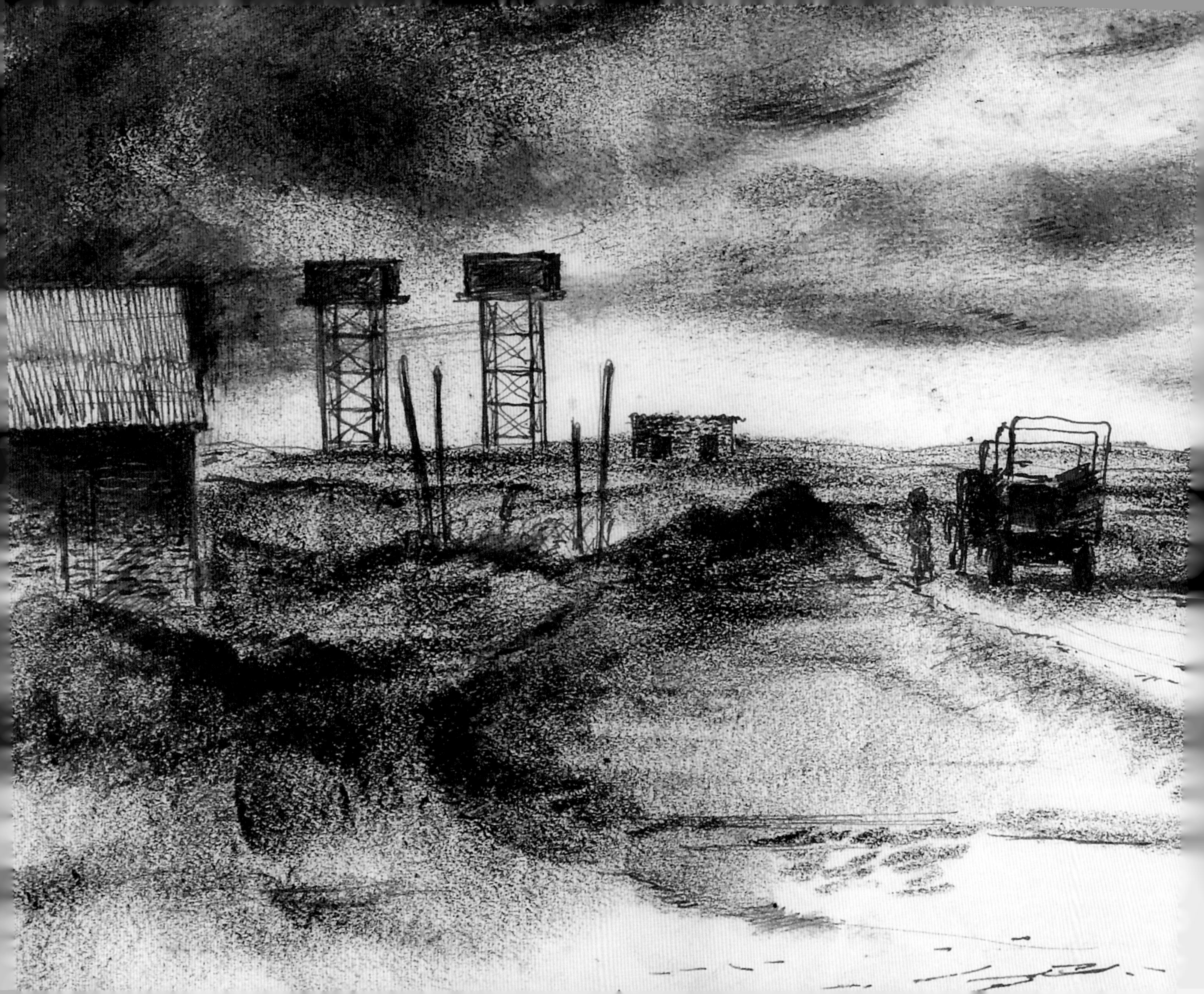

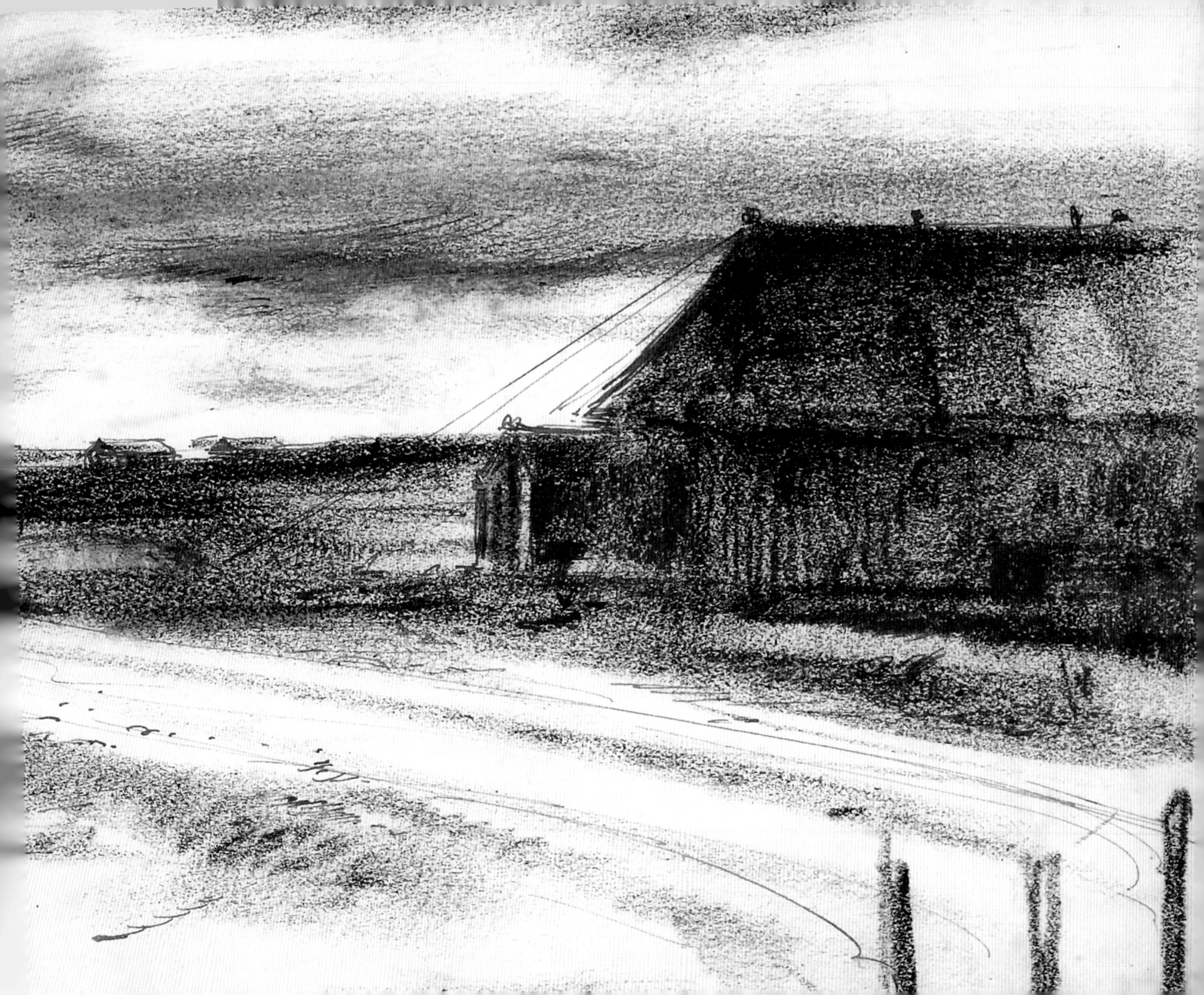

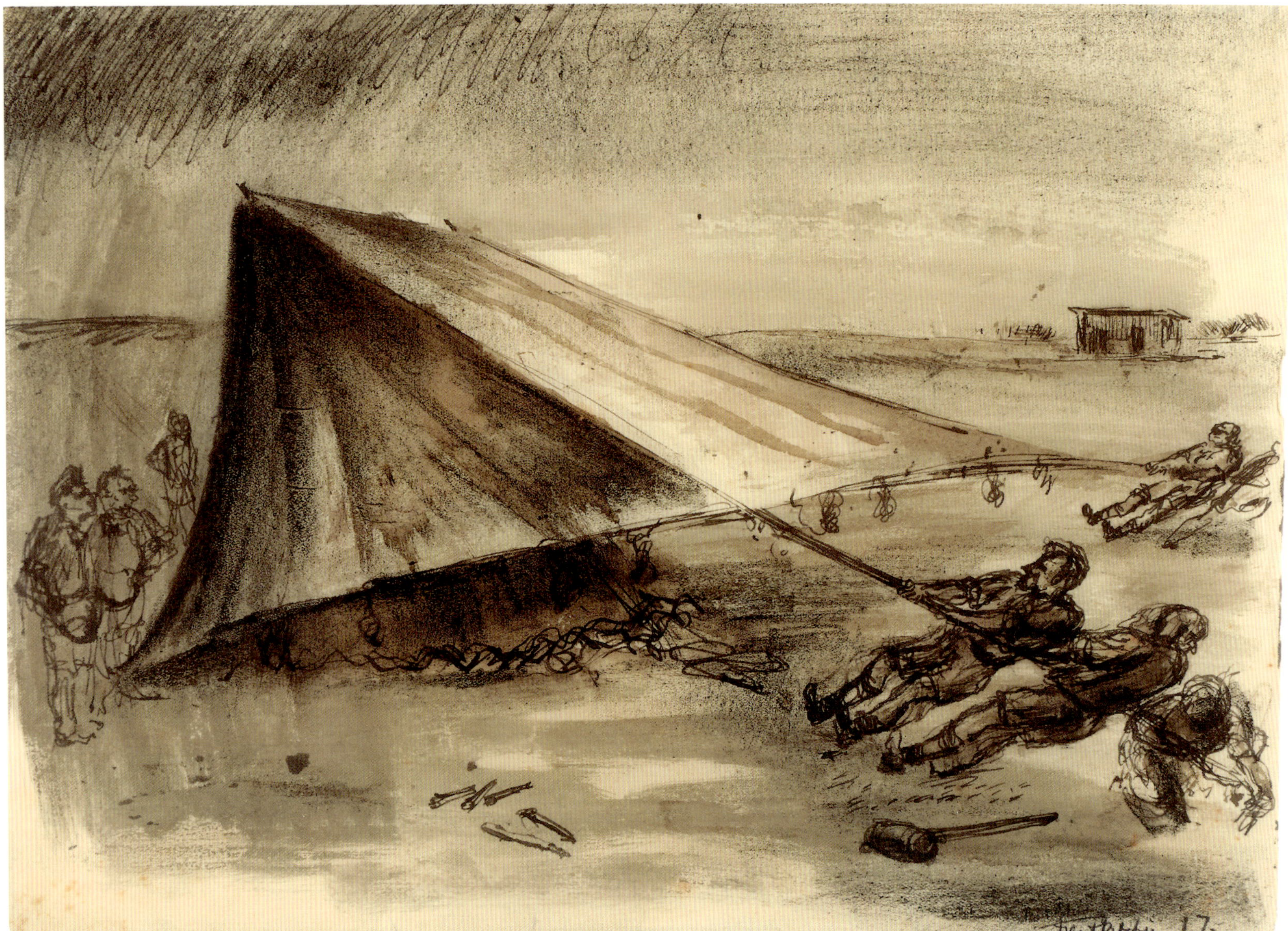

Left **Tent Pitching**

Opposite **The Hospital Site**

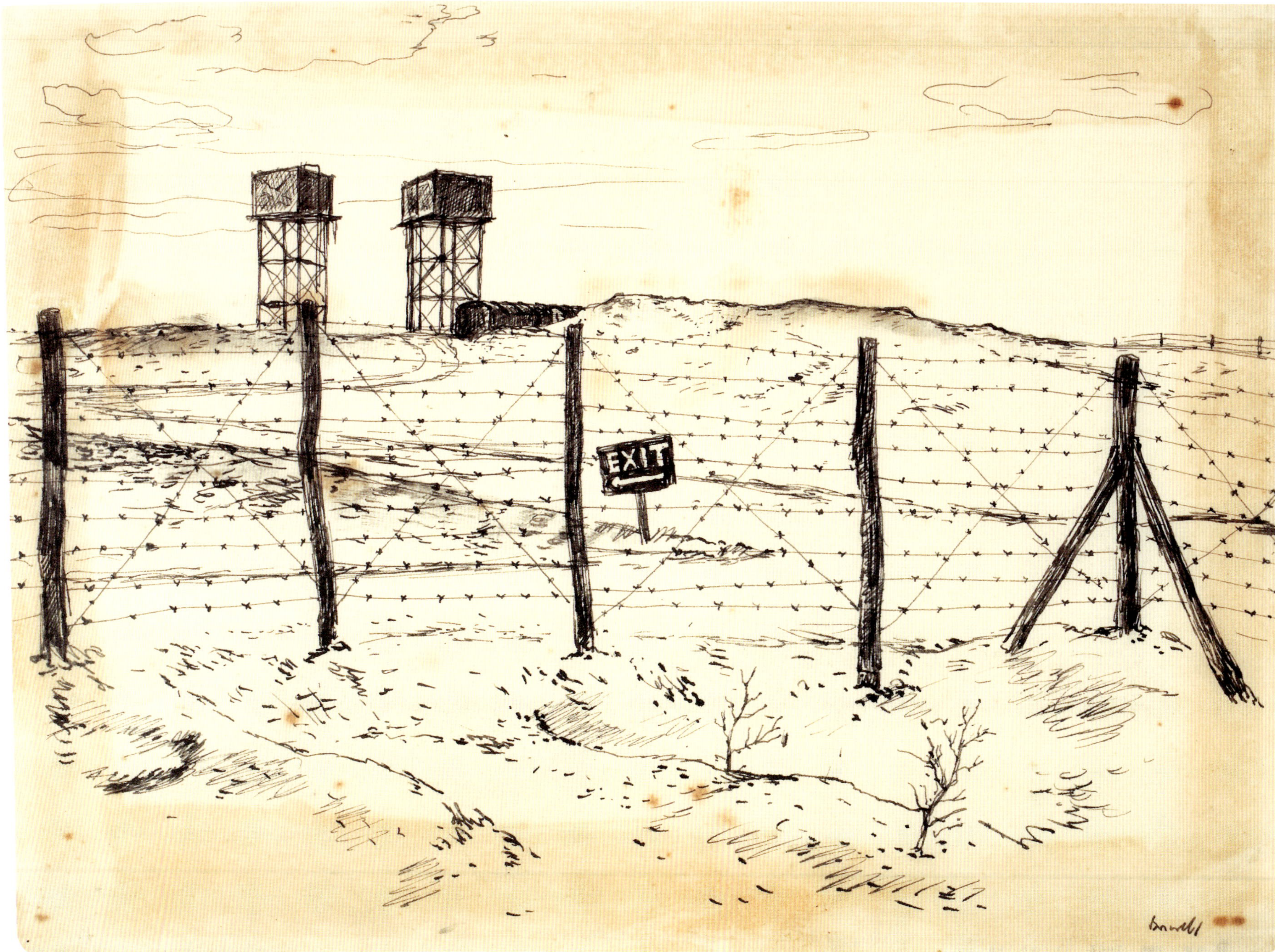
EXIT

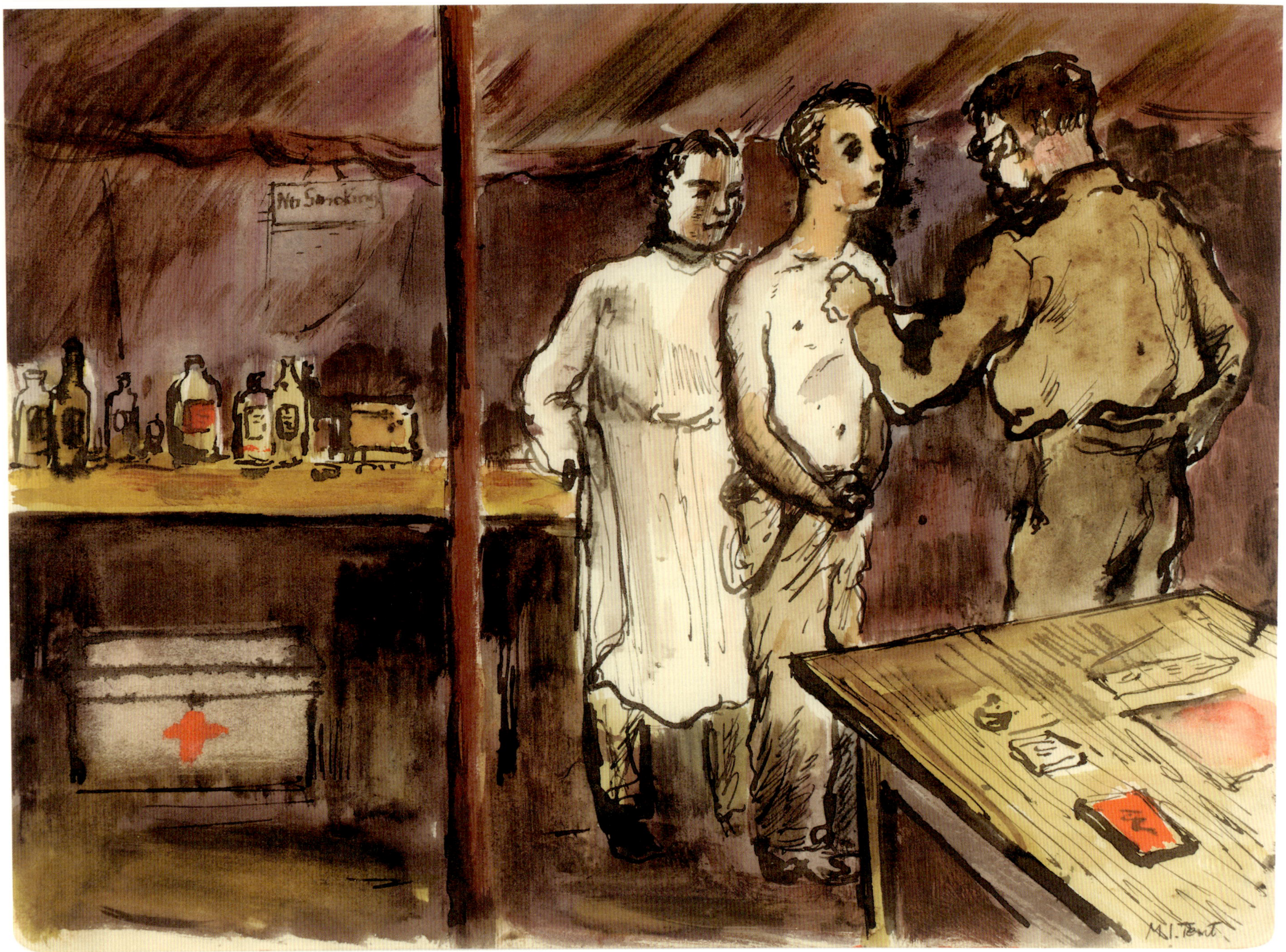
No Smoking
M.I. Tent

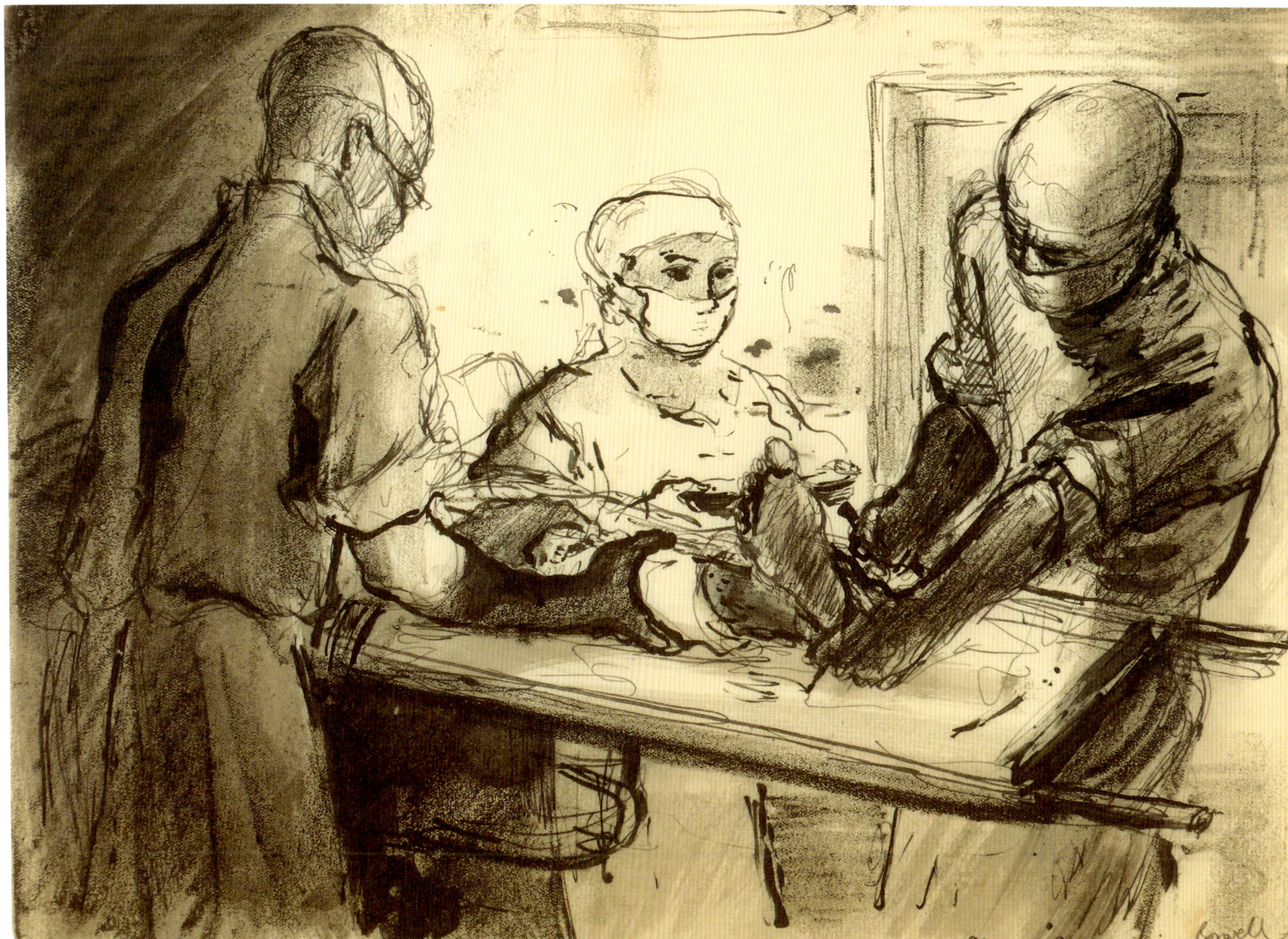

Opposite **M.I. Tent**

Right **Steinman Pin Going In**

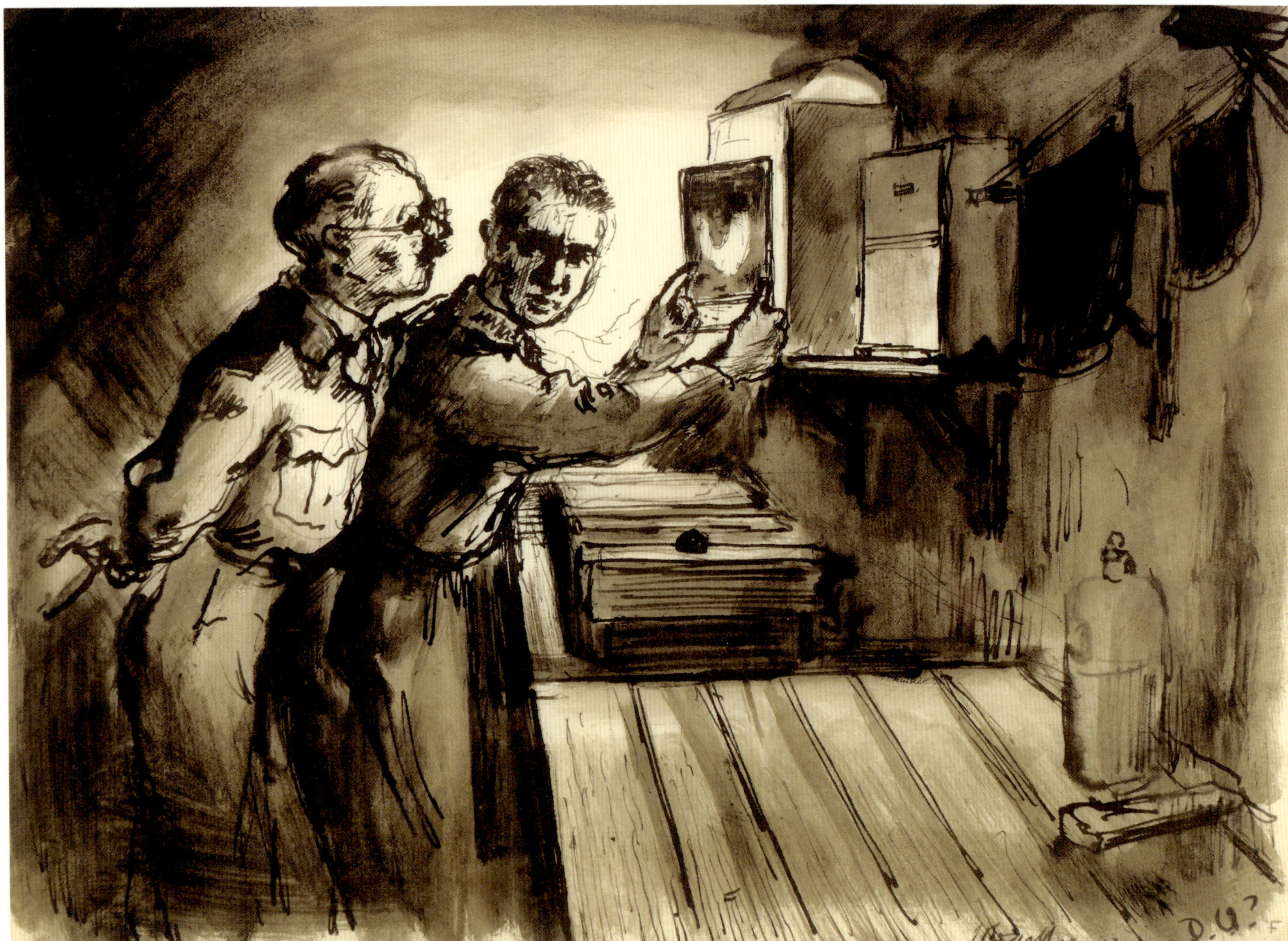

Left **X-Ray at the Divisional Unit**

Opposote **Casualty**

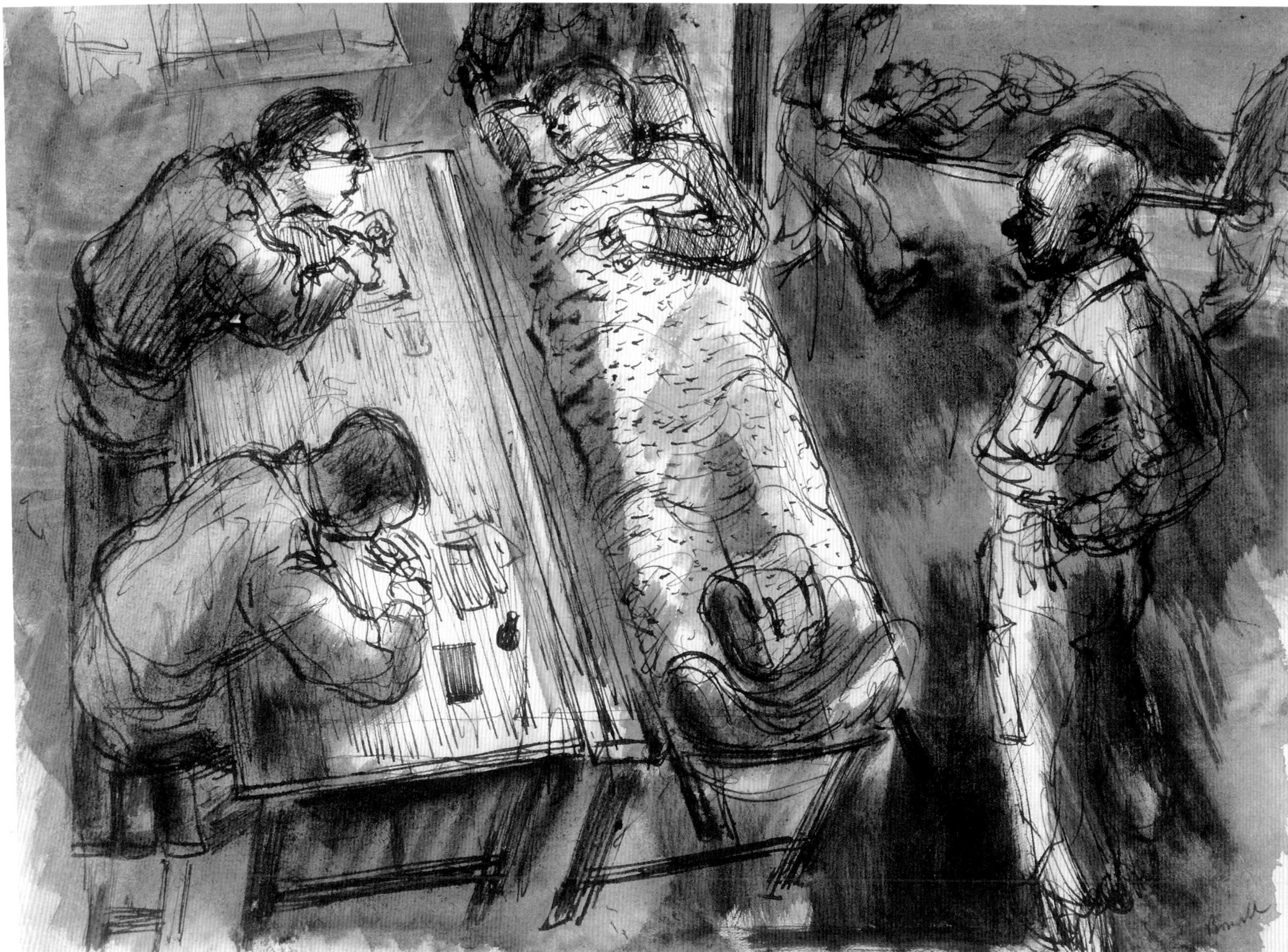

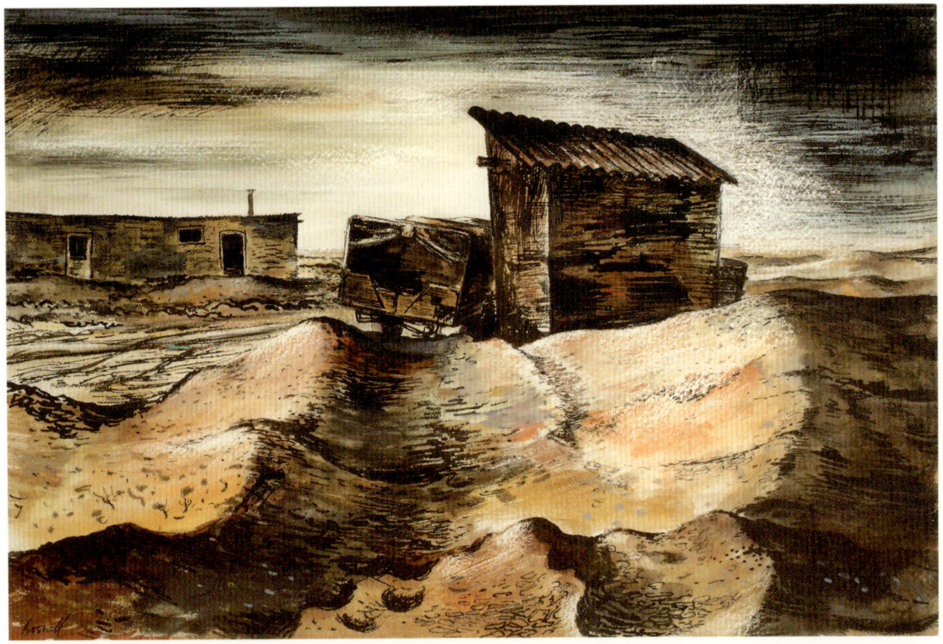

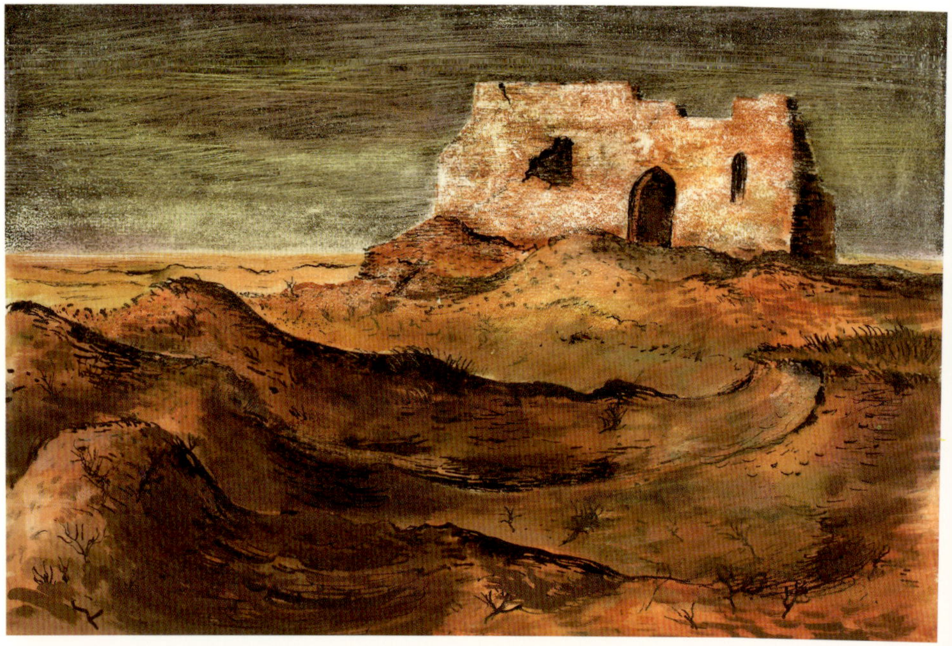

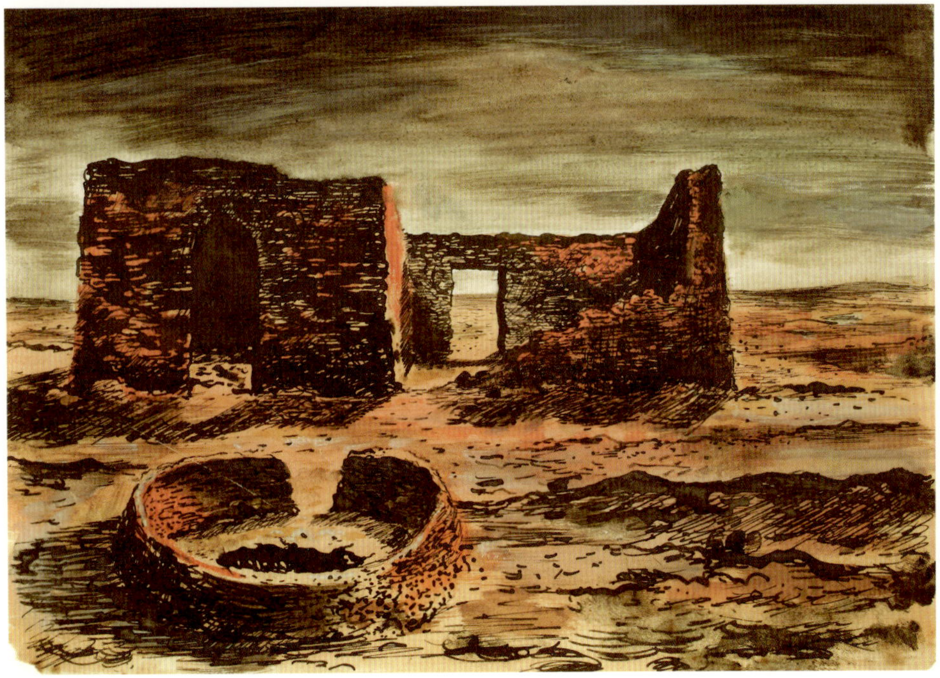

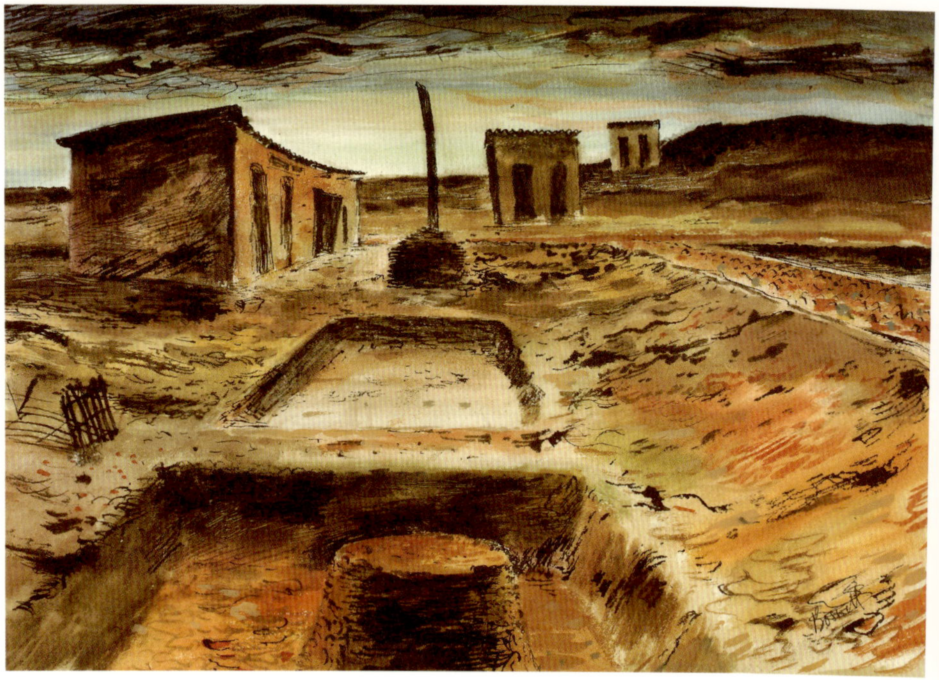

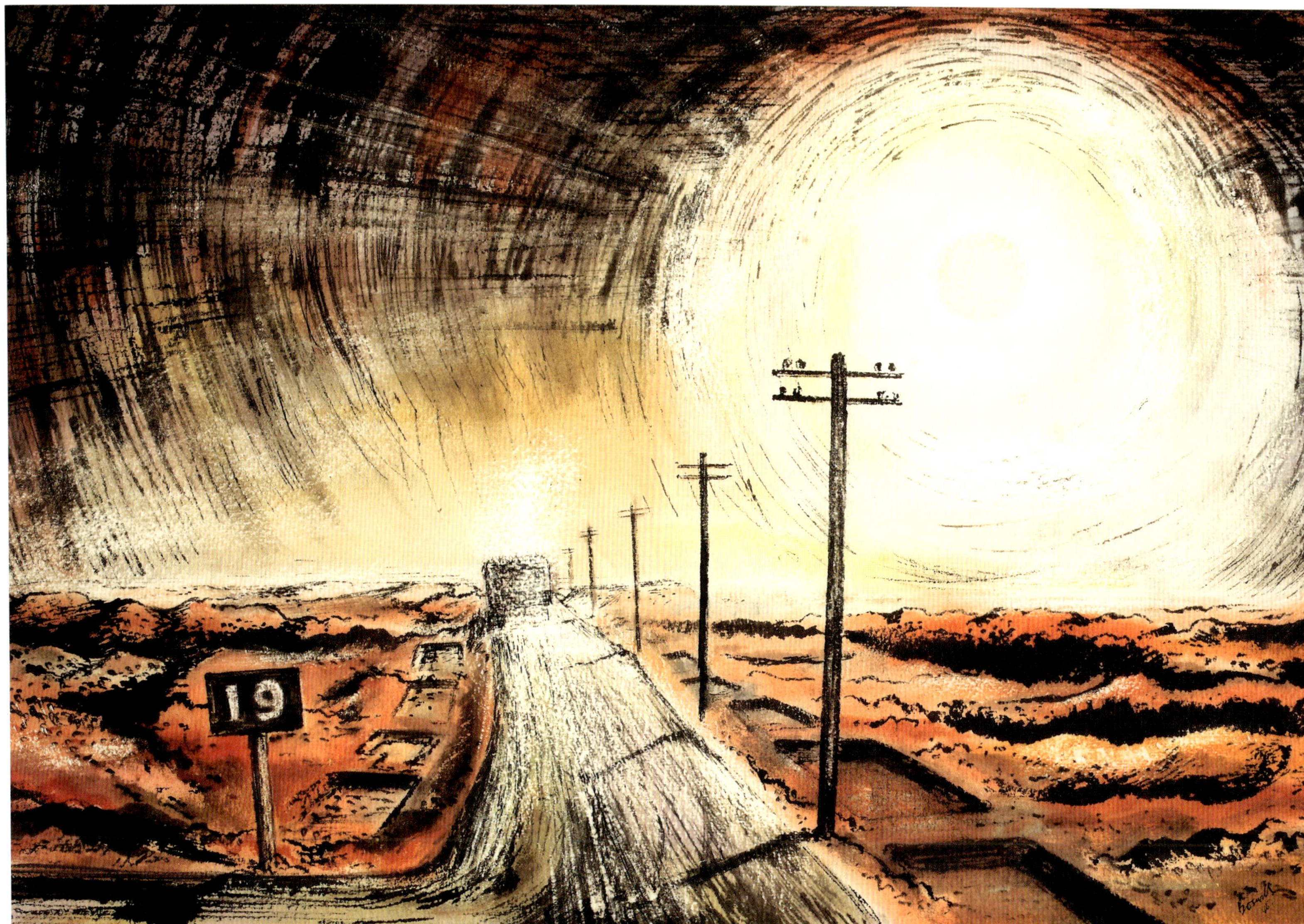

Opposite

Top left **Moonlight**

Bottom left **Red Desert, Iraq**

Top right **Red Desert**

Bottom right **Camp 17**

Right **Burning Sun**

Overleaf **V.C. Mound Shaiba**

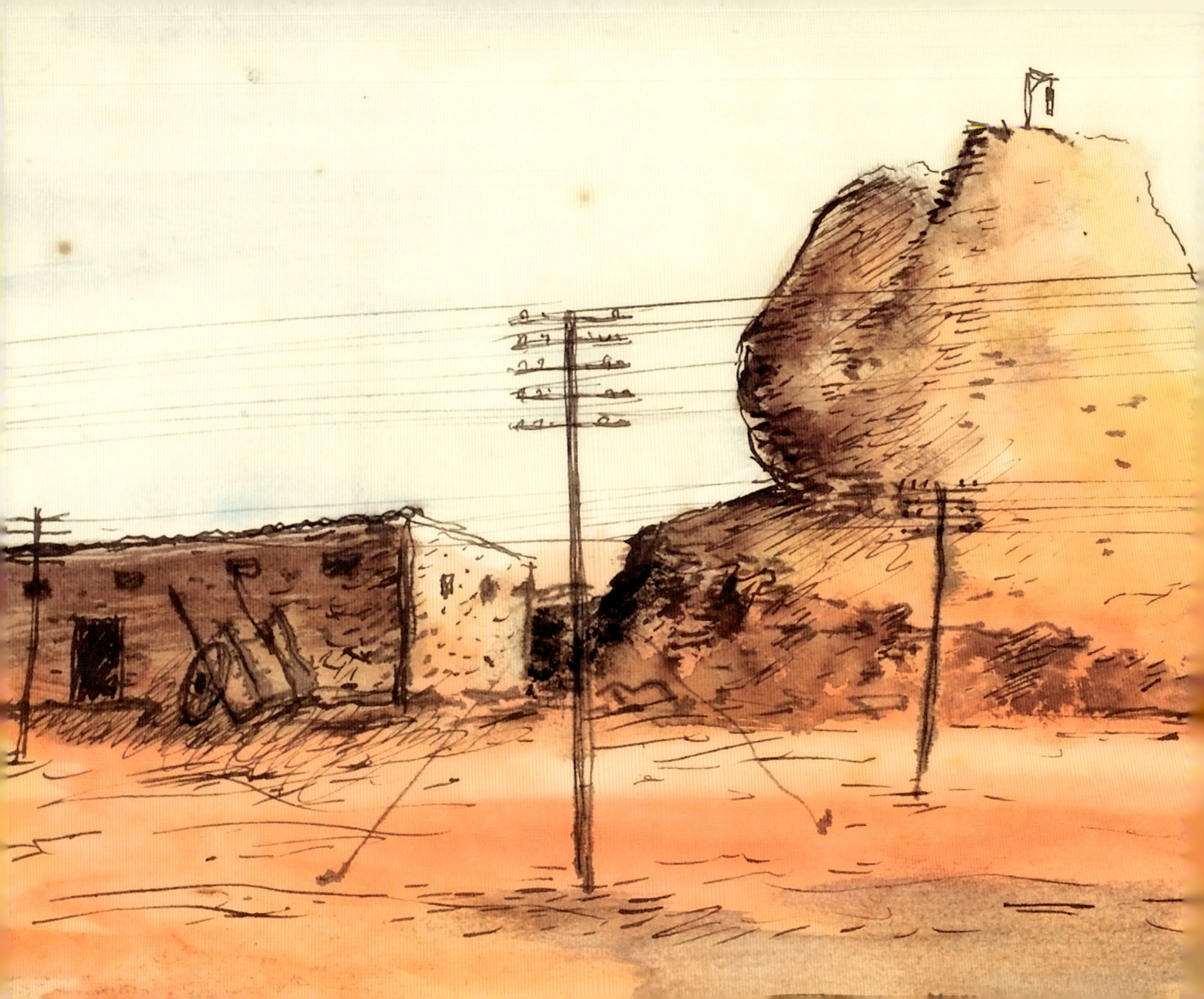

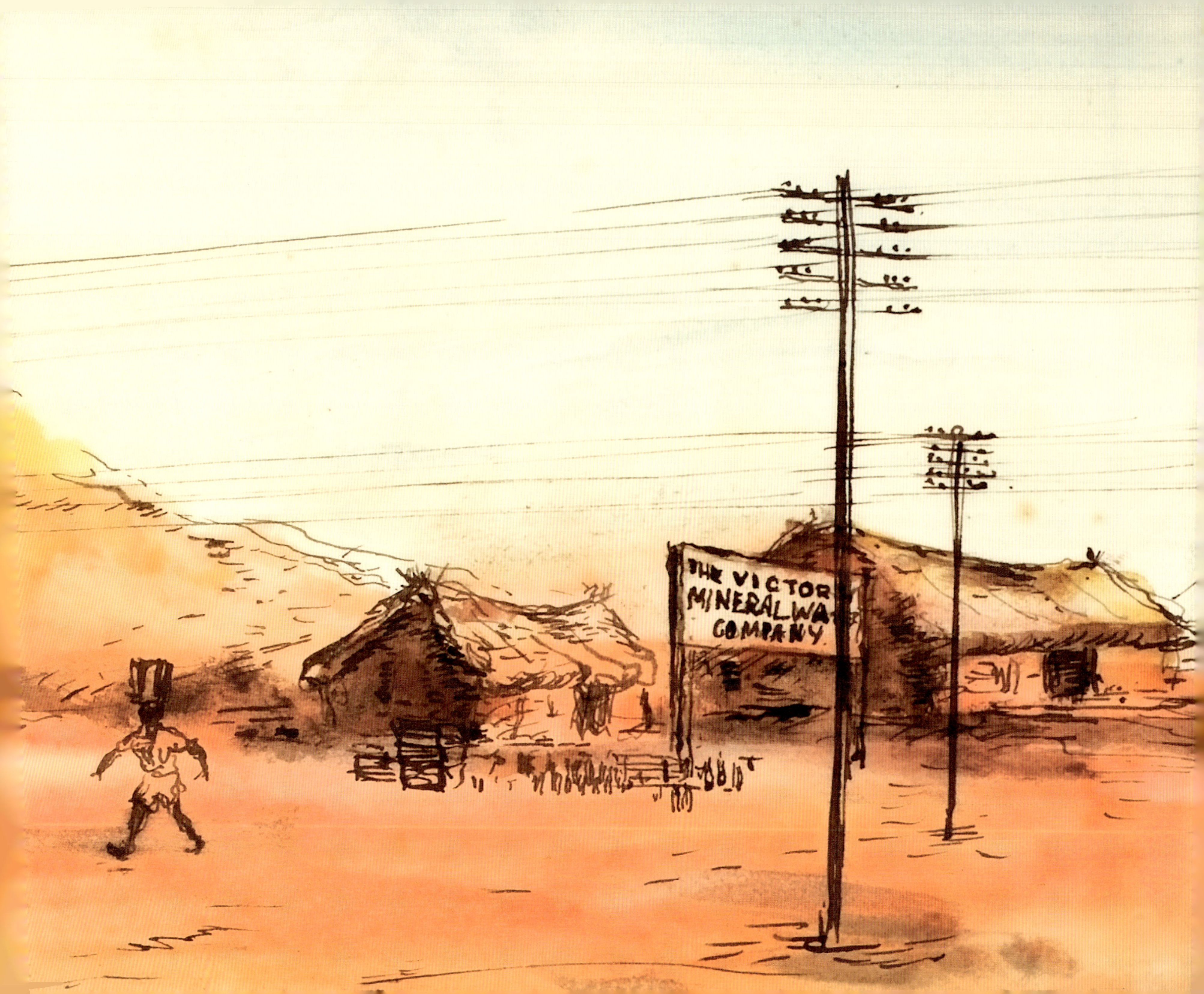
THE VICTOR
MINERAL WA
COMPANY

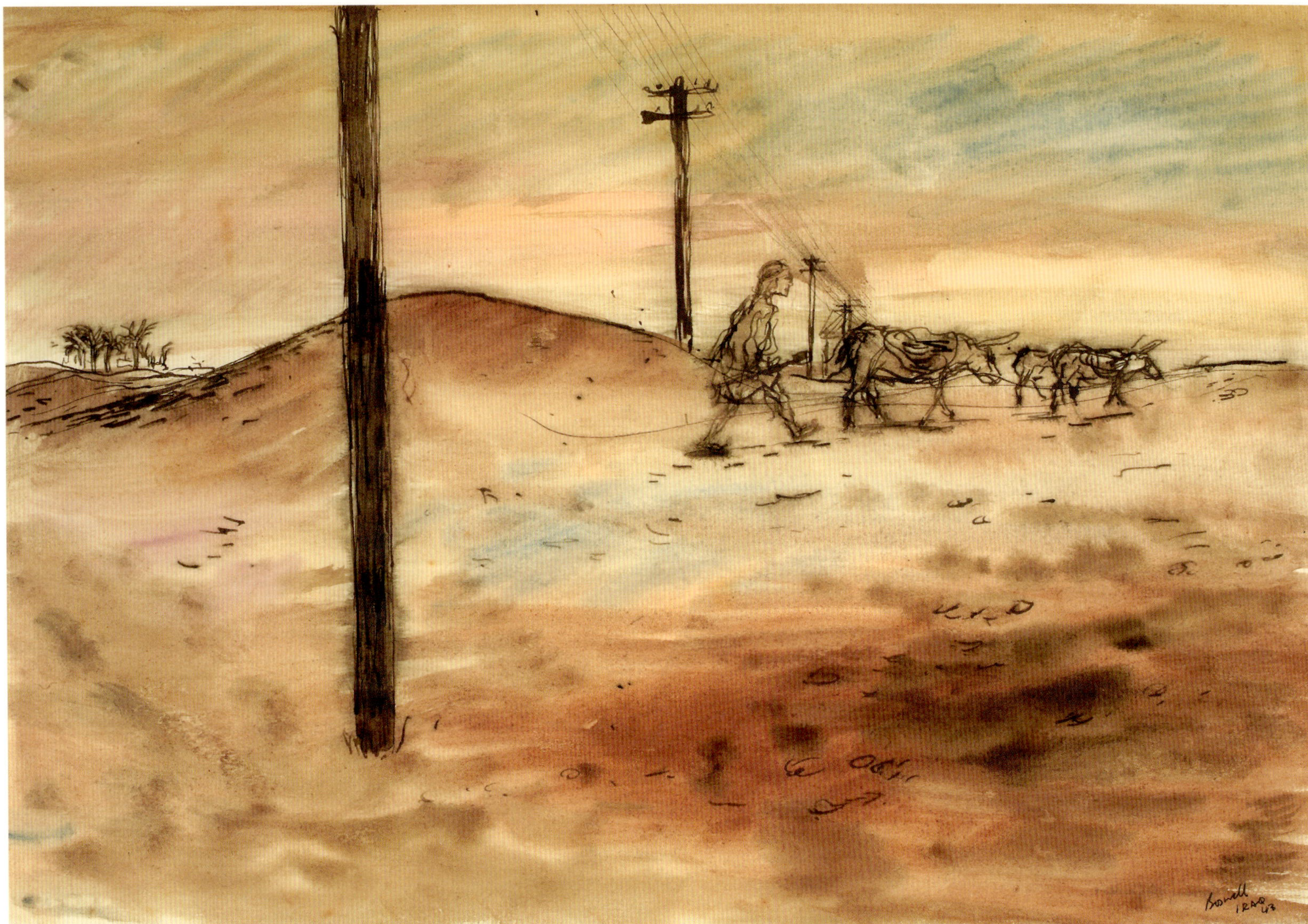

Left Going Places

Opposite The Company Cookhouse

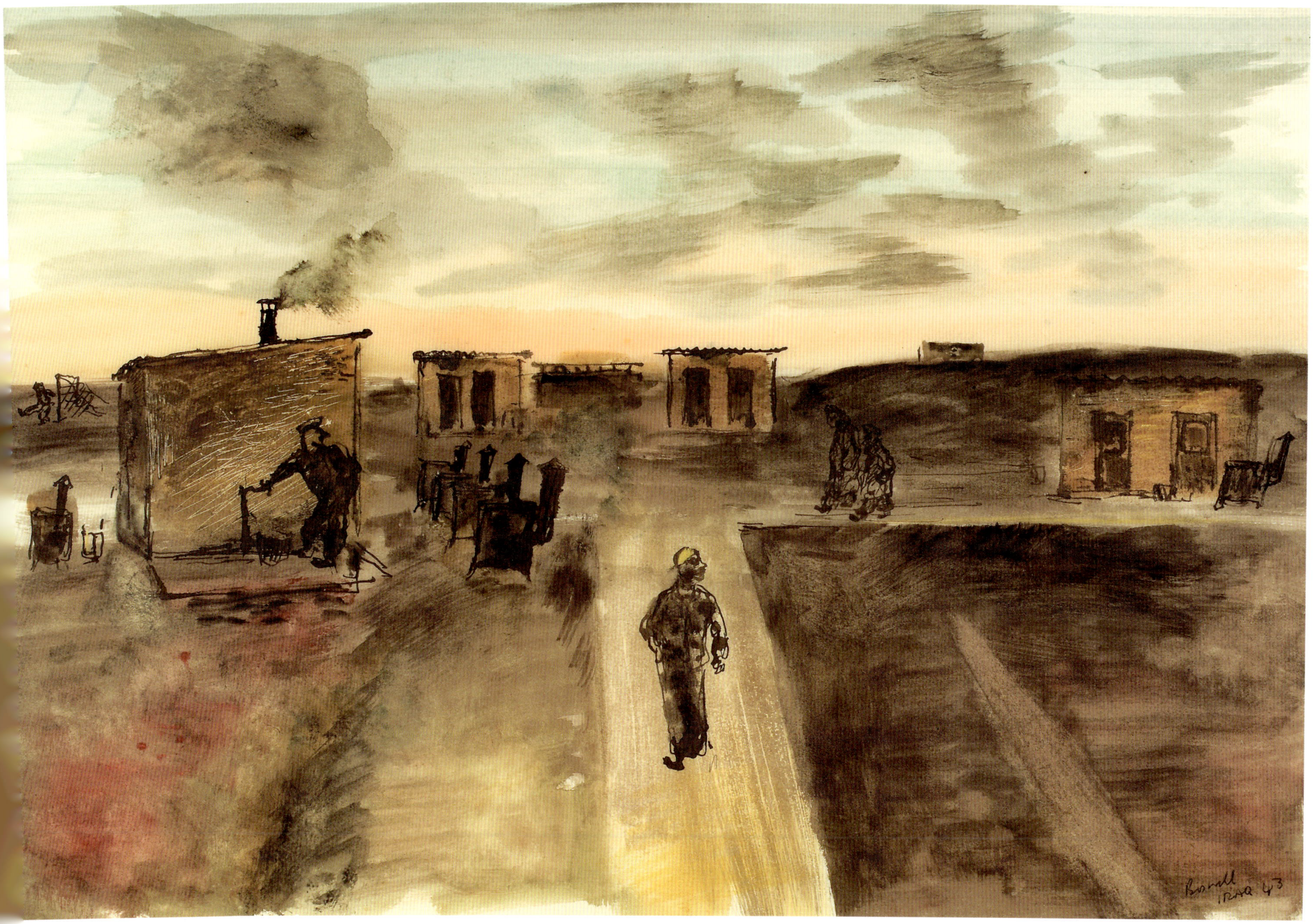
IRAQ 43

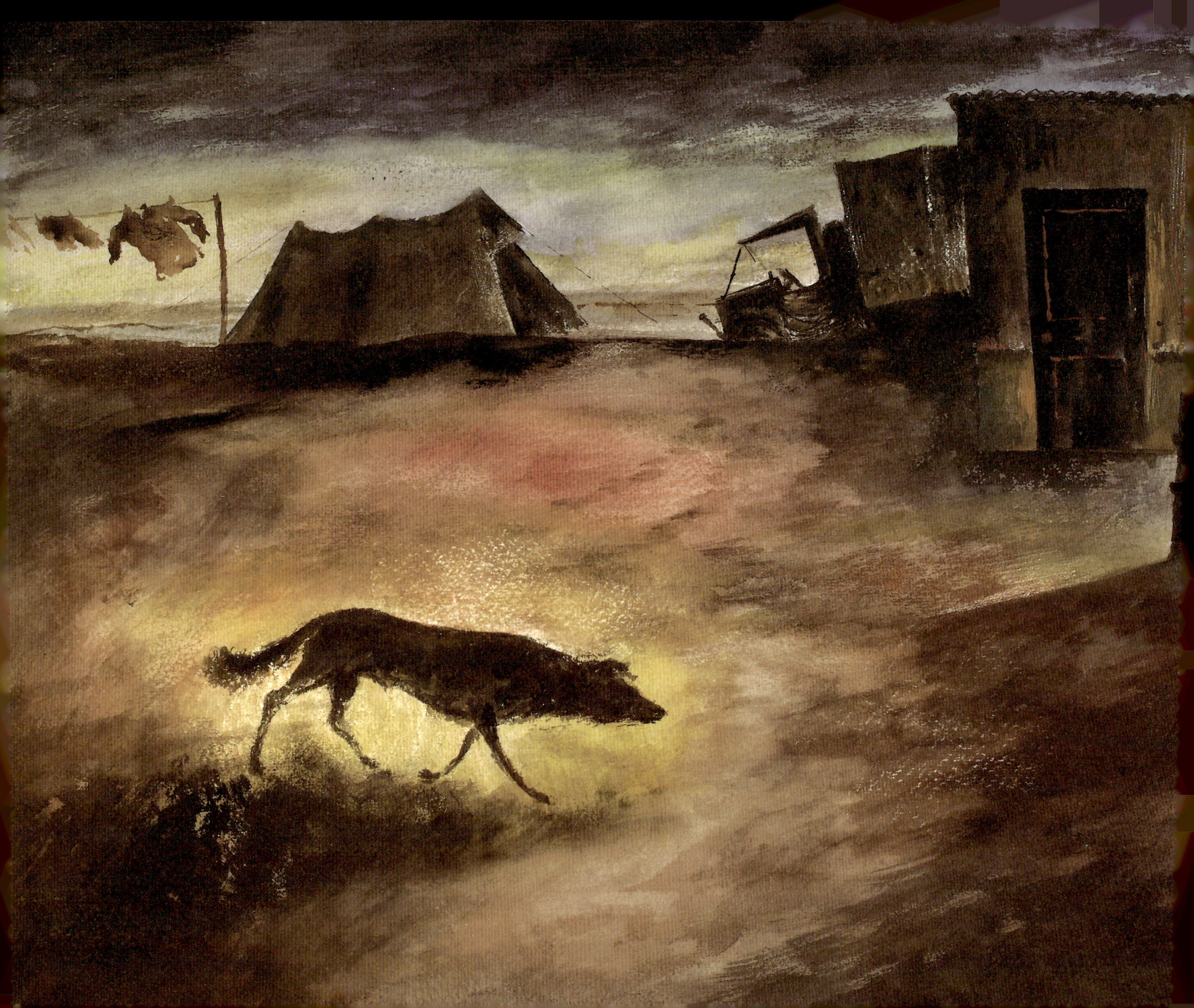

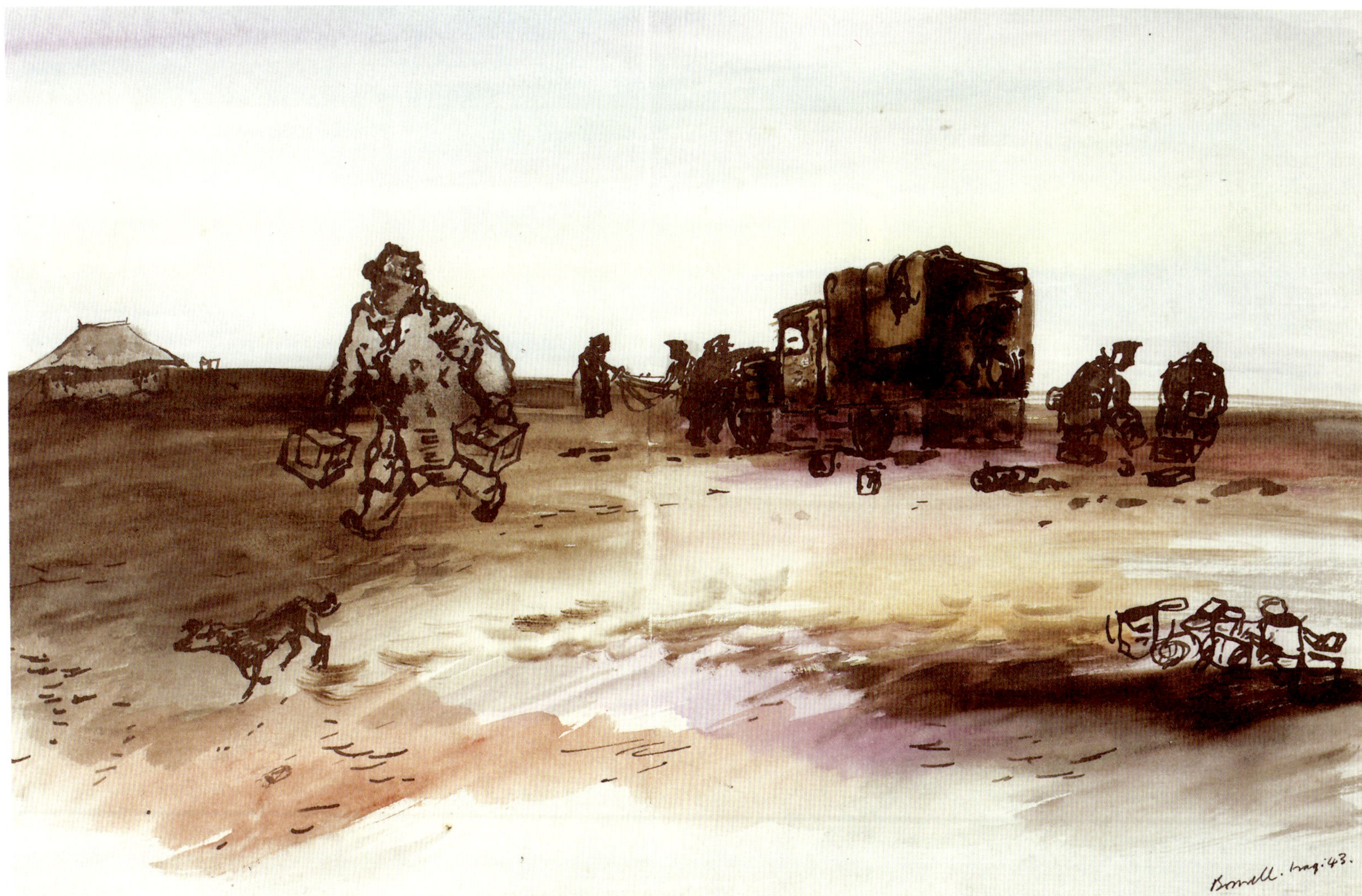

Opposite
7 Reinforcement Camp

Right Stop for Char

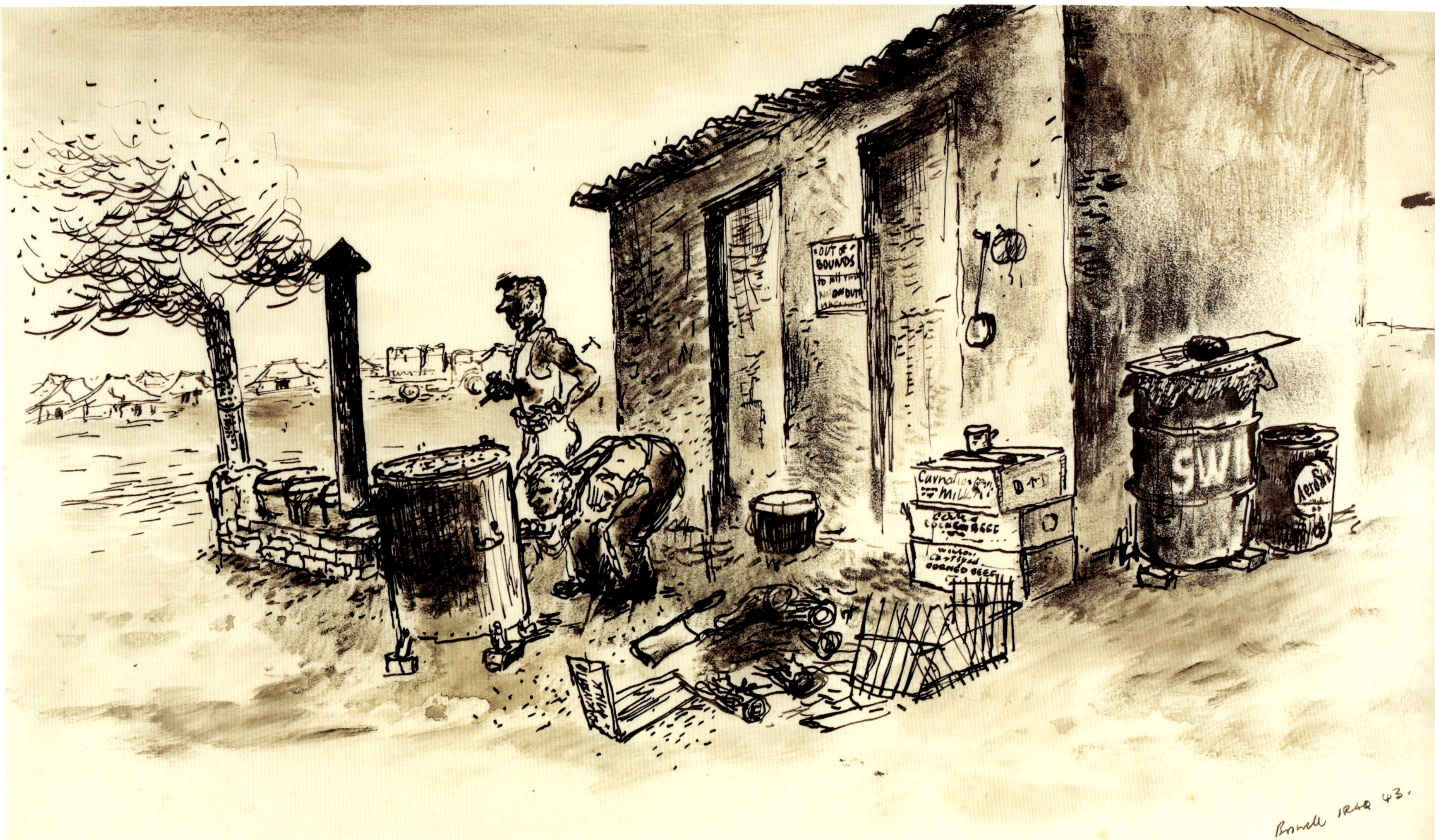
OUT OF
BOUNDS
Carnation
MILK
CORNED BEEF
SWI
Boswell IRAQ 43.

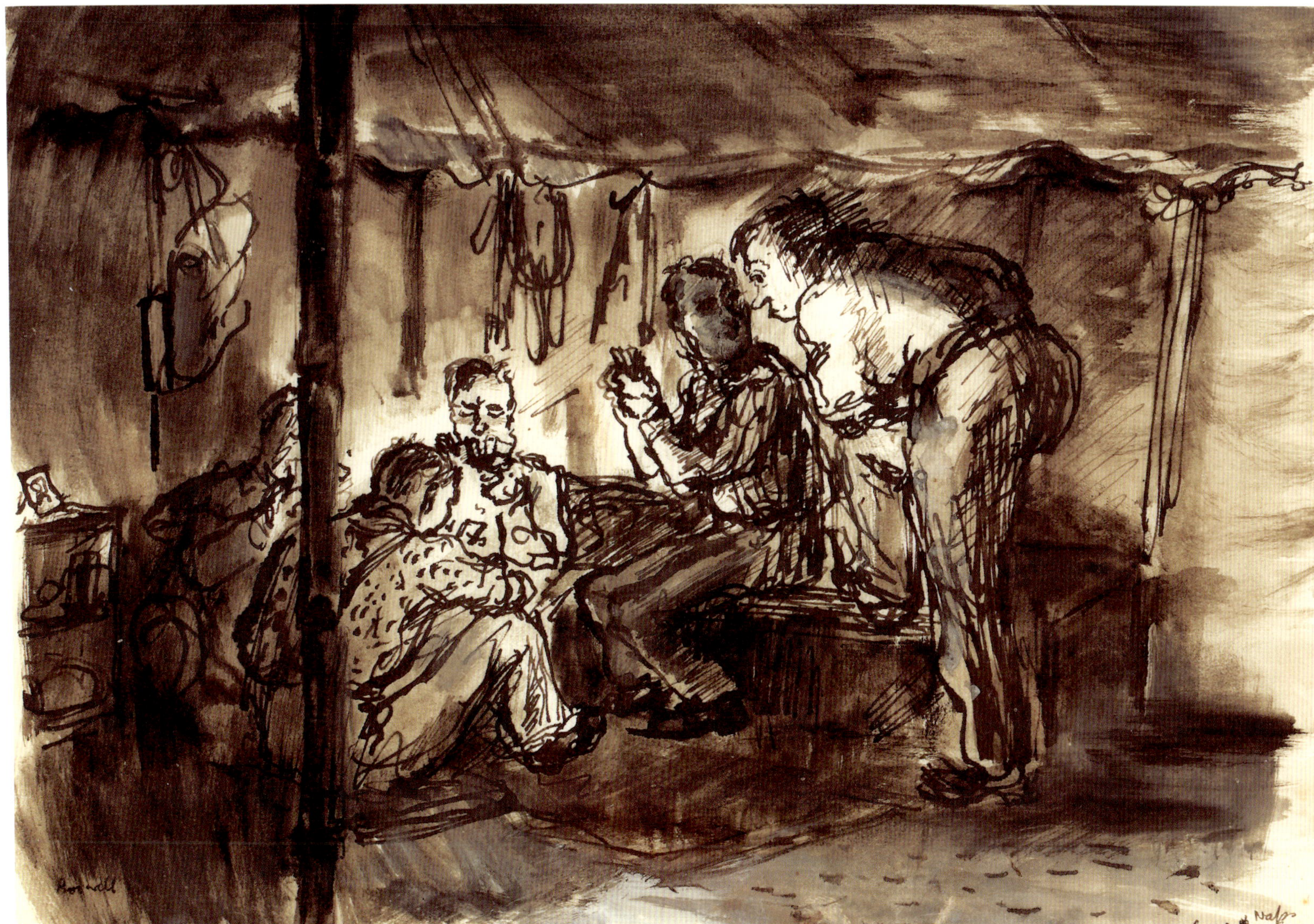

Opposite The Sergeants' Mess Cookhouse

Right Games and Naps

Overleaf *Lilliput*, September 1944

ENDURANCE

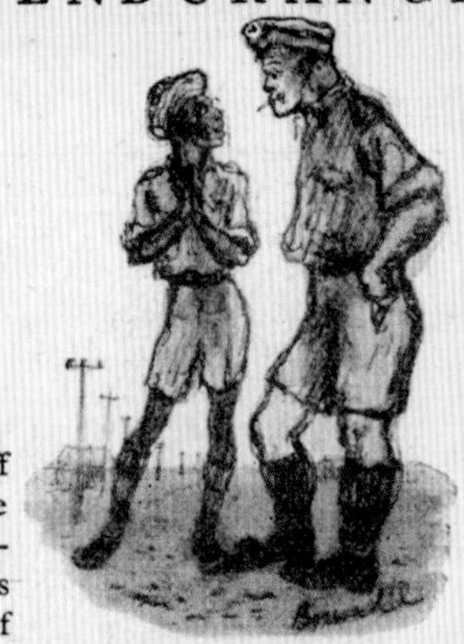

by James Boswell

The Land of the Scorpion

THE Middle East hit the new arrival right between the eyes. It staggered him with new smells, new people, new ideas. Two years ago our armies, streaming back to the canal zone, packed the camps, canteens and cities. Kiwis, Indians, Negroes, Afrikanders, Greeks, Poles, French and English jostled each other over crown-and-anchor boards, filled Shafto's ramshackle cinemas, and drank the Naafis dry. Threaded through this cosmopolitan mass, and giving it unity, ran the Rommel legend.

At every table and in every tent, the talk came round to Rommel; to his generosity to prisoners, his wisecracks about the British, his dash and skill and cunning. A few months later the legend was dead. And the tales told were about Monty's skill and dash and cunning.

But for us in Iraq, who left Egypt hurriedly to set up a hospital, the victories over Rommel were something we read of in out-of-date newspapers, or heard in bits and pieces when we could get the wireless to work. Heat, dust and boredom were our enemies, and transit camps were our homes while we waited for the hospital site to be made ready.

Where the lorries dropped us in the sand, there were a couple of sheds built of mud and wicker, and a tap that stemmed off the water-pipe we had followed across ten miles of barren sand. Grey-green tamarisk scrub grew patchily around the camp where Indian pioneers were putting up our tents. The sun climbed swiftly up the sky, spreading an eye-searing heat that drove us all to shelter before midday. We made our beds and put up nets to keep off the flies, and then we lay and sweated like rashers in a frying-pan.

* * *

WE stayed there ten weeks—maybe it was longer—we forgot days and dates, and each day at ten o'clock we went to our beds and lay sweating and cursing softly at the heat. Some slept. We told each other the stories of our lives, raking through dusty sheives of memory for fresh tales, to spin out the paralysing tedium of the siesta. In the evenings, when the moon hung improbably large above us, we sat around and tried to write home. We paid calls on neighbouring tents, and, if we were lucky enough to get the transport, a truck took us ten miles to the open-air cinema, to see a three- or four-year-old film. Through the flickering beams of light from the projection room, bats flew swiftly to and fro, dodging the changing rays and throwing

F 201

LILLIPUT

sudden shadows on the screen.

At night scorpions crept under our ground-sheets and into our empty boots. One day the men caught a spider. A colossal chap, "a tarantula!" Maybe it was. Anyhow it was big and hairy, green, the colour of the tamarisk, and with a reputation for being poisonous.

The corporal called me over to have a look. A scorpion lay, still and braced in the corner of a petrol can. The spider moved a little to the left and to the right, not fast, but like a boxer who weaves to conceal his next blow. Then he leapt. One swift scurrying wrench, and out again. The scorpion had lost a claw, and his tail curved up over his body stabbing absurdly towards his missing limb. The spider leapt again, and tore off the other claw. The third time he went in to kill, and after the kill he ate the scorpion.

Ten minutes later he killed and ate another, and four shiny black claws lay around him, but he didn't try to eat them. The third scorpion was too good for him. He was getting slow. It stung him swiftly and retired to another corner. The spider didn't move much after that. Just lay and curled up slowly. The corporal shook the tin and he rolled over.

"He had it that time," he said.

Behind us someone said "Same as the dogs, see. Can't do anything on a full belly. Pound o' steak will lose you any race."

When the heat began to ease off, the dust came. At first, sharp little scurrying gusts, that whipped up fine sands and sifted it through the windows and crevices of the tents into the eyes and nostrils. Then, later, a steady pressure of wind that bore a

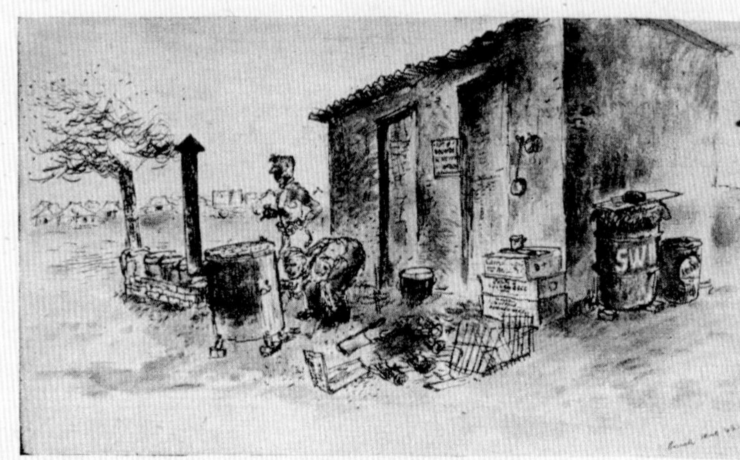

Outside the cookhouse: "Greyhounds for dinner"

202

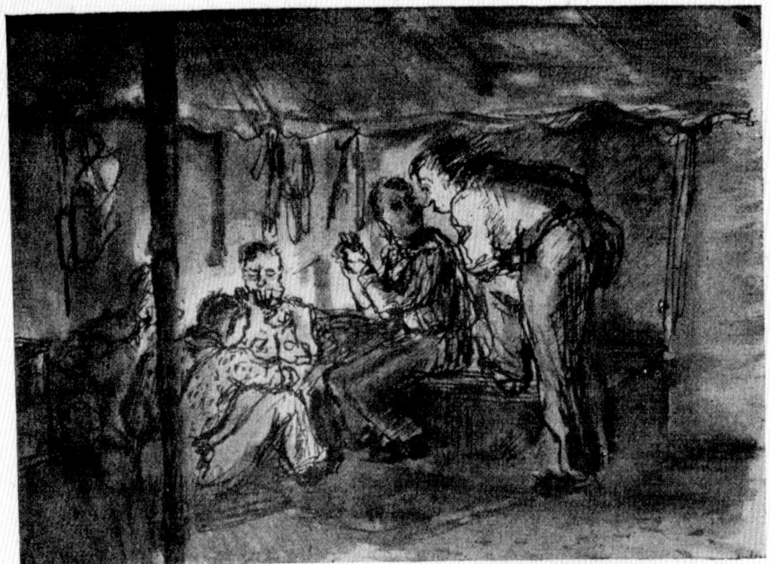

Visiting another tent "Telling each other the story of our lives"

burden of fine grey dust filling the air all day. The sun became a butter-coloured disc, shadows disappeared, colour died, and at times a dim tangible dusk came down across the desert. Dust seeped steadily through us. It sought out every entry to our tents, stuck on our sweating skins, caked our faces, filled our hair, and, with a gentle interminable pressure, wore our tempers to a thin fragile membrane of sense.

* * *

EACH morning a thirty-hundred-weight pulled into camp, and three of us, from the ration store, climbed in. The Corporal rode in front. He knew the way and, though he couldn't speak a word of Urdu, he usually managed to guide the Mahratta driver to the depot. In fact he usually managed to get most of the things he wanted, and carried on a diplomatic offensive on behalf of the unit that kept us better-fed than we deserved.

We bumped along the desert track, marked out sketchily by old petrol cans with palm leaves sticking out of them. Behind us our dust cloud rose billowing in the upward currents of hot air.

After about forty minutes' run we hit the depot. Tents, brick sheds, mud huts, wicker herds, miles of basted wire fencing, pipelines for water, light-gauge railways, straggle over the level impersonal sand, in no recognisable pattern. Arab road-making gangs work casually, and beside a mud hole a

brickmaker is slapping *motti* into a mould, and tipping out brick after brick in long rows. Inside compounds piled with stores Indian sentries keep watch from tall wicker-roofed platforms.

Our driver nosed his way down deep-rutted sand tracks, into the compound where we drew our vegetables. Aubergines, cucumber, bhindi, cans of dehydrated potatoes that rattle drily as you lift them. Archie disappeared round the back of the tent, and turned up again with a buckshee melon. Archie has a talent for getting buckshees. Sometimes I wandered round and watched him show his enormous biceps and barrel chest to the delicately-built Indians. They would come forward shyly and touch him—I was never very sure whether the melons were offered in admiration or conciliation.

In the butchery we stood and watched little, long-haired Indians at work in the slaughter-house. Their loincloths hung down, slack and heavy with sweat and blood. And from the shed, darkened to keep the flies away, their teeth gleamed white as they grinned back at us.

We drew half-a-dozen carcasses, so thin and small that we could take one under each arm. Sometimes we got Australian beef, and the truck drivers would go glum and silent on us when they saw it go on board. But nearly always it was mutton, and the cooks would greet us with bitter disgust when they saw the rigid carcasses under the net covers. "Christ, greyhounds again!"

* * *

Month after month, in one place or another, the wide-curving circle of sand circumscribed our lives, setting a pattern for their monotony and helplessness. The future and the past became remote but infinitely desirable, as we learnt to live on our own resources, making the best we could of the present. And if there is any comfort in the thought, we knew, before long, that nothing we could do would change the austere face of the desert, and, soon after our departure, wind and sand would once again impose their shape on the deserted landmarks of the Army.

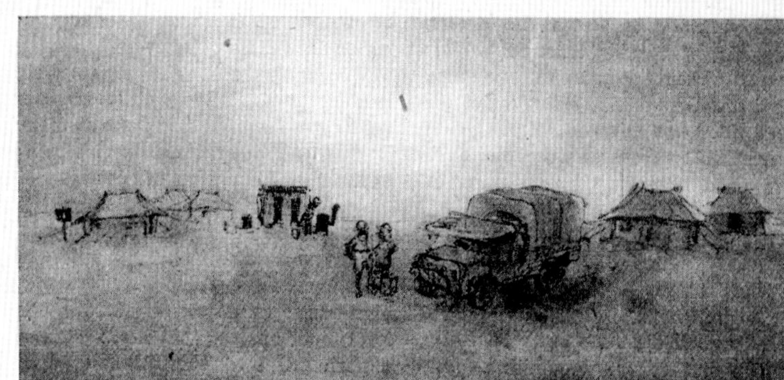

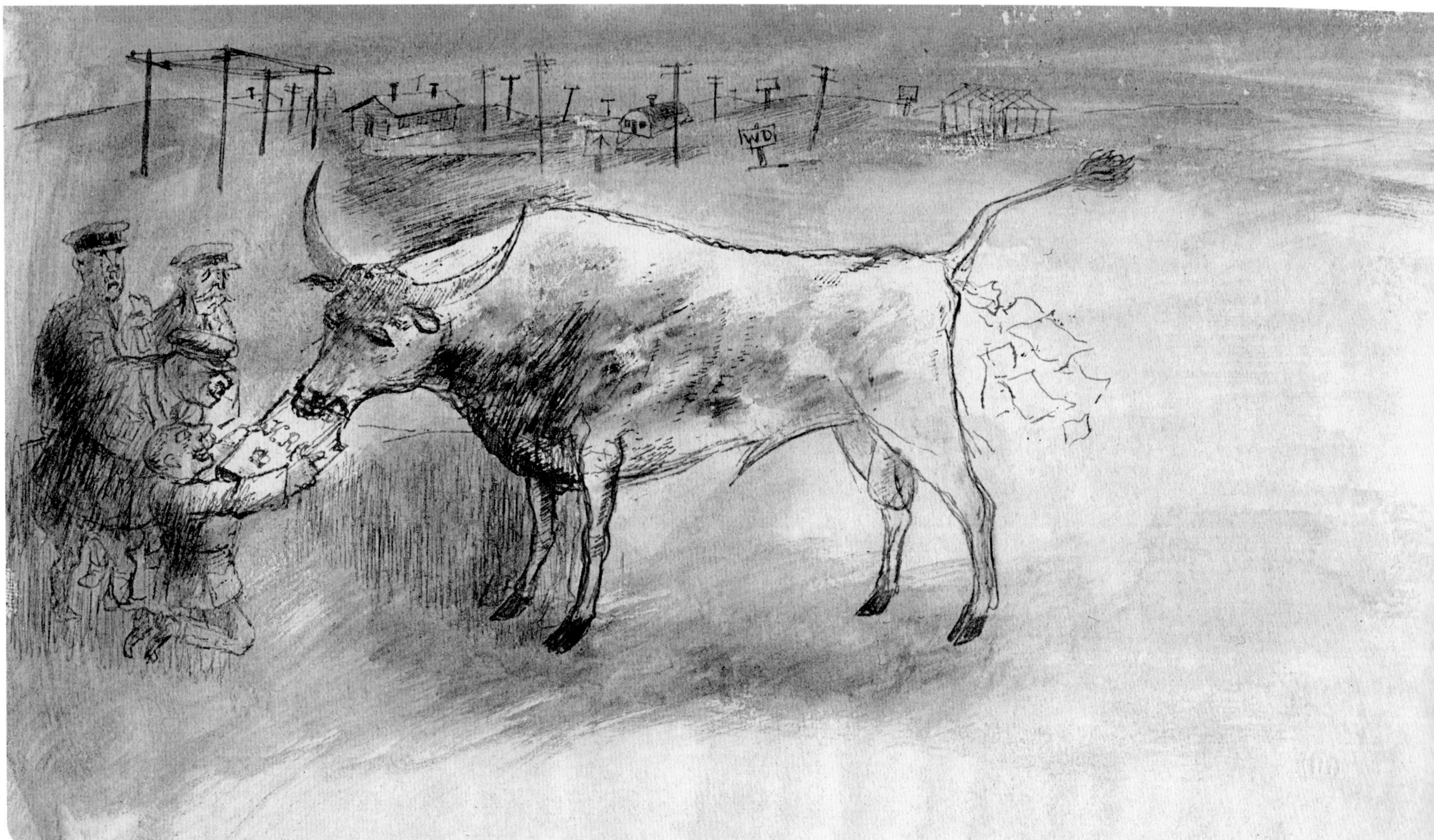
WD

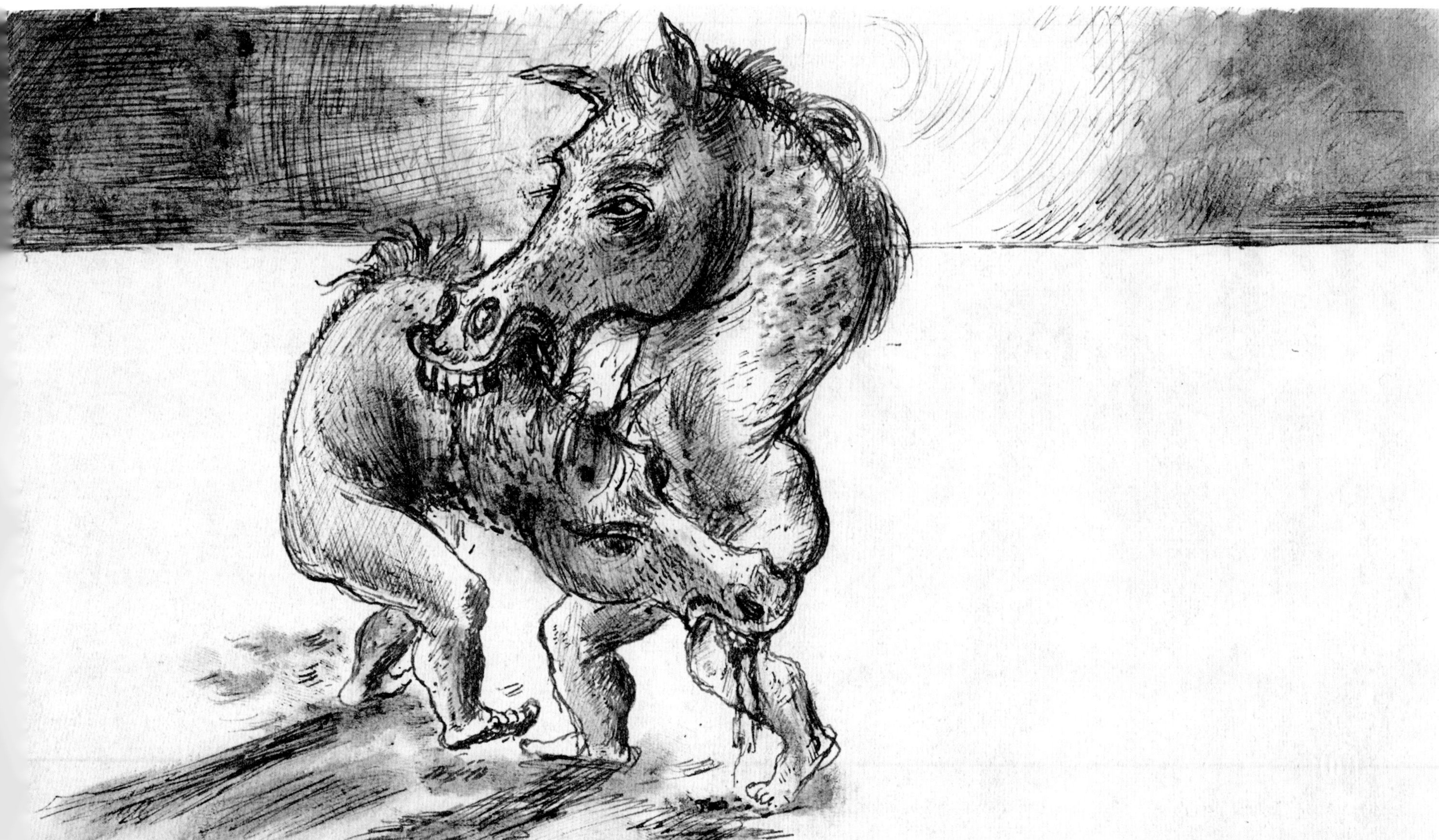

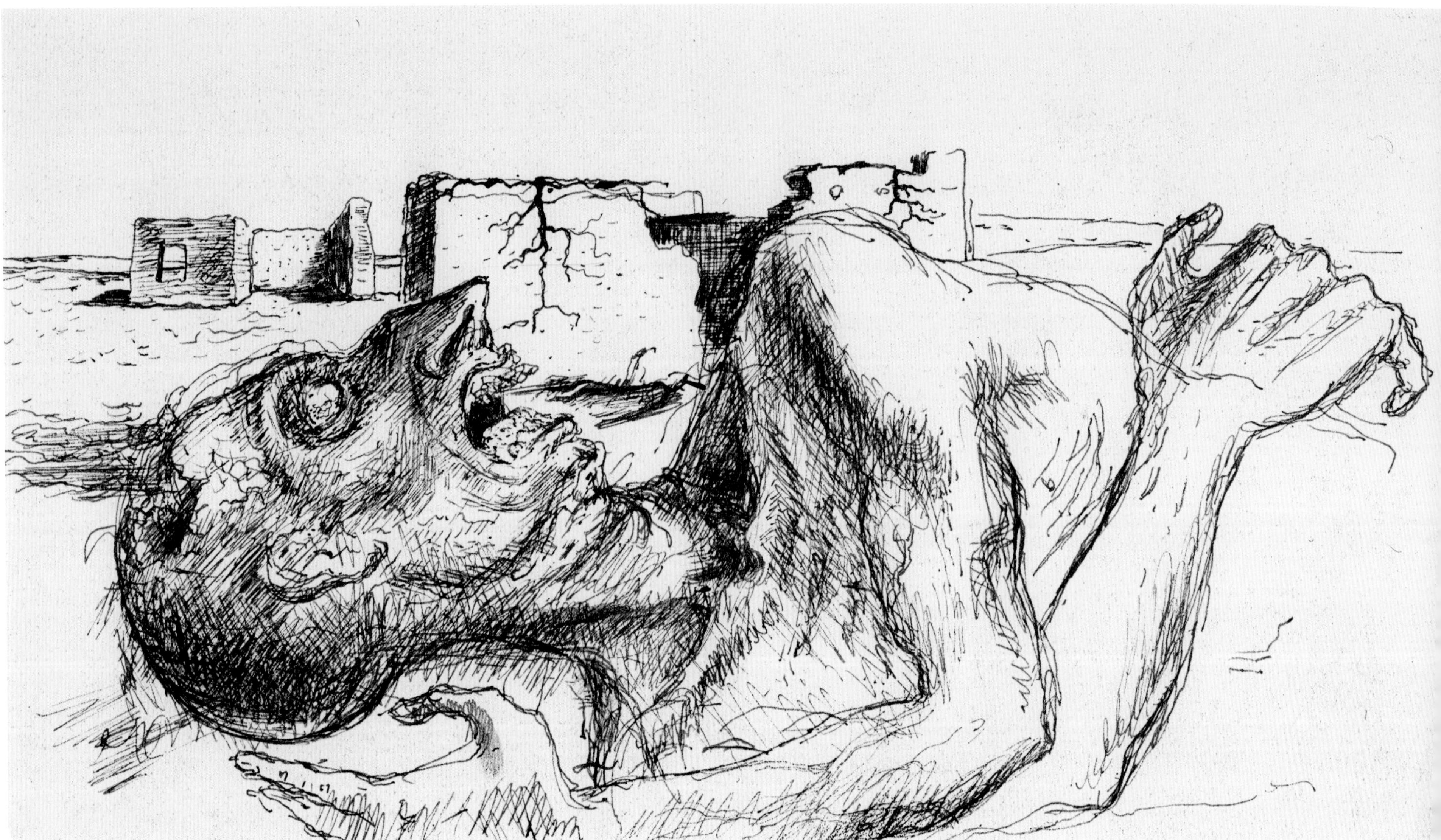

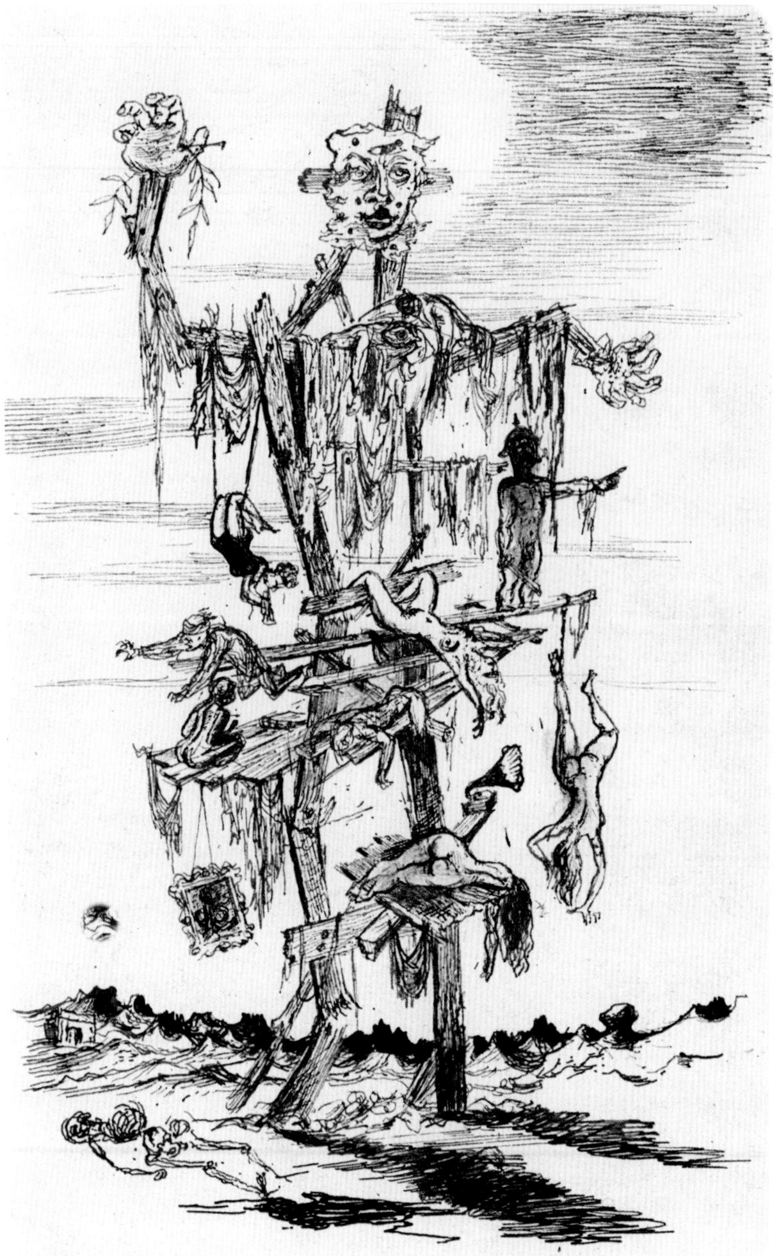

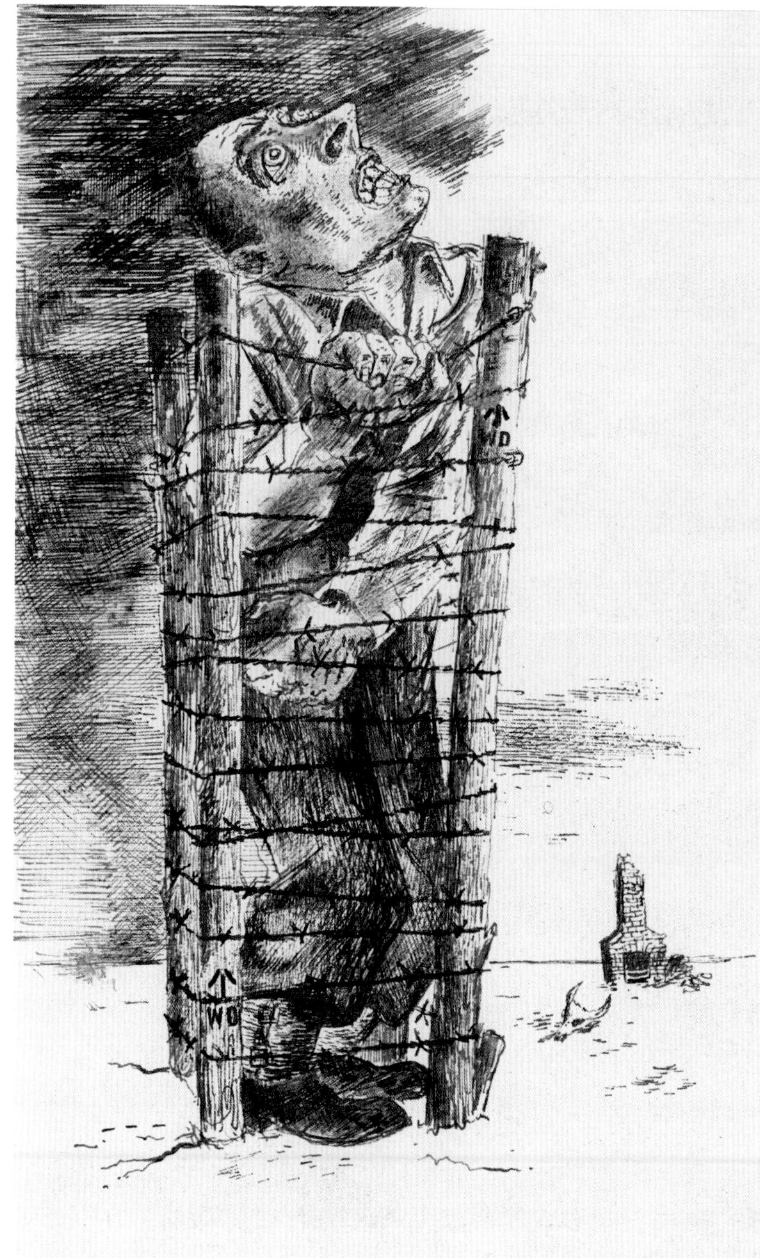
WD
WD

LONDON 1945

'The British artist at his best is fascinated by his subject-matter', Eric Newton said in his introduction to *War Through Artists' Eyes*, a picture survey published towards the end of the war in Europe. ('As I write, our armies are gathering along the frontiers of Germany. New fields to experience and record are opening up.') Being neither an official war artist nor yet recognised as a significant unofficial one, Boswell was not included; others, who had seen action or at least worked in theatres of war busier and even more far-flung than Iraq, had more obviously fascinating subject-matter for the book. Edward Ardizzone had been present at both the evacuation of Dunkirk and the landings in Sicily; his genial manner veiled horrific incidents, rendering them not harmless exactly but visually tolerable; Eric Ravilious had witnessed battleships in action, guns flowering flame, propellers generating clean wave patterns, before he disappeared off Iceland in 1942; Anthony Gross had splashed ashore on D-Day holding a pack of watercolour paper above his head; Albert Richards parachuted into Normandy and drew on the landing beaches only to be killed crossing a minefield in March 1945. Given all this, it is not surprising that drawings of not much happening on remote army bases were not in demand or, if known about at all, not particularly appreciated.

In 1944 Boswell was switched from radiography to army education and given a commission. Captain, later Major, Boswell transferred to the Army Bureau of Current Affairs where he joined Richard Bennett, whom he had first met on *Left Review*. The desk job enabled him to renew his artistic connections. He was elected Chairman of the AIA and held a one-man show, *On Duty in the Desert*, at the Charlotte Street Centre.

The war in Europe ended in May 1945 and British party politics officially resumed. 'There's a General Election on its way,' was the pay-off line in the June 2nd 1945 issue of *Current Affairs*', a fortnightly ABCA periodical issued for the instruction and edification of troops due to be released onto civvie street once the rest of the war, in the Far East, was over. That fortnight's topic was *The Artist and the Public*, hardly the most engaging concern with which to slake demob impatience three weeks on from VE Day. The three contributors however – Boswell himself, John Piper and Carl Giles – addressed it as entertainingly as they could, using ABCA guidelines to identify themes ripe for group discussion by 'your

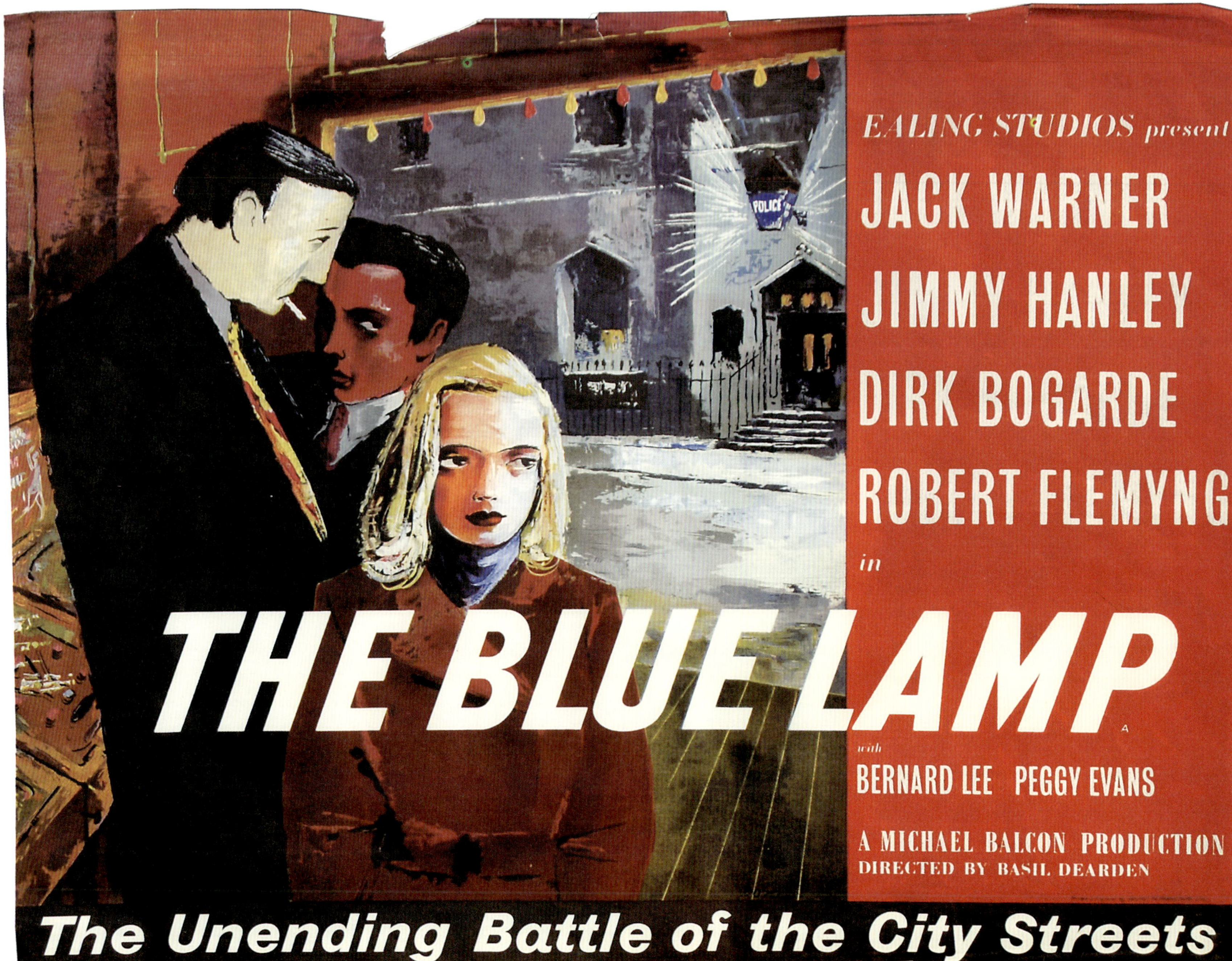
EALING STUDIOS present
JACK WARNER
JIMMY HANLEY
DIRK BOGARDE
ROBERT FLEMYNG
in
THE BLUE LAMP
A
with
BERNARD LEE PEGGY EVANS
A MICHAEL BALCON PRODUCTION
DIRECTED BY BASIL DEARDEN
The Unending Battle of the City Streets
POLICE

men', ie: those now being encouraged to think for themselves and vote.

'In the past 'hate' pictures have by no means always been bad pictures, but today the artist, in so far as he is a leader, has an urge to counterbalance, rather than to increase, hatred', Piper wrote, his geniality an expression of the high-hat taste that elevated Henry Moore to the status of ideal representative of the human race on a mission to another planet, as Kenneth Clark was fond of saying. On the other hand Giles who, as temporary Captain Giles, had been a cartooning war correspondent attending the liberation of Belgium and the Netherlands, stressed the virtues of ridicule. 'Take that Musso. By causing people to laugh at such a creature, I think a cartoon fired a good shot at making them realise in a cheerful way the futility and stupidness of Fascism.' He rejected the assumption that *The Artist and the Public* was a matter of Us and Them.

'Nearly everybody still seems to like jokes about sergeant-majors. For some reason it is funny to see the 'Schweik' of your company being bawled at by the sergeant-major, and much funnier to hear what your 'Schweik' says about the sergeant-major afterwards.'

Boswell, whose sympathies lay somewhere between Giles's buoyant popularism and Piper's pleasing aesthetic, talked about 'the great body of artists whose work we see daily without being particularly aware of its existence', unlike 'the 'pure' artist (concerned) not with an abstract thing called 'beauty' but with the inter-play of our emotions and the world around us.' An admirable reconciliation of these two strands of creativity, it so happened, was the sequence of drawings that he himself produced for the 1946 ABCA calendar, a wall chart listing key dates from the war years. He headed each month with a rear-view mirror image of people's lives on various fronts, home and abroad, generations emerging from a now distant Chamberlain era and advancing into the brave new age of the Welfare State.

'Something has happened in the past six years that has changed the artist's world. The war has given him a public', Boswell wrote in *The Artist's Dilemma*, the first in a series of short monographs on *New Developments*, published in 1947. 'For all that the pressure of war gave the artist a socially useful task, the purpose was in itself a temporary one on which he could not build to last. All that he could do was to learn that given a purposeful task he can do it.'

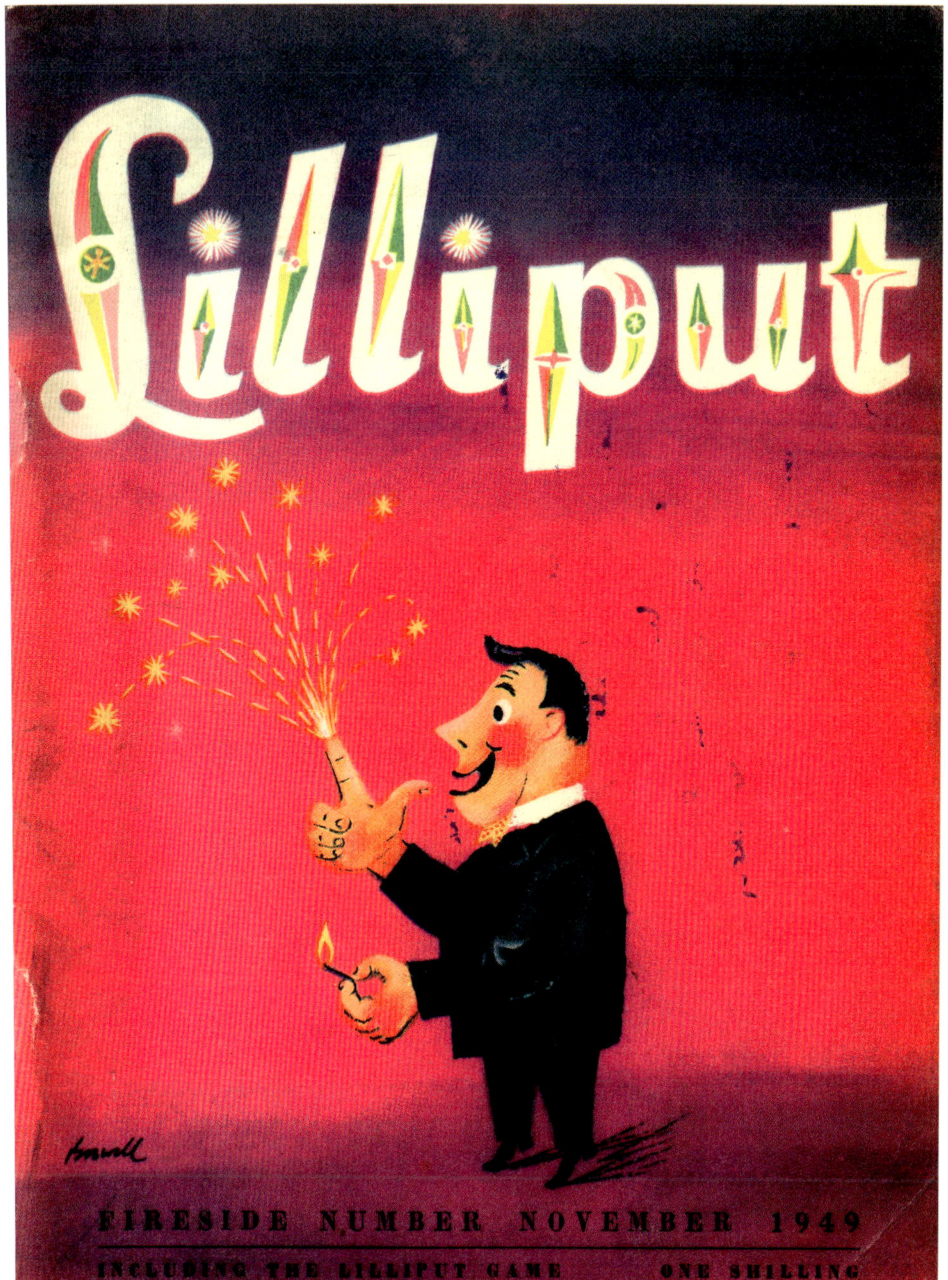

Chapter opener *The Blue Lamp*, film poster. Ealing Studios, 1950

Right *Lilliput*, November 1949

Discharged from the army Boswell returned to Shell but couldn't settle. He left and spent 'four very crazy drunken years in Fleet Street' as art editor of *Lilliput* (The Monthly Magazine for Everyone), under its new editor Richard Bennett. This for a while suited his purposes ideally. He stirred *Lilliput's* visual mix, employing the best artists of what proved to be a brief golden age of English illustration. Among them were Edward Bawden, Edward Burra, John Minton, Mervyn Peake and Ronald Searle, whose feral St Trinians schoolgirls were the popular antidote to Henry Moore humanism. *Lilliput* carried photo essays by Bill Brandt and others, a sufficiency of female nude studies and colour reproductions of paintings by a variety of painters ranging from Poussin to Burra. There were articles too on Daumier and Cruikshank, 'concerned with things and people rather than with any aesthetic cult.' Subject was foremost.

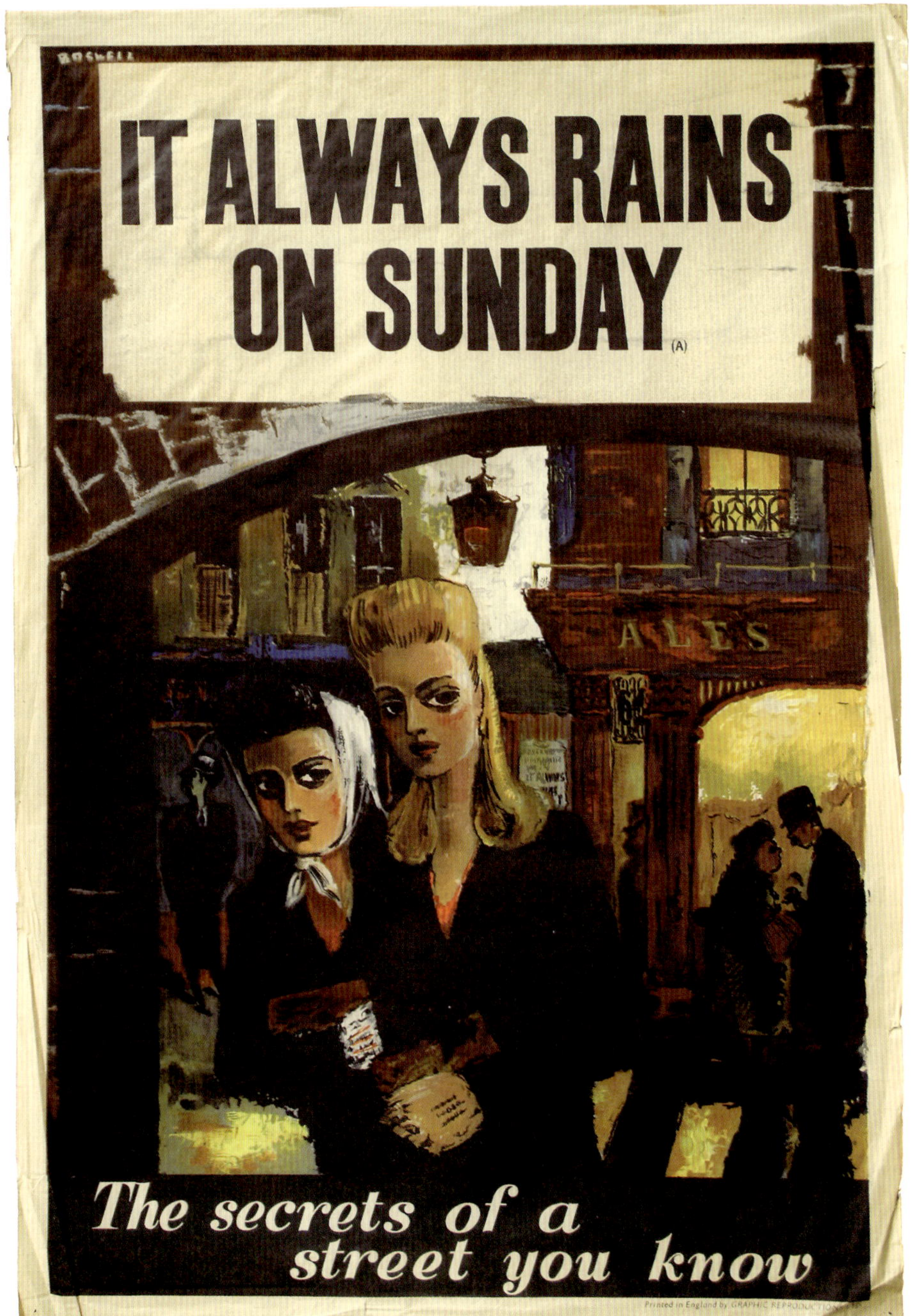

It Always Rains on Sunday, film poster. Ealing Studios, 1947

Boswell himself contributed drawings, some derived from the wartime sketchbooks, some demonstrating his appetite for post war London, its grottiness charming, even dazzling, to his eyes after service life and the desert confines of Iraq. In April 1947 he published *Portrait of a Neighbourhood*, consisting of four pictures of Camden Town, painted by him in a vertical format to suit the magazine page. Here were old haunts revisited: the shored-up Café Rouge from his 1940 lithograph *Quiet Evening*, barrage balloons gone, two storeys missing and the 'Rouge' bit dropped from the sign. To the soldier returned, the open door of the corner shop (*Little Gold Mine*), the light from the pub spilling across the pavement (*Saturday Night*) and even the dodginess of the spiv at the fruit and veg stall spelt robust expectations. The left wing historian Eric Hobsbawm supplied a commentary. Noting that Camden Town's inhabitants were 'practically all shockingly housed', he argued that the district's ordinariness is slightly démodé', still 'stuck fast in the period when Sickert painted it.' That helped place Boswell in an impressive order of succession: Cruikshank, Sickert and now him.

No doubt a good few of the 97 suicides (40 by gas), the 3 murders and 2 manslaughters of St Pancras, in the last year when they counted such things, belonged to Camden Town', Hobsbawm remarked. When Boswell reworked *Saturday Night* into the poster for the Ealing Studios thriller *It Always Rains on Sunday*, glamorising the hairstyles and street lighting, he created a Camden melodramatic enough to sustain its own brand of film noir.

For the magazine, which prided itself on the sophistication of its ridicule, Boswell developed bug-eyed characters tapering head to toe, a livelier, seedier, and more rounded bunch than Chamberlain and his pre-war gang. They were the recently-demobbed, let loose in Lilliputian London. Face to Face: *Nine Interviews with a Mirror*, published in 1949, involved a good selection of these self-deluding types, among them the social climber, the acne victim, the tireless raconteur and the pub bore. Boswell showed them examining themselves and commented that reflections tend to pander to the reflected eye. 'The mirror cannot lie, but to the frankly hopeful question it will do its best to return the agreeably dishonest answer.'

'How unnecessary', he wrote, 'to go through the looking-glass when on this side of it we are already in a different and more amiable world.' This world was no longer the unreservedly black and white one that had so exercised him in *Left Review*. Under its Labour government post-war Britain was broke but engaged in social reform and Boswell, who had let his Communist party membership lapse, recognised that the old Realist/Surrealist polarities and solidarities no longer applied.

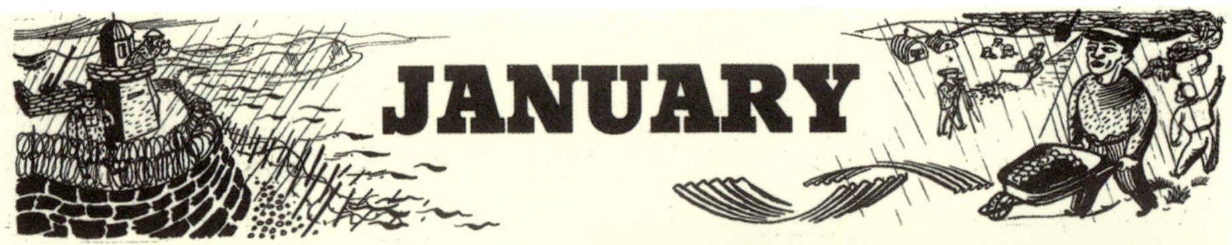

JANUARY

Sun.	-	6	13	20	27
Mon.	-	7	14	21	28
Tues.	1	8	15	22	29
Wed.	2	9	16	23	30
Thurs.	3	10	17	24	31
Fri.	4	11	18	25	-
Sat.	5	12	19	26	-

1940

Tension and military preparations in Belgium and Holland. Mr. Churchill broadcasts appeal to all neutrals to stand with Britain and France against aggression.

Foreign Legion formed in Finland.

1941

Desert offensive goes well, many thousands of prisoners. Bardia surrenders (5th), Tobruk captured (22nd), Derna (30th).

Imperial forces enter Eritrea and Italian Somaliland. Hailie Selassie re-enters Ethiopia.

Dive-bombing attacks on Malta begin.

Civilian air raid casualties in Britain for month : 1,648 killed, 4,864 seriously injured.

1942

Day and night bombing of Malta. R.A.F. continuously attacks Libya supply bases.

Japanese begin invasion of Netherlands East Indies, advance in Malaya, invade Burma.

First U.S. troops arrive in Northern Ireland.

Marshal Timoshenko advances into Ukraine.

1943

Russians drive Germans back in Caucasus, capture Field Marshal von Paulus and sixteen generals at Stalingrad, raise siege of Leningrad.

President Roosevelt and Mr. Churchill at Casablanca for the " unconditional surrender " meeting.

8th Army enters Tripoli. Pursuit of Rommel continues.

U.S. heavy bombers make their first raid on Germany (27th).

1944

General Montgomery arrives in England to be C.-in-C. British Group of Armies. General Eisenhower assumes duties as C.-in-C. Allied Expeditionary Force.

British troops capture Maungdaw in Burma (10th).

5th Army land south of Rome, occupy Nettuno and Anzio (22nd). Gustav Line broken north of Cassino.

U.S. forces launch amphibious attack on Marshall Islands.

1945

German forces in Ardennes flung back to original positions.

Russian winter offensive. Fall of Warsaw (16th), Cracow and Lodz (18th). Russians reach Gulf of Danzig and break into Brandenburg. Reach Landsberg 68 miles from Berlin.

14th Army advances on Mandalay. Akyab captured.

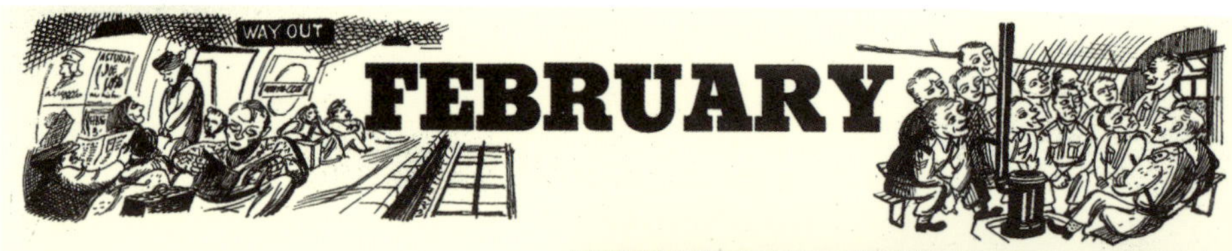

FEBRUARY

Sun.	-	3	10	17	24
Mon.	-	4	11	18	25
Tues.	-	5	12	19	26
Wed.	-	6	13	20	27
Thurs.	-	7	14	21	28
Fri.	1	8	15	22	-
Sat.	2	9	16	23	-

1940

Heavy fighting in Finland. Mannerheim line entered. Russians advance on Viipuri.

H.M.S. *Cossack* releases prisoners from German ship *Altmark* in Norwegian waters.

1941

Desert victory. Benghazi captured (6th). El Agheila on Cyrenaica frontier occupied (8th).

" Give us the tools and we will finish the job "—Mr. Churchill's broadcast (9th).

British paratroops raid Calabria. Genoa bombarded by Royal Navy.

Civilian air raid casualties in Britain for month : 859 killed, 2,037 seriously injured.

1942

Fall of Singapore (15th). Japanese advance on Rangoon. Battle of the Java Sea followed by Japanese landings in Java.

1943

General Russian advances. Final capitulation of Germans at Stalingrad. Rostov recaptured.

Germans attack in Tunisia, capture Gafsa, heavy fighting for Kasserine Pass.

R.A.F. begins round-the-clock bombing (25th).

1944

Major German offensive against Anzio beach-head. Fighting in streets of Cassino. Monastery of Monte Cassino bombed and shelled.

Japanese cleared from Ngakyedyauk Pass in Burma. 14th Army mopping up in the Arakan.

1945

Marshal Stalin, Mr. Churchill and President Roosevelt meet at Yalta (4th-12th).

Allies pressing Germans back to Rhine.

Fall of Manila (3rd). The assault on the Ryukyu Islands (4th-12th). Americans land on Iwojima (18th).

Burma Road open to convoys.

1946 ABCA War Calendar designed and illustrated by Boswell for the Army Bureau of Current Affairs

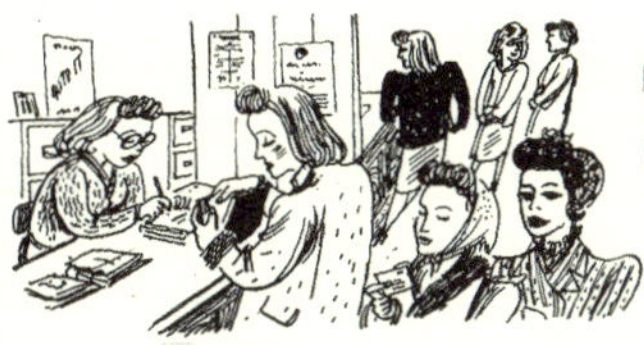

MARCH

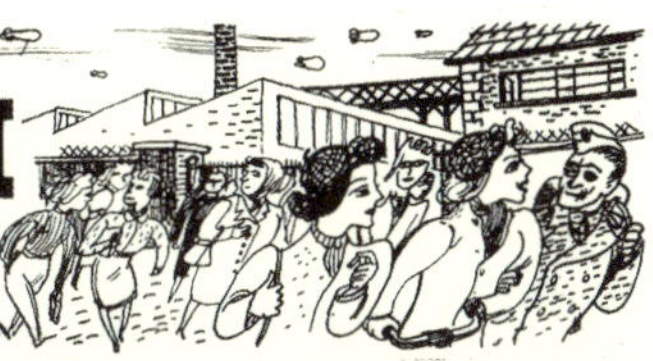

Sun.	-	3	10	17	24/31
Mon.	-	4	11	18	25
Tues.	-	5	12	19	26
Wed.	-	6	13	20	27
Thurs.	-	7	14	21	28
Fri.	1	8	15	22	29
Sat.	2	9	16	23	30

1939

Czech President Hacha summoned to Berlin. Slovakia declares her independence. Hungary invades Carpatho-Ukraine. German troops cross Czech frontier and on 15th Hitler declares the "Protectorate of Bohemia and Moravia."

Lithuania cedes Memel to Germany after ultimatum.

British and French guarantees to Poland.

1940

Mr. Chamberlain states that Allies would respond to Finnish appeal for military aid.

Russo-Finnish peace signed in Moscow (12th).

M. Daladier resigns, succeeded as Prime Minister by M. Reynaud.

1941

Lease-Lend Bill signed by President Roosevelt (11th).

British Somaliland regained. Siege of Keren (1st-27th). Enemy recapture El Agheila.

Yugoslavia revolts against signing of Tripartite Pact.

Civilian air raid casualties in Britain for month : 4,613 killed, 1,054 seriously injured.

1942

General MacArthur arrives in Australia to take up Allied Command.

1943

Japanese convoy in Bismarck Straits destroyed by Allied bombers. 22 ships, 10 warships, 12 transports sunk or left sinking.

Rommel attack on 8th Army held. 8th move against Mareth Line initial penetration held, attack El Hamma, force Rommel to withdraw from Mareth Line.

1944

Ground lost at Anzio regained. 1,400 tons of bombs dropped on Cassino. Allies hold three quarters of town.

14th Army cross Chindwin at several points. Airborne forces landed in Central Burma. Major-General Wingate killed.

Russians force River Pruth, enter Rumania (31st.)

1945

American 1st Army captures Cologne, crosses Rhine at Remagen and establishes bridgehead (7th). American 3rd Army crosses Rhine south of Mainz (23rd).

Field Marshal Montgomery's 21st Army Group forces the main crossing of the Rhine on 25 mile front north of the Ruhr (24th).

14th Army captures Mandalay (20th).

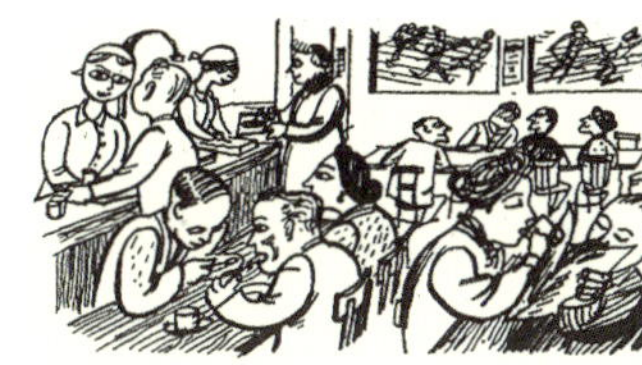

APRIL

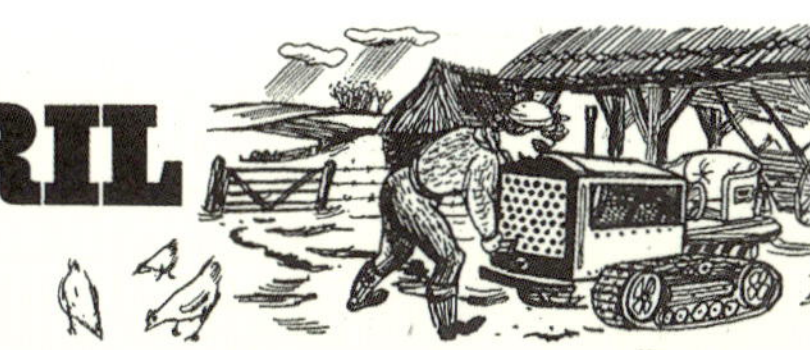

Sun.	-	7	14	21	28
Mon.	1	8	15	★22	29
Tues.	2	9	16	23	30
Wed.	3	10	17	24	-
Thurs.	4	11	18	25	-
Fri.	5	12	★19	26	-
Sat.	6	13	20	27	-

★ Easter

1939

Italy invades Albania (7th).

Hitler denounces Naval Agreement with Britain and non-aggression pact with Poland. Demands Danzig and road through Polish corridor.

Mr. Chamberlain announces compulsory military training.

1940

Germans invade Denmark and Norway (9th). British Expeditionary Force lands in Norway at Namsos and Narvik (15th-18th). British attempt to reach Trondheim fails.

Belgium cancels army leave.

1941

British withdraw in desert. Benghazi evacuated (3rd). Bardia lost, Tobruk encircled. Germans and Italians cross Egyptian frontier at Sollum (26th).

Soviet-Yugoslav pact of friendship and non-aggression signed (5th).

Imperial troops enter Addis Ababa (5th).

Germans invade Greece and Yugoslavia : Belgrade heavily and repeatedly bombed. Bulgaria invades Yugoslav territory. British and Imperial forces in action in Greece. Yugoslav army capitulates (17th). Evacuation of Imperial forces from Greece begins (22nd). Civilian air raid casualties in Britain for month : 6,475 killed, 5,023 seriously injured.

1942

U.S. forces in Bataan forced to surrender. Siege of Corregidor begins.

First air raid on Tokyo by U.S. bombers (18th).

1943

Heavy raids on German targets on all but ten days of month. 900 tons of bombs on Essen (3rd-4th). 1,300 tons on Duisburg (26th-27th).

1st Army launches offensive in Tunisia.

1944

81,000 tons of bombs dropped on Germany and Western Europe.
Russians recapture Odessa.

1945

Reichswehr broken, Allies advance on all fronts. Fierce fighting in Berlin.

Vienna falls to Russians (13th).

Mussolini caught and shot by Italian partisans while attempting to flee the country.

Death of President Roosevelt (12th). United Nations Conference opens in San Francisco (25th).

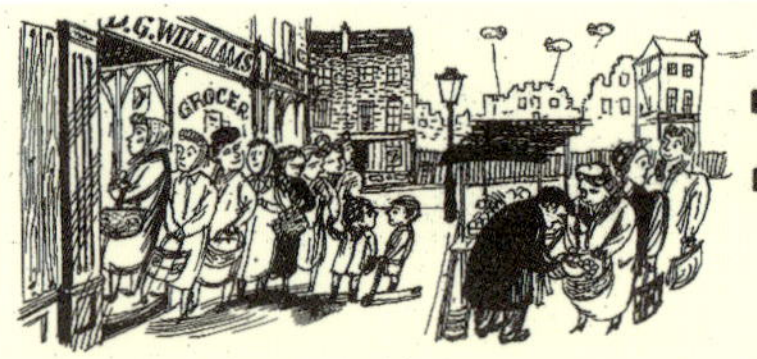

MAY

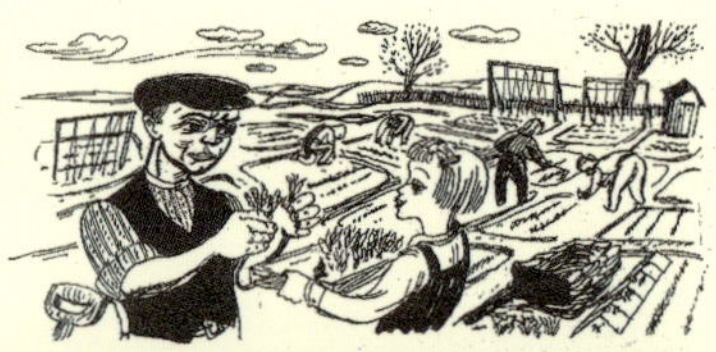

1939

Italo-German alliance signed in Berlin.
Denmark signs non-aggression pact with Germany.

1940

In Norway Germans reach Andalasnes. Allied forces embark at Namsos.
Germany invades Holland and Belgium, over-runs Luxemburg (10th).
British and French troops enter Belgium.
Mr. Chamberlain resigns and Mr. Churchill becomes Prime Minister and forms War Cabinet (10th).
Dutch C.-in-C. orders fighting to cease (14th).
Mr. Eden calls for " Local Defence Volunteers."
B.E.F. withdrawn west of Brussels. Germans drive for the Channel ports.
Belgian Army capitulates (28th). B.E.F. begins evacuation through Dunkirk (30th).

1941

Rudolf Hess, Hitler's deputy, parachutes into Scotland (10th).
Germans invade Crete by air (20th).
H.M.S. *Hood* sunk in *Bismarck* action (24th). *Bismarck* sunk (27th).
Civilian air raid casualties in Britain for month : 5,612 killed, 6,669 seriously injured.

1942

British evacuate Mandalay, withdraw over Irrawaddy.
Battle of Coral Sea (4th). Japanese Fleet withdraws after sustaining severe losses.
British land on Madagascar (5th).
Twenty-year Anglo-Soviet treaty signed in London (26th).

1943

Tunis and Bizerta captured (7th). Axis forces in Tunisia surrender (13th), 291,000 prisoners.
Mr. Churchill in Washington, addresses both houses of Congress.

1944

5th and 8th Armies open Gustav Line offensive. Cassino town and monastery captured. Patrols link up with Anzio.

Sun.	-	5	12	19	26
Mon.	-	6	13	20	27
Tues.	-	7	14	21	28
Wed.	1	8	15	22	29
Thurs.	2	9	16	23	30
Fri.	3	10	17	24	31
Sat.	4	11	18	25	-

Russians recapture Sevastopol, liberate Crimea.

1945

Berlin falls to Russians (2nd).
Unconditional surrender of German forces in Italy, Tyrol, parts of Styria and Carinthia to Field-Marshal Alexander (2nd).
Field-Marshal Montgomery receives unconditional surrender of all German forces on his front, to become effective on 5th.
Final surrender of Germany (7th).
Fall of Rangoon (3rd).

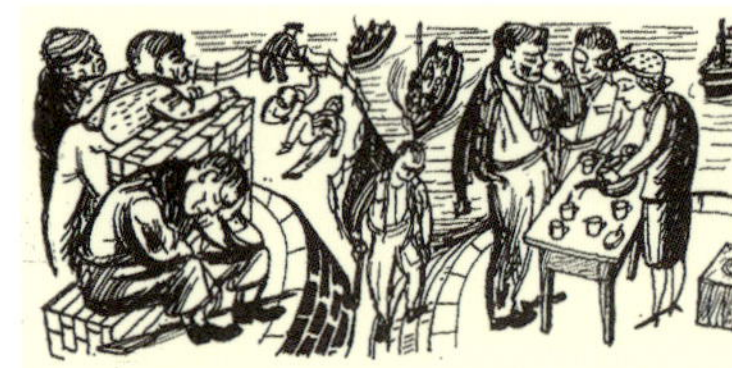

JUNE

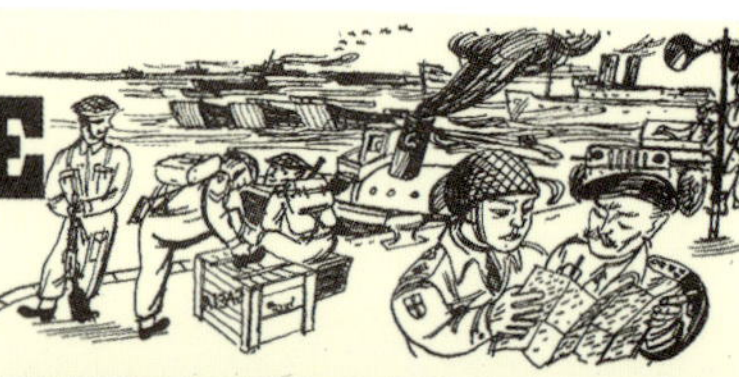

1939

Discussions in London with Polish and Turkish military missions.

1940

Dunkirk evacuation completed (3rd-4th).

Battle of France. German tanks break through French line.

Italy declares war (10th).

Germans enter Paris (14th). Marshal Pétain forms cabinet, announces that France has asked for terms (17th).

French receive armistice terms at Compiègne (21st). Hostilities in France end (25th).

1941

Imperial forces withdrawn from Crete.

Twenty consecutive heavy R.A.F. raids on Ruhr, Rhineland and ports in north-west Germany. Daily R.A.F. sweeps over Channel and northern France.

Germans invade U.S.S.R. (22nd) and make rapid gains.

1942

Rommel offensive in Libya. Battle of Knightsbridge. Imperial forces withdraw to Egyptian frontier. Germans capture Tobruk (21st), advance into Egypt.

1943

Pantellaria and Lampedusa occupied. Raids on Sicilian airfields.

1944

D. Day (6th). Landings in Normandy. Beach-heads consolidated.

Bayeux liberated (8th). Cherbourg (26th).

Sun.	-	2	9	16	23/30
Mon.	-	3	★10	17	24
Tues.	-	4	11	18	25
Wed.	-	5	12	19	26
Thurs.	-	6	13	20	27
Fri.	-	7	14	21	28
Sat.	1	8	15	22	29

★ **Whit Monday**

Advance in Italy continues. 5th Army enters Rome. 8th take Perugia.

First V.1 flying bombs on Southern England (13th-14th).

1945

Okinawa finally cleared of Japanese (21st). Australian landings in Borneo.

World Security Charter signed by fifty nations at San Francisco (26th).

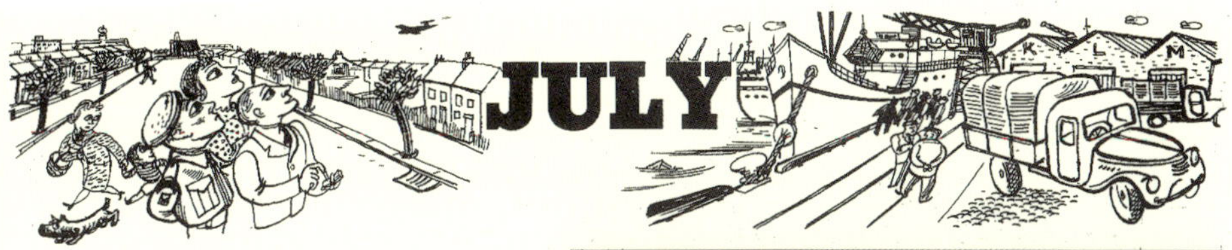

JULY

Sun.	-	7	14	21	28
Mon.	1	8	15	22	29
Tues.	2	9	16	23	30
Wed.	3	10	17	24	31
Thurs.	4	11	18	25	-
Fri.	5	12	19	26	-
Sat.	6	13	20	27	-

1939

United States denounces trade treaty with Japan.

1940

British attack French Fleet at Oran and Mers-el-Kebir. Pétain government breaks off diplomatic relations with Britain. Marshal Pétain becomes "Chief of the French State."

1941

Stalin calls for total effort, advocates guerrilla warfare and scorched earth policy.

Anglo-Soviet agreement signed in Moscow for mutual assistance against Germany with no separate peace.

Vichy France cedes Indo-Chinese bases to Japanese. Great Britain denounces all trade treaties with Japan.

Allied forces occupy Syria.

1942

Rommel held at El Alamein and withdraws.

Fall of Sevastopol (1st). Russians retreat at Kursk and Bielgorod. Germans cross the Don.

1943

U.S. airborne forces and British paratroopers spearhead landings in Sicily (9th-10th).

Rome bombed. Hitler and Mussolini meet at Verona. Mussolini resigns, is arrested and Badoglio takes over government (25th). Martial law in Italy.

1944

Caen captured (9th). U.S. break-through north of St. Lô. British 2nd Army attacks round Caumont.

Civilian air raid casualties for month in Britain: 2,441 killed, 7,107 injured.

1945

Japanese mainland shelled by Allied warships. Heaviest air raids of the war on Japan.

Mr. Churchill, President Truman and Marshal Stalin hold first session of Potsdam Conference (17th).

Result of General Election in Britain (26th). Mr. Churchill resigns, Mr. Attlee, Prime Minister.

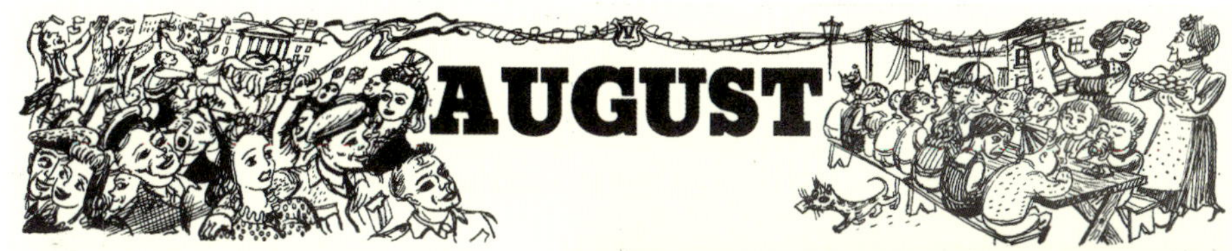

AUGUST

Sun.	-	4	11	18	25
Mon.	-	★5	12	19	26
Tues.	-	6	13	20	27
Wed.	-	7	14	21	28
Thurs.	1	8	15	22	29
Fri.	2	9	16	23	30
Sat.	3	10	17	24	31

★ **August Bank Holiday**

1939

British-French-Soviet staff talks in Moscow.

Soviet-German non-aggression pact signed in Moscow (23rd). Anglo-Polish alliance signed (25th).

Queen Wilhelmina and King Leopold offer mediation.

Final British note to Hitler (30th).

1940

Battle of Britain begins. Heavy German air attacks on ports and shipping and on airfields. Croydon airport bombed (15th), 182 German planes destroyed over Britain (15th). First bombs on Central London (24th). First R.A.F. raid on Berlin (25th). First all-night raid on London (26th).

1941

Mr. Churchill and President Roosevelt meet off Newfoundland. Atlantic Charter signed.

U.S.S.R. announces evacuation of Smolensk. Heavy fighting for Leningrad. Russians withdraw over Dneiper and destroy Dneiper dam.

British and Russian forces enter Persia.

1942

U.S. forces land on Guadalcanal.

Germans drive into Caucasus. Mr. Churchill meets Marshal Stalin in Moscow (12th).

General Sir Harold Alexander, appointed C.-in-C. Middle East and Lieut.-General Sir Bernard Montgomery Commander of 8th Army.

The Dieppe raid. Heavy fighting ashore for nine hours (19th).

1943

Russians recapture Orel, Bielgorod, Kharkov, Taganrog.

All enemy resistance in Sicily ends (17th). Italian mainland shelled.

Mr. Churchill and President Roosevelt meet at Quebec Conference.

1944

Hinged on Caen, U.S. armour sweeps across Brittany. Germans retreat from Normandy. Falaise gap closed. F.F.I. liberate Paris (23rd). New landings in south of France.

Rumania accepts armistice terms. Bulgaria gives in.

1945

Atomic bombs dropped on Hiroshima (6th) and Nagasaki (9th).
U.S.S.R. declares war on Japan (8th). Russians cross into Manchuria and Korea.

Japanese surrender broadcast from Tokyo (10th), Allied reply (11th). Terms accepted (14th).

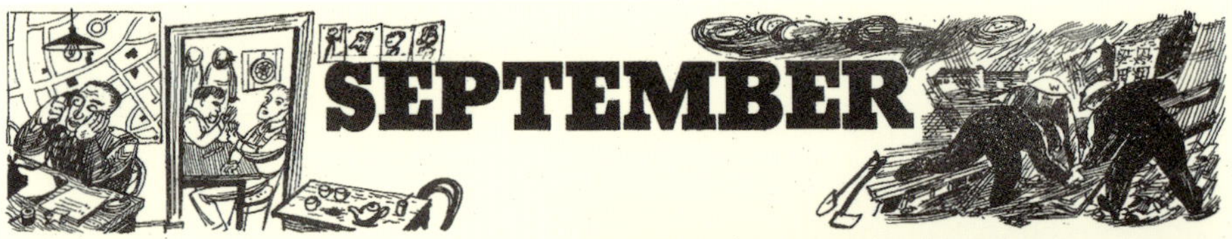

SEPTEMBER

Sun.	1	8	15	22	29
Mon.	2	9	16	23	30
Tues.	3	10	17	24	
Wed.	4	11	18	25	-
Thurs.	5	12	19	26	-
Fri.	6	13	20	27	-
Sat.	7	14	21	28	-

1939

Germans invade Poland. Warsaw bombed. British and French demands on Germany (1st).

Ultimatums expire. Britain and France at war with Germany (3rd).

Dominions declare war: Australia and New Zealand (3rd), South Africa (6th), Canada (10th).

B.E.F. lands in France. Conscription in Britain for men 18 to 41.

German "blitzkreig" cuts through Poland. Soviet troops enter Eastern Poland (17th). Warsaw surrenders (27th). Poland partitioned between Germany and U.S.S.R. (29th).

1940

Beginning of London "blitz." Civilian casualties in Britain during month: 6,968 killed, 10,615 seriously injured.

Conscription in United States.

British bases leased to U.S. in return for 50 destroyers.

Japanese forces enter Indo-China.

1941

Germans capture Kiev after forty-five days' battle (19th).

1942

Violent fighting in suburbs of Stalingrad. German advance held. Russians advance between Don and Volga.

1943

8th Army crosses Straits of Messina and lands in Italy (3rd). General Eisenhower announces unconditional surrender of Italy (8th). 5th Army lands in Naples area (9th).

Germans occupy northern Italy and Rome. Mussolini rescued by German paratroops. Patrols of 8th and 5th Armies link-up.

Sweeping Russian advances. Entire Donetz Basin re-occupied. Smolensk recaptured.

1944

Channel ports taken. Allies cross into Belgium. Brussels liberated (3rd). Antwerp (4th). 2nd Army crosses Dutch frontier. U.S. 1st Army enters Germany near Aachen.

1st Allied Airborne Army drops in Holland. Link up with ground forces at Nimejen. Withdrawal from Arnhem after heroic defence.

Mr. Churchill and President Roosevelt meet at Quebec.

First V.2 rockets on Southern England (8th).

1945

Japanese forces in S.E. Asia surrender to Admiral Mountbatten at Singapore (12th).

Council of Foreign Ministers meets in London (11th).

End of Lend-Lease. Anglo-American trade and financial discussions begin in Washington.

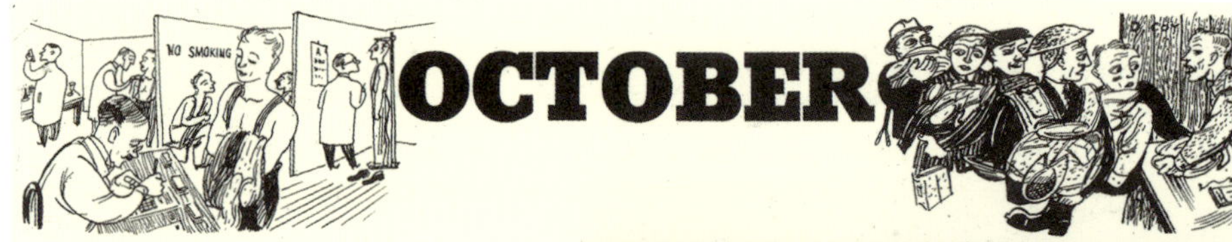

OCTOBER

Sun.	-	6	13	20	27
Mon.	-	7	14	21	28
Tues.	1	8	15	22	29
Wed.	2	9	16	23	30
Thurs.	3	10	17	24	31
Fri.	4	11	18	25	-
Sat.	5	12	19	26	-

1939

Mr. Chamberlain rejects Hitler peace proposals.

M. Molotov reaffirms Soviet neutrality.

1940

Hitler and Mussolini meet on Brenner (4th). Italy invades Greece (28th).

Civilian air raid casualties in Britain for month: 6,313 killed, 8,695 seriously injured.

1941

Battle of Moscow begins. Hitler issues order of day to troops facing Moscow: "Today is the beginning of the last great decisive battle of this year" (2nd).

Russians evacuate Orel, Bryansk, Marulpol, Odessa and Kharkov.

Germans break through into the Crimea.

1942

8th Army offensive opens in Egypt (23rd). German counter-attacks repulsed.

Australians halt Japanese advance on Port Moresby in New Guinea and advance. Naval battles off the Solomons.

1943

Fall of Naples (1st). 5th Army opens offensive on Volturno river (13th). Italy declares war on Germany.

Russian offensive sweeps on. Dnepropetrovsk recaptured. Break-through between Lower Dneiper and Sea of Azov.

1944

Fierce fighting in Scheldt pocket. British cross Lower Rhine west of Arnhem. Maas reached and bridgehead established.

14th Army captures Tiddim (19th).

Russians open new offensive in Latvia. Capture Kirkenes in Norway.

Mr. Churchill and Mr. Eden in Moscow.

British airborne troops land near Athens. City cleared of enemy by partisans.

U.S. forces land on Leyte in Philippines.

1945

Indonesian nationalists declare war on Dutch. British and Indian troops in clashes in Java and Indo-China.

Laval executed.

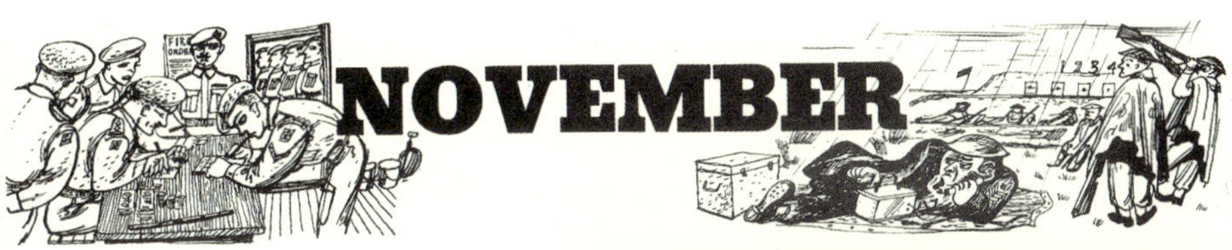

NOVEMBER

Sun.	-	3	10	17	24
Mon.	-	4	11	18	25
Tues.	-	5	12	19	26
Wed.	-	6	13	20	27
Thurs.	-	7	14	21	28
Fri.	1	8	15	22	29
Sat.	2	9	16	23	30

1939

U.S. Neutrality Bill signed.

U.S.S.R. invades Finland after demands for withdrawal of Finnish troops from border regions.

1940

Fleet Air Arm cripples Italian Fleet at Taranto (11th-12th).

Dusk-to-dawn raid on Coventry ; heavy damage (14th-15th). Civilian air raid casualties in Britain for month : 5,004 killed, 7,949 seriously injured.

1941

R.A.F. daylight offensive over Northern France, the Channel and occupied territory begins. Heavy night raids on German and Italian targets.

Germans capture Kerch. Russians lose and retake Rostov.

Imperial forces attack in Libya. 8th Army under General Cunningham advances fifty miles in day (18th). Great tank battle round Sidi Rezegh.

1942

Axis forces in Egypt begin retreat westwards. Tobruk and Benghazi recaptured. Prisoners include General von Thoma, commander of the Afrika Corps. Montgomery chases Rommel.

The Allies land in North Africa, under command of General Eisenhower (8th). British First Army enters Tunisia.

German troops take over Vichy France. French scuttle warships at Toulon as Germans enter port.

Russian counter-offensive at Stalingrad.

1943

Russians recapture Perekop, cut German land communications with Crimea. Kiev, Gomel recaptured.

President Roosevelt, Mr. Churchill, and Generalissimo Chiang-Kai-Shek meet in Cairo (22nd-25th).

8th Army cross the Sangro in strength.

Teheran Conference opens 28th.

1944

British assault troops land on Walcheren (1st). Fall of Flushing (3rd). Geilenkirchen, Metz, Strasbourg captured.

14th Army take Mawlu and Kalemyo.

Russians cross Danube.

All Greece cleared of enemy.

1945

Trial of major Nazi war criminals opens in Nuremburg (21st).

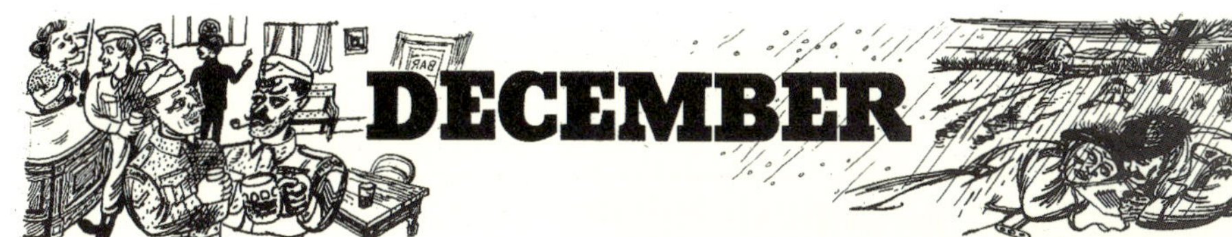

DECEMBER

Drawings by James Boswell

Sun.	1	8	15	22	29
Mon.	2	9	16	23	30
Tues.	3	10	17	24	31
Wed.	4	11	18	★ 25	-
Thurs.	5	12	19	★ 26	-
Fri.	6	13	20	27	-
Sat.	7	14	21	28	-

★ Christmas

1939

U.S.S.R. expelled from League of Nations.

Graf Spee scuttled off Montevideo after Battle of River Plate.

1940

Wavell's desert offensive opens (9th). Sidi Barrani and Sollum captured.

President Roosevelt's broadcast : "We must be the arsenal of democracy" (29th).

Fire "blitz" on City of London (29th-30th). Civilian air raid casualties in Britain for month : 3,988 killed, 6,247 seriously injured.

1941

Japanese bomb Pearl Harbour ; cripple U.S. fleet (7th). President Roosevelt orders mobilization.

Raids on Singapore. Japanese landings in Siam, Malaya and Philippines. H.M.S. *Prince of Wales* and *Repulse* sunk off Malaya by Jap air attack (10th). Hong Kong surrenders (25th).

Italy and Germany declare war on United States (11th).

Germans in retreat along entire Eastern Front. Hitler takes over command of German Army (19th).

Fluctuating fighting in Libya. Imperial forces retake Benghazi.

Women in Britain conscripted for National Service.

1942

Extensive Russian advances. Violent German counter-attacks.

Capture of El Agheila : Rommel begins retreat to Mareth Line

1943

Saturation raids on Berlin.

8th Army captures Ortona.

New Russian offensive in Kiev salient.

1944

Germans launch Ardennes offensive, penetrate 40 miles.

Allied advances in Italy and Burma continue.

1945

Preparatory commission of United Nations Organisation meets in London.

Anglo-American financial agreement signed in Washington.

Mr. Bevin, Mr. Byrnes and M. Molotov confer in Moscow.

'Without some conviction of purpose and sense of stability and permanence the artist founders in frustration.'

Boswell left *Lilliput* in December 1950 and immediately set to work on a 20ft by 50ft mural for the *Sea and Ships* pavilion in the 1951 Festival of Britain's South Bank exhibition, a commission secured through James Holland who was the design co-ordinator. Bawden, Piper, Moore, Sutherland and Fitton were among the many other artists involved in what was intended to be a massive demonstration of the efficacy – in a thoroughly modern context – of murals and public sculpture. Boswell's *Drifters* and another mural in the same building by Josef Herman, were moderately well-received. 'Some success', *Architectural Design* acknowledged, 'though neither is intrinsically very remarkable.' From Lilliputian to gigantic in one go was, perhaps, too big a leap.

A decade later however Boswell was to achieve immeasurable public success devising the look of the Labour Party campaign for the 1964 election. Twenty six years on from *Design for Dying*, twenty years on from the 'badly-done stage setting' of southern Iraq, from drawings of inaction acutely observed, his dashing *Let's Go with Labour* on pamphlets, billboards, buses and bus shelters, in newspapers and on TV, proclaimed a sense of purpose and retaliation, for the time being.

JAMES BOSWELL (1906–1971)

1906 Born 9 June at Westport, New Zealand.

1917 Family moved to Auckland where he attended Grammar School.

1924 Studying at the Elam School of Art, Auckland.

25–29 Studied at the Royal College of Art, London.

926 Met the New Zealand-born artist, Fred J. Porter (1883–1944), who taught him 'la belle peinture'.

927 First exhibited at the London group. Continued to exhibit paintings (mostly landscapes) in mixed exhibitions in London for the next five years. Also showed lithographs at the Senefelder Club.

928 Met Montagu Slater, left-wing journalist, poet, novelist, editor; and a little later Edgell Rickword, Marxist poet, critic and editor.

932 Gave up painting, joined the Communist Party and took to illustration and graphic design.

933 Founder- member of the Artists International Association (AIA); other artists included Clifford Rowe, Misha Black, Pearl Binder, James Fitton and James Holland.

934 Exhibited with the AIA.
In October *Left Review* was launched. For the next four years Boswell was to be one of its major illustrators. Also contributed anti-fascist drawings to the *Daily Worker* under the pseudonym of Buchan.

936 August: Became Art Editor of the Publicity Department of Asiatic (now Shell) Petroleum Company.

6–39 Took part in AIA anti-war and anti-Fascist exhibitions, showing reportage and satirical drawings.

939 Visit to Paris where he produced series of drawings of the brothel, *Le Sphinx*.

40 Still working for Shell. Undertook ARP duties. Did many drawings of the Blitz. Contributed illustrations to *Poetry and the People*.

1941 January. Called up in early part of the year as a private in RAMC. Went to Crookham, near Fleet, Hampshire.
Sent to Millbank barracks during the first half of the year and started his radiography training.
In the autumn went to Peebles, Scotland.

1942 Left Peebles for Iraq.

1943 Most of year in Iraq
Travelled back to Britain via Malta and Sicily, arriving in London on 16 December.

1944 Joined OCTU at Wrotham; moved to Lincolnshire, then in summer to Perth.
By the winter joined Richard Bennett as writer and illustrator, under pen name of Buchan, on *Current Affairs*.
Exhibition of drawings *On Duty in the Desert* at Charlotte Street Centre.
Elected Chairman of AIA.

1945 Demobilised and returned to Shell.

1947 Resigned from Shell. Joined Richard Bennett on *Lilliput* as Art Editor.
Illustrators included Ronald Searle, Gerald Hoffnung, James Fitton, James Holland and Paul Hogarth.

1948 Exhibited small drawings and paintings at Wolf Mankowitz's gallery, Piccadilly Arcade.
Visited Australia.

1950 December: Left *Lilliput*.

1951 Commissioned by Basil Spence to paint large Mural (20ft x 50ft) for the *Sea and Ships* Pavilion in the Festival of Britain.
Became Editor of the house journal of J. Sainsbury Ltd. In 1969 he wrote and edited the centenary history of the firm.

52–59 Exhibited at many mixed exhibitions – Royal Academy, London Group, Paris Salon and John Moores, Liverpool.

1954 Visited Paris; spent many hours looking at Monet's *Nympheas* in the Orangerie. Also studied the stained glass at Chartres.

1957 Deeply impressed by exhibition of American Abstract Expressionism at the Tate Gallery – especially by Jackson Pollock.

1958 The *New Left Review* organized exhibition of *Left Review* drawings at the Partisan Coffee House, Soho.

1962 One man shows at Drian Gallery, London and County Town Gallery, Eastbourne.

1964 Designed the poster *Let's Go With Labour* and the entire publicity campaign for the Labour Party for the General Election which swept Harold Wilson to victory.

1965 One-man show at New Vision Centre.

1967 Exhibition at Commonwealth Institute, London.

1969 Wrote, illustrated and edited *A History of J Sainsbury* for their centenary

1968 Commissioned to paint a large mural *The Golden Day*; for the new BP House, Wellington, New Zealand.

1970 Publication of *Social Realism and The Arts* by Donald Drew Egbert with extensive material on Boswell and reproduction of drawings.

1971 15 April: Died in London.

DRAWINGS IN PRINT

Left Review

Our Time

Lilliput

Seven

The Daily Worker

The Daily Mirror

The Artist and the Public (Boswell, Piper, Giles), ABCA Current Affairs, June 1945

The Artist's Dilemma, by James Boswell, London 1947

James Boswell A New Zealand Artist in London, by Herbert Roth, Auckland City Art Gallery Quarterly no 65 1977

James Boswell Drawings, Illustrations and Paintings, Nottingham University Gallery 1976

Boswell's London, intro William Feaver, London 1978

Indigo Days, by Julian Trevelyan, London 1957

War Through Artists' Eyes, by Eric Newton, London 1945 Thirties,

British Art and Design before the War, Arts Council of Great Britain, 1979

Projecting Britain: Ealing Studios Film Posters, Ed David Wilson, London 1982

AIA: The Story of the Artists International Association, ed Lynda Morris and Robert Radford, Oxford 1983.

Art for a Purpose, the Artists International Association 1933-1953 by Robert Radford, Winchester 1987

The Artist as Reporter, by Paul Hogarth, London1986

Edward Bawden War Artist, Ruari Mclean, 1990

James Fitton RA, exhibition catalogue Dulwich Picture Gallery, London 1986

To the Kwai and Back, by Ronald Searle, London 1986

Giles: Fifty Years at Work, intro William Feaver, London (British Council) 1994

CATALOGUE

The British Museum

page 12 left 1983,0723.24
right 1983,0723.22
page 14 2000,1125.6
page 15 1983,0723.20
page 25 left 1992,0404.103
right 2000,1125.18
page 28 2000,1125.23
page 30 1992,0404.105
page 31 1973,0225.98
page 32 top 2000,1126.10
bot. 2000,1125.12
page 33 1992.0404.108
page 34 1992,0404.11
page 36 2000,1125.24
page 37 1992,0404.109
page 38 bot. 1992,0404.102
page 39 left 1992,0404.106
page 40/41 1992,0404.112
page 42 2000,1125.17
page 43 top 1992,0404.107
bot. 1992,0404.139
page 44 1983,0723.19
page 53 1992,0404.113
page 54 2000,1126.9
page 57 2006,3031.35
page 59 1992,0404.110
page 73 2000,1125.15
page 85 left 1992,0404.123
right 1992,0404.134
page 94 2000,1125.19
page 95 t. left 1992,0404.115
b. left 2000,1125.20
t. right 1992,0404.136
b. right 1992,0404.140
page 98/99 1992,0404.126
page 101 2000,1125.10
page 106 t. left 1992,0404.132
b. left 1992,0404.124
t. right 1192,0404.131
b. right 1992,0404.127
page 107 1992,0404.130
page 108/109 1992,0404.125
page 110 1992,0404.120
page 111 1992,0404.118
page 112 1992,0404.133
page 113 2000,1125.16
page 114 1992,0404.121
page 115 2000,1125.22

Photography: Julian Nieman

Imperial War Museum, London

page 19 left Art LD 2022–75
right Art LD 1883–2
page 21 Art LD 2022–1924
page 26 Art LD 2022–58
page 29 Art LD 1883
page 35 left Art LD1883–14
right Art LD 1883–7
page 38 Art LD 2022–20
page 39 Art LD 1883–31
page 44 bot. Art LD 2022–16
page 45 top Art LD 2022–32
bot. Art LD 2022–13
page 46 left Art LD 2022–27
right Art LD 1883–8
page 47 left Art LD 2022–1
right Art LD 2022–29
page 48 Art LD 1927
page 49 Art LD 1927
page 50 left Art LD 2022–10
right Art LD 1883–40
page 51 Art LD 2022
page 52 Art LD 1926
page 56 Art LD 1883–10
page 57 Art LD 2022–52
page 58 Art LD 1883–13
page 60 Art LD 2022–5
page 61 Art LD 2022–5
page 66 Art LD 2022–53
page 67 left Art LD 2022–41

Tate Gallery

Frontispiece
page 20 8224–17–3
page 62 top & bottom
page 63 top 8224–17
bottom
page 67 right
page 70 8224–16–50
page 78 left8224–17–63
centre 8224–17–50
right 8224–17–51
page 80 left 8224–16–13
right 8224–16–26
page 81 8224–17–34
page 83 left 8224–16–16
right 8224–16–14
page 85 8224–16–21
page 86 8224–16–31
page 87 left 8224–16–32
right 8224–16
page 88 8224–18–16
page 89 8224–18–17
page 90 8224–16–37
page 91 8224–18–11
page 92 top left 8224–129
b. left 8224–16–14
t. right 8224–16–36
b. right 8224–16–46
page 93 8224–16–45
page 96 top 8224–17–67
bot. 8224–17–33
page 97 left 8224–16–20
right 8224–16–45
page 100 8224–16
page 102 8224–16–33
page 103 8224–18–13
page 104 8224–18–4
page 10 58224–18–19
page 118 8224–19
page 119 8224–19
page 120/121 8224–19